NEW YORK'S Most Sensational Vice Trial

THE CASE AGAINST LUCKY LUCIANO

ELLEN
POULSEN

The Case Against Lucky Luciano: New York's Most Sensational Vice Trial
©2007 by Ellen Poulsen

Clinton Cook Publishing Corp.
P.O. Box 640356
Oakland Gardens, NY 11364-0356
www.lucianotrial1936.com

Cover design: www. lightbourne.com
Interior design: www.folio-bookworks.com

Cover Photo of New York's Woolworth Building courtesy of NYC Municipal Archives.

Luciano mug shot on front cover courtesy of NYC Municipal Archives.

Women's Court photo on page ix courtesy of the Photography Collection, Miriam and Ira D. Wallach Division of Art, Prints and Photographs, The New York Public Library, Astor, Lenox and Tilden Foundations.

Eunice Carter photo on page 55 courtesy of the Photographs and Prints Division, Schomburg Center for Research in Black Culture, The New York Public Library, Astor, Lenox and Tilden Foundations.

ISBN-10: 0-971-7200-1-0
ISBN-13: 978-0-9717200-1-5
e-book: 978-0-9717200-2-2

Printed in Canada

Publisher's Cataloging-in-Publication
(Provided by Quality Books, Inc.)
Poulsen, Ellen, 1953–
The case against Lucky Luciano : New York's most sensational vice trial / Ellen Poulsen.
   p. cm.
   LCCN 2006909212
   ISBN 0-9717200-1-0
   ISBN 0-9717200-2-9

   1. Luciano, Lucky, 1897–1962. 2. Criminals—New York (State)—New York —Biography. 3. Organized crime—New York (State)—New York. 4. Trials (Prostitution)—New York (State)—New York. 5. Dewey, Thomas E. (Thomas Edmund), 1902–1971. 6. Mafia trials—New York (State)—New York. I. Title.

     HV6248.L92P68 2007   364.1'092
                                          QBI06–700242

THE CASE AGAINST LUCKY LUCIANO

ELLEN POULSEN

Clinton Cook Publishing Corp.

Little Neck, New York

DEDICATION

To My Mother,
Joan,
Who taught me to love New York.

CONTENTS

Part III
Recantment

FOREWORD

Salvatore Lucania, a.k.a. Charles "Lucky" Luciano. Millions of words have been written about him, including even a posthumous memoir attributed to him (though it reads like the lurid invention of a Hollywood screenwriter and some historians have suggested that's just what his so-called "Last Testament" is). He's become a mythical Mafia Superman.

The organizer of organized crime. Al Capone's secret boss (yeah, right — try saying that in Chicago with a straight face!). Mastermind of a worldwide dope cartel and Boss of All Bosses of the Cosa Nostra. He's alleged to have paved the way, from a prison cell, for the Allied invasion of Sicily and one novel depicts him heroically parachuting onto the island as a prelude to this. His alleged autobiography paints Luciano in the best possible light and, of course, innocent as a lamb of that most dastardly of charges, White Slavery. Before he gets too mythologized, it might be time to reexamine the landmark case that broke Luciano's luck, something not attempted since Hickman Powell's 1939 book, *Ninety Times Guilty*, which tells only Dewey's side of the case and is also hampered by its lurid, melodramatic style, and the moral constraints of the period.

Comes now Ellen Poulsen, a cop's daughter and a dedicated researcher blessed with acute investigative and sociological instincts; and her book, *The Case Against Lucky Luciano: New York's Most Sensational Vice Trial*, is an instant classic and a trailblazer for future historians. Poulsen's goal here is more objective: not to deflate the Luciano myth (nor to explore the complex structure of Cosa Nostra for a post-Valachi audience) but to detail the workings and political motivations of both the "Bonding Combination" and Tom Dewey and his investigative staff, and most of all, the women of the case: Peggy Wild, Nancy Presser, Gashouse Lil, Jennie the Factory, and Cokey Flo — the madams and hookers who were alternately exploited and victimized by both sides. Ellen also authored *Don't Call Us Molls: Women of the John Dillinger Gang* and finds some interesting parallels between the FBI's treatment of gang molls and the interrogative methods used by Dewey and his staff on the madams and whores of the Luciano case.

Luciano comes across neither as innocent nor as guilty as previously pictured, but he clearly wasn't the victim of a frame-up, either. Along the way, too, we are introduced to fascinating characters such as Eunice Carter, the African-American woman on Dewey's staff who discovered that organized crime controlled and extorted from much of New York's prostitution industry, and Tommy "The Bull" Pennochio, the Luciano lieutenant who served as treasurer of the Bonding Corporation, and a longtime narcotics dealer with ties to the Chinatown Tongs. Also explored is the Hot Springs connection and the incredible measures utilized by Dewey to extricate the fugitive crime boss from that wildly corrupt citadel of the South.

No dry rehash of the often questionable stuff armchair Mafia fans have already seen in a hundred other books, this is a classic case history of the trial that launched both Luciano and Dewey into U.S. history. Utilizing original sources, Ellen Poulsen has produced a groundbreaking book that will raise eyebrows in the true crime community and provide a fertile field for future researchers.

– **Rick Mattix**
Coauthor, *The Complete Public Enemy Almanac*

Author's Preface

By the mid-1930s, remnants of Tammany Hall had survived the wrecking ball of the Seabury Hearings. Replacing corruption with homey, urban comfort was Mayor Fiorello LaGuardia. He was a reform mayor, with family values. He read Little Orphan Annie on the radio. Righteousness was starting to replace wickedness as society's convention. Morality became an important, overlooked value.

Yet, despite the new, soft edges, New York was jaded. A vice scandal couldn't ruffle a pigeon's feathers in Prospect Park. The Luciano trial proved that. The Vice Czar had plastered the tabloids for one month in May 1936. While the trial dominated the headlines, the *Daily News'* "Voice of the People" featured one mere suggestion that New York needed a red light district. As though to break the silent yawns of the public, Thomas E. Dewey, the special prosecutor, announced that he had no interest in stopping prostitution. He only wanted the racketeers behind the vice syndicate.

Judge Philip McCook's gavel fell in June of that year, with convictions and prison sentences for Luciano and his co-defendants. The glowing constellation of the trial's prosecutors would fly toward the future. Thomas E. Dewey, Murray I. Gurfein, Sol Gelb, Barent Ten Eyck, Eunice H. Carter, and Frank S. Hogan took on new rackets' investigations. They tackled the successors to the Dutch Schultz restaurant rackets; the conviction of James J. Hines and the ousting of Tammany Hall's Al Marinelli; and the investigations into the trucking and garment industry rackets. At the same time, Dewey's staff members defended the appeals brought by Luciano's attorneys after the convictions. By 1939, Luciano had exhausted his legal redress. The appeals, with dubious witness recantments, embalmed a story that was dead and forgotten.

The vice trial had braved public unease with prostitution. The prostitutes, who testified against their former boyfriends and pimps, displayed a show of guts that earned the grudging respect of tabloid journalists. With the passage of time, though, the imprint left by the witnesses disintegrated and the bravery of these street women lost its appeal. In the retelling, their courage and strength would be replaced with lesser traits of stupidity, syphilitic ravishment, and drug addiction. Nancy Presser is best remembered as pinched in a direct hit during the sensational raids of Saturday night, February 1, 1936.

When accused of being a whore, she allegedly said, "The word is prostitute."[1]

What was in a word, anyway? Presser dwelled in a night world where madams called themselves Nigger Ruth and Sadie the Chink. These words were jargon. They were trade names. Presser's semantics served her dumb blond mystique, etching it in stone.

Prostitutes didn't fit into a comfortable category. They weren't molls. In the 1930s, they were consigned to the darkest side of town. During the vice trial, news blackouts prevented photographers from taking pictures of them. Ostensibly for their protection, the only images allowed were drawings.

On the day of their release from the Women's House of Detention, the material witnesses paraded before Judge Philip McCook. The women discussed their collective futures. One by one, each assured the judge she would go home; she would attend Mass or go to Temple. A group of social workers waited in the next room, hoping to reform the prostitutes. The rotund veteran of the old dancehalls, Jennie "the Factory," laughed. "I'm too old for social services," she sneered.

Desperate to be released, many of the departing girls agreed to attend worship services. Even though Peggy Wild promised to go home to "St. Ann's Parish in the Bronx," she knew it was impossible. "What is your plan?" Judge McCook asked another departing prostitute. "I'll go crazy if I stay here; that is one plan," the girl replied.[2]

The two key witnesses, Mildred Balitzer and Florence "Cokey Flo" Brown, tried to escape the life and go straight. Nancy Presser and Thelma Jordan heard a rumor that they were slated for death by the underworld. They fled to Europe, hoping to escape their fate as sacrificial lambs, who would be slaughtered for the sins of those who helped convict Luciano.[3]

The assumption of Luciano's guilt was first developed in Thomas Dewey's office through the use of grand jury revelations of bookers Louis "Cockeyed Louie" Weiner and his son, "Dumb" Al Weiner. Later, bookers who had worked for the Mott Street Mob implicated Luciano and his co-defendants through hearsay revelations.[4] Their collective testimony established a deeper, albeit circumstantial, link to connect Luciano to the bonding combination. The association of Tammany Hall district leader Al Marinelli as lender to combination boss David "Little Davie" Betillo, and as a fixer in combination enforcer Ralph Liquori's robbery case, is significant given Marinelli's close association with Luciano. Yet, these facts will stand on their own merits—or demerits, depending on how easily one is swayed by the evidence.

The witnesses were male and female, imprisoned and free. They risked their lives to testify. With the exception of one hotel thief, the imprisoned men were bookers who turned state's evidence. Joe Bendix, Pete Harris, Dave Marcus, Danny Brooks, and Dumb Al Weiner have been forgotten. The twenty-eight imprisoned women who took the stand have been condensed, like a can of soup, to three prototypes: Cokey Flo, Mildred Balitzer, and Nancy Presser. In truth, the witnesses who implicated Lucky Luciano fit into assorted criminal patterns. From Joe Bendix, who wrote plaintive letters to his wife from prison, to the popular booker Jack Eller, who changed his plea to guilty mid-trial, they suffered their own silent agonies.

The madams and prostitutes received no further witness protection. Two round-trip transportation tickets bought Presser and Jordan a hiatus to Europe, with no guarantee of safety upon their return to the United States. Brown and Balitzer opened an automobile service station in California. When they went bust, their requests for money were ignored. Reparation had been paid by Dewey's office, and it bought them nothing. They were dumped, left homeless with no handsome district attorneys, no magazine ghostwriters, and no guardian angels.[5]

Thomas Dewey moved to new campaigns and political aspirations. The bookers and witnesses, including Joe Bendix, remained in bitter, protective, solitary confinement. The New York trial-of-the-century was forgotten. As a cult figure, Cokey Flo would go on to elicit contempt among crime buffs as a stoned hooker, the stuff of inside jokes and knowing guffaws. The eternal shame of the harlot, at once biblical and secular, put the Luciano trial witnesses outside the gates of history.

Acknowledgments

No research project can be undertaken without the help of the dedicated people who preserve America's history. For this project, I depended heavily upon the efficiency of the chief archivists, Kenneth Cobb and Leonora Gidlund, at the New York City Municipal Archives.

My deepest appreciation goes to Brian Beerman, John Binder, Reno Dakota, Patrick Downey, Mario Gomes, Rose Keefe, Allan May, Charles Molino, Steve McCormick, Richard McDermott, Rick Porrello, Jim Sanseverino, Patterson Smith, Tom Smusyn, and Tony Stewart.

Special thanks to William "Bill" Helmer, for his help with the title of this book, and Rick "Mad Dog" Mattix, who provided constant guidance in the development of the bibliography.

Thanks to Liz Tufte for typesetting and design, and Sharon Young for editing.

Thanks also to my friends in the fascinating world of 1930s crime history research. Without the help of my fellow researchers, this book could not have been written.

– Ellen Poulsen

Photo on opposite page: Jefferson Market Women's Court (NY Public Library)

PART I

The 1933 Prostitution Bonding Combination

CHAPTER 1

THE INDIVIDUALISTS

You ain't no better than anybody else.
– Jimmy Fredericks

Dago Jean never used her real name. Her sobriquet was the patent she'd earned from years of operating houses of prostitution. In the Depression, a New York madam wore her name like a shingle. It made good business sense to have a brand. Reputations garnering thousands of customers could be built on one established alias. Dago Jean, who also went by the name Jean Lamar, competed for the $2 house trade with Jennie "the Factory" Fischer. The two women nursed their mutual grudges, with some vendettas stretching back twenty years.

In spite of their differences, they shared the same concern. A new mob combination, seeing prostitution as a lucrative racket, was extorting weekly payoffs for protection. Madams were opening their doors to enforcers bearing lead pipes and torches. With this new bonding combination threatening their lives, a few began to join forces. The majority already had joined the bonding syndicate. But Dago Jean, along with a few old-school individualists, had held out for the right to operate without payoffs to the racket.

One night in 1933, Dago Jean opened her door to two men. They had the right password and were good for the money. They weren't rubes. Yet, she knew something was wrong. From her experience, johns came in and looked for girls like cats after a mouse. But this pair didn't cast their eyes hungrily around the room. They fixed their hardened eyes on her. They advanced forward. One of them pinned her down. Before her startled eyes, the other opened the linen closet and threw in a lit book of matches. The fire quickly spread throughout the room. While her furnishings and carpets burned, she escaped with her girls. After that, her colorful name took on a new meaning. It was used as a lesson for the others.[1]

Joan Martin wasn't stupid, and she didn't look it, either. At 41, she wore thick, round-framed glasses, which gave her the wary face of an owl. Since emigrating from Eastern Europe years before, she'd run her houses independently. With only one or two girls in her brothel, she had to compete in buildings that housed other $2 joints. The competitors often fought dirty. Rival madam Nigger Ruth kept calling the police, informing them of Joan's location in hopes of running her out. But Joan had bribed the building super as a shield against detectives making inquiries.

"Every superintendent in New York takes money," she later testified. She paid her super $10 a week. It was part of the overhead that had also included payoffs to bookers. A booker was the go-between who acted as a hiring agent between the madams and the prostitutes. Yet, a booker was not a pimp, and had no dominion over the prostitutes.

Bookers had lucrative places in the prostitution racket. They paid a high percentage to the new combination for preemptive bail insurance (which they called bonding), which the bookers had joined after being persuaded by death threats, punctuated by sniper's bullets. The madams were a different story. They were cagey and accustomed to working independently. Madams had dealt with bail bondsmen for decades and saw no reason to change over to a new system that would eat into their profits.

Some time after the enforcers set fire to the linen closet in Jean's apartment, they visited Joan Martin. The madam looked through the peephole. She didn't recognize the men standing in the corridor of her building.

"Police," they barked like the howl of a wolf pack. Beneath the eye-level spyglass, the marauders held lead pipes and switchblades.

Reluctantly, she allowed them entry. She was surprised when Charlie Spinach, her booker, followed them in. Accompanying him was Abe Wahrman, an enforcer. Charlie Spinach did the talking. "You have to join the combination," he stammered. "In case of a pinch, the combination takes you out of jail."

"Nothing doing," said Joan. "I won't join it. I don't see no percentage in it for me."

Spinach tried to soften the madam by explaining things. "You pay ten dollars for each girl and five dollars for yourself, each week," he said, softly and distinctly. "If the girl gets pinched, the combination puts up half the bail," he added, suddenly speaking more quickly. "You pay the other half. If you get arrested, we put up all the bail and you have to pay it back," he concluded. "You have to join or you can't get girls."

Abraham "Little Abie" Wahrman, Combination Enforcer
(NYC Municipal Archives)

"I'll get my own girls," Joan Martin replied.

Abe Wahrman turned to the posse. "Then take the joint apart. Give her the works."

They lifted the couch, ripping the upholstery away from the springs, while cutting the carpet with the switchblades. The men broke other pieces of furniture with the lead pipes. Their work done, they ran out into the street.

The next day, Charlie Spinach returned. This time, he brought Jimmy Fredericks. The general manager of the bonding combination, Fredericks was a loud-mouthed, volatile boss. He practiced duplicity with women, pretending to be tender when it suited him. Florence "Cokey Flo" Brown, his otherwise perceptive girlfriend, believed he was gentle. She would swear under oath that Fredericks hated using force on women. Now, to Joan Martin, he tried to sweeten the deal.

"It wasn't my men who wrecked your place," he said earnestly, shaking his head sadly at the mess. "But if you join the combination, you'll get protection with the bond."

Joan Martin
(Author's Collection)

For the first time, Joan paid up. She gave Fredericks $15, on the spot, for one girl. Then, to her disbelief, he raised the stakes.

"And there's the two hundred and fifty security for the girl and one hundred fifty for you."

"I don't have the money."

"Then we'll put you on the installment plan." For a few weeks after that, Joan paid her dues. As madams frequently did, she moved. But this madam left no forwarding address.

Having no alternative but to trust Charlie Spinach, she continued to book with him. Rather than

Jimmy Fredericks, Combination Enforcer
(NYC Municipal Archives)

protect her, he notified Jimmy Fredericks of her whereabouts each time she disappeared.

In five days, Fredericks visited her again. His polite demeanor was gone. Once inside the new apartment, Fredericks aimed his gun at her dog. She rushed to the animal, lifting him protectively in her arms.

"Lay off the dog," she yelled. Rushing to the bedroom door, she threw the dog into the room. She turned to face Fredericks.

"You'll take my orders or else," he leered, and lifted a blackjack. Before going unconscious, Joan saw the savage weapon. It dangled from a short strap, the kind you'd see on a woman's purse. It was wrapped in black electrical tape.

"I was blood from top to toe," she later testified. Her frightened maid, with the help of Joan's one prostitute, turned to the speechless john for help. With the help of an elevator operator, they carried Joan Martin from the house. A cabbie took her to a local hospital, where doctors sewed ten stitches into her scalp.

After recovering from her wounds, she moved again. Jimmy Fredericks' next step was to send Ralph "The Pimp" Liquori, a brothel stickup artist, to the address furnished by Charlie Spinach. With his men surrounding him, Liquori covered her with his revolver. His men then emptied coffee cans and sugar bins, looking for cash. They took her watch and $36 from her wallet. The finishing touch was to steal coins from her girl's purse.[2]

That's how the bonding combination broke Joan Martin. After that, she always paid. She changed bookers, leaving Charlie Spinach for Pete Harris. He, too, like Charlie Spinach before him, reported her every move to Jimmy Fredericks.

She got to know all the members of the combination after that. While she moved once every two weeks, they always found her.

Peggy Wild, real name Margaret Ventimiglia, was a notorious throwback to old New York's sporting underground. Civil reformers, like New York's Committee of 14, had monitored Peggy Wild since she'd started her business with call houses in 1924. Privatized investigators from the Committee of 14 had stalked her operations in Manhattan, Brooklyn, Queens, and Long Island, where she'd operated on the Nassau County border.[3]

Peggy Wild was not weak like the frightened bookers. She was a Trojan horse. The madam, who had run joints in Saratoga, had entertained Vincent Coll. Wild had hosted "Dutch" Schultz, "Legs" Diamond, and "Lucky" Luciano. Wild's sporting establishment had been a favorite haunt of Hyman, Joey, and Louis "Pretty" Amberg. She had once admitted to blackmailing her clients.[4]

In 1933, when Peggy Wild met the obnoxious Jimmy Fredericks, her instincts said the combination boss was not in the same class as her old friends and customers. The madam had entertained mobsters of higher ranking than Fredericks. It now felt ludicrous to accept his authority. At the same time, she'd heard there'd be violence. By this time, she was not willing to endure vandalism meted out by sadistic mobsters. In spring, 1934, after moving to 110 W. 55th Street, and booking with Pete Harris, she asked him for advice. She discovered that the bookers all talked the same talk.

"You have to bond," Pete Harris said. "We won't be able to give you girls."

Harris, a booker who had relinquished his authority to the combination, took his orders meekly. He'd been threatened with death, and told to get out of town, unless he joined the combination. Like Charlie Spinach, he would provide no counsel and would turn her in to Fredericks if she went outside the combination.

For a time, Peggy Wild spread the word that she was closed. She tried running a place across the hall, in secret. But she was soon found out. Her act of deception earned her an unwelcome nickname among the bookers and combination heads. They called her a wise guy.

Knowing she was backed against a wall, she tried to organize the madams. She called upon three tough competitors: Pearl Woods, Betty Winters, and Jennie the Factory. Jennie was a heavy, 57-year-old madam, who had run her houses since 1915 without bookers or bonding combinations. She "got girls" through word-of-mouth. She would operate for a while and then go out of business while she lived on her accumulated capital. Fischer believed that the large number of available girls made bookers unnecessary.

Around 1930, while working in the Coney Island section of Brooklyn, she started booking girls with Cockeyed Louie Weiner. By the summer of 1933, with the rest of the madams caving into the pressures of the bonding combination, Jennie opened a house on West End Avenue and 85th Street. Except for a short period when she booked with Nick Montana, Jennie continued to do business independently. She stayed on West End Avenue for one year. As was her custom, the rotund, old-fashioned madam decided in the summer of 1934 to live off her earnings. She had a pleasant summer, visiting Coney Island with her family. Between Thanksgiving and Christmas, she returned to her profession in time for the holidays. While booking with Pete Harris, she opened up on 97th Street between Broadway and Amsterdam Avenue.

Right before Christmas, Jimmy Fredericks came to her door and stood in the hall. She looked through the peephole.

"Open the door," said Fredericks. "I thought you were in trouble; I came to bail you out."

"Nobody's in trouble," Jennie retorted. "Get out of here."

Jimmy Fredericks began yelling and banging on the door. Jennie, concerned that the super would throw her out of the building, put on her hat and coat and agreed to meet Fredericks downstairs.

"You know," said Fredericks, "you have to bond every girl and give ten bucks a week. That will include protection, and nobody will bother you; and if you get arrested, I'll help you."

"I have no money now," said the indignant Jennie. "You just give me a few days to think it over."

"You better think it over and make your mind up," concluded Fredericks. "You ain't no better than anybody else."

The first thing Jennie did was to call Peggy Wild.

"What's this all about?" the aged madam asked her old colleague.

"I don't know myself," Peggy admitted, "but don't be in a hurry. Wait a couple of days."

Jennie moved a few blocks away and set up a house at 140 W. 86th Street. Fredericks, hot on her trail, showed up at the door. Fischer finally agreed to bond when Fredericks, accompanied by stick-up man Santos "Chappie" Selafani, pulled a gun on her at that location.

"Everybody has to bond and you do, too," he said, the revolver pointed at her stomach. Jennie, who paid on the spot, later related the chilling story.

"When I first heard about the combination, I thought it was a few bums used to come to doors to try to shake you down. But I didn't believe it was really the truth."

Jennie Fischer convinced Peggy Wild she'd have to bond. "You better, because everybody else gives and we can't get away with it," she said simply.

By summer 1934, Peggy Wild paid Pete Harris through his collector, Joseph "Jo Jo" Weintraub. Confident she was protected under the new system, she went to Saratoga. There, her reputation for operating houses was solidly established.

The following spring, on March 15, 1935, in a raid at 158 W. 58th Street, Peggy Wild was arrested and taken to the usual destination,

Jefferson Market Women's Court. There, she gave the standard defense, claiming she was a housewife. She embellished the story by saying that the girls were visitors to her home. As promised, the bonding combination furnished the girls' bond.

Peggy Wild paid her own counsel, Max Rachlin and Abraham "Abe" Karp, two disbarred lawyers who acted as informal attorneys and bail bondsmen in Women's Court.

After the experience in Women's Court, Peggy became depressed. Fearing the onset of a nervous breakdown, she went briefly to Rye, north of New York City. But her fortunes took a turn for the worse when, on September 17, she returned to the city and was arrested for the eleventh time at 853 Seventh Avenue.

This time, she didn't get the same treatment. With a rap sheet longer than ticker tape, Wild was held on a $2,500 bond as a habitual criminal. Nobody was willing to pay her bail. Beneath the gothic towers of the Women's Court, she spoke with Jesse Jacobs. An unlicensed bondsman, Jacobs refused to post her bond. According to him, Peggy Wild had defaulted in her payments to the combination.[5]

"Why didn't you pay the bail?" she asked. After all, she had paid the sum of $250 a week to the combination for her own protection. Now, she was being kept in jail, friendless and unconnected.

Jesse Jacobs' answer astounded her. "You're too well known."

Peggy was infuriated. The madam and the bondsman went back a long time, to the mid-1920s. For many years, the Jefferson Market Women's Court had one door, and that door revolved. Jaded bail bondsmen like Jesse Jacobs, Max Rachlin, and Abe Karp had been dependable. But that was before the bonding combination had come along to change the rules.

CHAPTER 2

DANCEHALLS AND BED HOUSES

Freedom of movement not to be found in the waltz.
—Dancehall Inspector, 1914

Jennie the Factory and Peggy Wild were career madams. Before the encroachment of the combination thugs, their biggest problem had been anti-vice reformers. An insidious group of covert watchdogs kept files on them. In folders, dog-eared and dirty, investigators chronicled vice and gambling. Some files went back twenty years. Madams who dodged police were less successful in avoiding reformers who visited their joints in disguise. The common wisdom prevailed that they were "safe with the police department, but powerless with the Committee of 14."

For over twenty-five years, the Committee of 14 kept a shadowy vigilance over New York's dance parlors and Raines Law hotels. In 1931, the Committee died of old age. The *New York Mirror*, a tabloid, took an editorial stand and declared, "People are, for some reason, against all organizations that pry into the affairs of others."

Its demise began with the stock market crash of 1929. After that, the cascading economic collapse overshadowed moral concerns. A watchdog organization suddenly seemed old-fashioned. It was easy to forget the deplorable conditions, such as Raines Law hotels that had brought the Committee of 14 into being in the first place.[1]

The Committee emerged in 1905 as a New York City citizens' group that advocated the elimination of vice—a generic term, which would condense the double threat of gambling and prostitution. The Committee engaged businessmen, bankers, and lawyers, who would visit dancehalls, pool halls, bars, disorderly houses, and tenements. The Committee also hired private investigators, posing as customers and patrons of the rowdy, underworld joints.[2]

Voyeuristic in its approach, the Committee should have come under more governmental control. Yet, its mission statement was carefully worded to sidestep accusations of prurient interest. Its objective was to employ undercover agents to study gambling—to root out the persons responsible, in a publicized report with recommendations. Agents would promote legislation to prosecute offenders. They hoped to simplify the vice laws. But beneath the rhetoric, its agents were mere actors in the lewd drama of sex and scandal.

The scheme to send civilian undercover agents developed after The Committee of 15, its parent organization, published its findings on the "bed houses" in 1902. This Committee blamed the Raines Law hotels for the spread of vice. The Raines Law, enacted in 1896, granted hotels the right to sell liquor on Sunday. It allowed proprietors to build rooms behind the store. Saloon owners started a building boom by converting upstairs lofts into impromptu hotel rooms. With the add-ons, saloons could then apply for the Raines Law liquor license by calling themselves "hotels." The extensions were then used for assignation, the place a prostitute brought a customer.[3]

The fallen women and girls who worked as prostitutes were called "working girls" in the first two decades of the twentieth century. They were professional hookers with many aces up their sleeves and ways to ply their trade. While the Raines Law hotels proliferated as public havens for gambling, sporting, and drinking bootleg liquor, the dancehalls provided privacy. Within the rooms of a dancehall, a paying customer could engage in wanton behavior without fear of exposure. Even Committee of

14 agents, acting undercover, chose not to reveal themselves to the players in the lewd events unfolding before their scandalized eyes.

The 1873 Society for the Suppression of Vice, a predecessor of the Committee, had also used undercover agents. They were scandalized by the Tango, a new dance craze.

"The chief characteristic is a freedom of movement not to be found in the old dances such as the waltz and the two-step," one Cleveland inspector wrote. "It permits dancers to introduce such steps and movements as please their own particular whim or fancy. It very clearly typifies the extreme care-free spirit which dances of this type inspire in some of our young people."

The dancing was merely a ploy to mask the real thing. In the "hostess racket," the customers were usually young men out for their first adult experience. By the end of the evening, their pockets were picked clean by the combined efforts of the taxi drivers, the hostesses, and the girls, who were called "entertainers." Pimps worked in "employment agencies." Scattered around the theater district, these agencies placed girls in the dancehalls.

The john was called a rube. He would find a dancehall by asking a taxi driver for a good time. Reformers called the drivers "vice steerers." They'd give the young rube a password in exchange for a high tip. Unknown to the unsuspecting rube, a driver would tip off the doorman, who then signaled the rooms upstairs. The hostess and orchestra members knew the signals and their meanings.

The rings had distinct meanings. One ring and the musicians would discard their tuxedo jackets and sit in civilian clothes. They would hide the liquor. This was in preparation for a raid. Two rings was another signal to the orchestra to play classical music to appear respectable. This was the ruse presented for the Committee investigators. Three rings meant the visitor was a rube or a "sucker," and four rings meant the visitor was returning and, therefore, was to be treated fairly. For a visitor, it would be an expensive night.

The first thing an "entertainer" did when greeting a guest was to sit on his lap. Treating it as a joke, she patted him down to find his cash.

Taking it out, ostensibly as a joke, she refused to return it. She pretended to want a present, as a reward for returning the man's money without a struggle. In order to get the man to spend his money at the bar, she then played the role of drinking buddy. The customer paid a high price for cocktails for himself and the girl, who drank only a concoction of sugar and water. The rube thought the girl was seriously drinking. If she did get hard liquor, she'd make a quick trip to the bathroom to vomit. That way, she could drink all night while her companion became intoxicated.

One undercover investigator said, "The men were drunk; they used the vilest kind of language," he reported. "The hostesses were supposed to tell rotten stories and all you heard was filthy jokes and profanity, and most of the men were intoxicated." One reported that "whites [were] dancing with yellows," which was a common occurrence. As a result of sensational headlines, an act was introduced to amend the greater New York charter. It would attempt to regulate the dancehalls, which numbered at least 1,400 by 1905.[4]

On January 17, 1920, the Volstead Act, which enforced the 18th Amendment, went into effect. The unpopular law prohibited the legal sale or consumption of alcohol. Prohibition altered the course of America's underworld by ushering in secret drinking establishments. Dancehalls went out of fashion as the proliferating speakeasies offered the services of prostitutes. Often, a girl got a job simply by walking into a speakeasy and offering herself for sale to the proprietor. In 1928, Jennie the Factory was discovered by the Committee of 14 to be operating a speakeasy at 343 W. 5th Street.

Speakeasies offered other ways for prostitutes to work. They often allowed girls to enter and pick up customers. At 117 W. 137th Street in Harlem, the Committee found that from 1922 to 1928, a mixed race house of prostitution offered "white girls for colored men." They also discovered speakeasies for gay men, who, by the epithet, were called "fairies."

While speakeasies were underground, employment agencies dotted the theater district around Times Square. A prostitute could find work in these agencies. The Roseland Dancing Academy and the Dreamland Dancing Academy were in operation until 1930.

Not all men wanted to take a chance at being arrested in a raid. For those looking for a sporting evening but fearing arrest, the Spirit of Paris Society offered a membership in a seemingly legitimate men's club.[5]

When prostitutes were arrested, they were not considered important. Predating the era when molls were taken seriously by police as witnesses, arrested prostitutes were usually taken to either Women's Court or to Welfare Island. Before fingerprinting, prostitutes were tracked and identified by the Bertillon method, which amounted to a physical description.

Women's Court cases were filed on cards listing the name, offense, age, place of birth, and the witness, who was usually a police officer. In many cases, the witness was a member of the family. In cases such as these, the family was concerned about the welfare of their "wayward girl," and misguidedly looked to the court system for help. When a woman first appeared in court, she was evaluated. Some of the classifications were non-infectious, mentally subnormal, drug addict, or infectious. Girls in their early teens were incarcerated.

Before its termination in 1931, the Committee of 14 was accused of supporting an untoward rate of conviction. Judge Samuel Seabury, who conducted the investigation into Women's Court corruption, criticized the Committee's fondness for convictions obtained without due process. The bad publicity was the kiss of death for the outmoded organization.[6]

After it disbanded, Committee of 14 officials joined other social service organizations. They remained available to detectives and prosecutors. Some would haunt the halls of the jails and courtrooms for years. In 1931, the moldy boxes holding their index cards and reports went to the archives of the Public Library. There, the records would lie before their later resurrection in the bonding combination case.

CHAPTER 3

The Doctor Called on Monday

It was because I needed money. . . .
– Mildred Curtis, Prostitute

I n 1933, "Dumb" Al Weiner, a prostitution booker, took over the family business from his father, Cockeyed Louie Weiner. Like his dad, Dumb Al started booking girls from the telephone at Wallack's Bar & Grill at 146 Rivington Street. In a wiretapped conversation, peppered with Yiddish, he took a routine order:

Female Voice: "I need a girl."

Weiner: "I have a girl. She can work to Thursday, when she gets her period."

Female Voice: "I have customers waiting. I don't know what to say to them."

Weiner: "Don't worry. She'll be there."

Female Voice: "Don't send any Hitler bastards over to my place. Them German girls are too smart and you can't rely on them."

At the end of every week, Al Weiner walked around the corner from his Rivington Street hangout to Delancey Street. Passing the peddlers hawking housewares and fabrics, he went into Ratner's Restaurant. There, in the shadow of the Williamsburgh Bridge that stretched heavily across the East River to Brooklyn, Al handed Jesse Jacobs a paper bag stuffed with $100 in cash.

Everybody paid Jesse Jacobs. The bondsman held the keys to the holding cells in Women's Court, and the adjoining Women's House of Detention. If arrested, the madam paid one-half, and Jacobs paid the other half. Before Cockeyed Louie handed over the business to his son, he said, "Expect to pay to Jesse Jacobs." Cockeyed Louie had explained the old system. Al Weiner later testified, and in his own words, related his father's advice.

"'This bonding is, that each place gives ten dollars for each girl. If there is any trouble, meaning, if there is an arrest, the madam pays half and the bonding pays half.' I says, well, 'Who is this bondsman?' 'Jesse Jacobs is the bondsman.'" [sic][1]

Jacobs wielded power in the combination. His name was even contingent on getting the nicest girls. A madam, who needed pretty, fresh faces, always told the booker, "Jacobs is my man."

In place before the combination, the old booking system had loopholes that allowed the madams to hide money. One scam, designed to

Al Weiner, a Booker, inherited the business from his father, "Cockeyed Louie" Weiner (NYC Municipal Archives)

Jesse Jacobs, Bondsman and Bagman (NYC Municipal Archives)

shortchange the bookers, was to move constantly. Madams went from one address to another. In doing so, they could take a girl the bookies overlooked. This movement characterized the New York system. This stark picture contradicts the image of the Chicago parlor houses, where a man had his choice of a room filled with women. It bore little resemblance, likewise, to the $2 cribs in Chicago to which a whore descended after she'd become too old for the parlor houses.[2]

In contrast, New York's $2 trade was not run in cribs. The system played itself out in "houses," which were apartments rented by madams for periods of only one or two weeks. Small and transient, they generally held one madam, one maid, and one to three girls.

If a madam successfully hid a girl from the booker, she could collect from the girl and pocket the money. During the Luciano trial, Betty Winters was the first madam to admit to booking with Cockeyed Louie Weiner. "Because he didn't know me very well," she testified, "I had to put up two hundred and fifty dollars for each girl."

If Betty Winters made it sound like it came out of her pocket, it didn't. Through a series of deductions made to their gross weekly earnings, the girls paid every penny.

The tawdry life of a syndicate prostitute was marked by addiction and sickness of body and mind. Often, a prostitute's life would end with suicide. Many, like Vivian Gordon, were murdered. They were young women hopeful that their youth, beauty, and sexual expressiveness would put them on "easy street." Most were runaways from home, never to return. The anonymity was compounded by the constant use of assumed names. The prostitute's use of an alias was a doubled-edged sword that made her more susceptible to victimization. Prostitute Vivian Gordon, the flamboyant con artist found murdered during the 1931 investigation into New York politics, was living under an assumed name.[3] It was unheard of for prostitutes to use real names. As a result, when they were killed, their families could not be notified.

Many prostitutes had been raised by alcoholic parents, with fathers or male relatives who had sexually assaulted them during their childhood. Prostitute Mildred Curtis, who had been a mistress to Thomas "Tommy the Bull" Pennochio, told her story to Judge Philip McCook. "How did you get into this way of life?" the Judge asked.

"Oh, it's a very long story," Mildred replied.

"You are pretty, that is one thing," said McCook. "That is one way you got into it, I know."

"No, it isn't that," Mildred replied. "It was because I needed money and I didn't want to go home; it was because my dad is too mean. If I ran away from home, and tried to go back, he would probably kill me. So I stayed here."

Yet, some of these women had left nice homes. For prostitute Nancy Presser, home was in a place far upstate, where her family had no idea that the money she sent home was blood money. Nancy's brother sent a letter to the district attorney after she was held as a material witness. "Nancy is a good girl," he wrote.

In spite of the denials of friends and family, the girls who drifted into prostitution had suffered trauma, either mental or physical in nature. During the 1930s, there was no help for psychological problems; no idea that there was an inner reason for self-destructive behavior. Yet, Judge McCook, who had an opportunity to observe the dozens of prostitutes who were held as material witnesses in the combination court case, observed a simple truth. Of one Jean Erwin, McCook said, "She is a very interesting case. She has what is either an inhibition, or a blocking, or a scar on her soul. There is something that is warping her, and injuring, something that she knows and will not tell."[4]

Whether the '20s roared or not, society considered it improper conduct for young ladies to aspire to lives outside the narrow perimeters of virtue and eventual marriage. In spite of the razzamatazz hype of the day, Victorian mores still formed borders around the parties and socials of the 1920s. Because of the influence of jazz age luxury items like radios, automobiles, and modern dresses, women wanted their beauty to be seen and admired by others.

Women living in the Midwest were drawn to Cleveland, Cincinnati, and Johnny Torrio's brothels in Chicago.[5] Those on the East Coast found their place in brothels in Philadelphia and New York. Prostitutes drifted through the cities, often while escorted by low-level syndicate pimps. This system came to be known as "white slavery" in 1910. The ambiguous term took over the imaginations of American citizens and became an instant metaphor for fear. The passage of the White Slave Traffic Act of 1910, otherwise called the Mann Act, which made it a Federal crime to bring a minor female over the state line for immoral purposes, did little to stop syndicate prostitution. The law was used into the 1930s as a way for state and federal prosecutors to pile charges upon indicted prisoners already facing prosecution for other alleged crimes. Most detectives believed that "white slavery" was a mere newspaper term.

White slavery was invoked in cases involving interstate movement of underage females. There were girls who had been duped into believing their pimps loved them. There were girls with huge regrets. There were Chinese immigrants, kept as indentured servants in San Francisco's notorious cribs.[6] This gave rise to the rumor that Chinese restaurants were fronts.

The mistaken notions abounded out of a lack of information. There was no intervention, no probation, no way for a girl to be lifted out of the life. The only professionals with weighted opinions were district attorneys, police officers, or judges. Those in law enforcement scoffed at the idea of a national syndicate forcing women into lives of prostitution.

For young, beautiful teenagers with talent, the Ziegfeld Follies or Broadway shows were a mighty goal. Showgirls frequently ended their evenings in parties marked by drug abuse with racketeers. With drugs lessening inhibitions and decreasing the natural beauty of these fresh-faced teenagers, prostitution loomed as another way to make a living. To a beauty starting to lose her looks, with drugs decaying her will, it was an easy choice to make.

It was impossible for these innocents to remain independent. Pimps would find them, and seduce them with charm. If that didn't work, they could always beat or terrorize them into submission. After the pimp knew he had the girl under his control, he withdrew all of the fabricated love he had shown her. From that point, under the domination of a pimp, a prostitute lost all control of her own life. Time was money for them both. The audacious term "white slave" was a pathetic euphemism for a living death. Rather than existing only as a veiled, elusive threat, prostitution robbed young women of their freedom, their self-respect, and often, their very lives.

A combination girl had to split her earnings in half at the end of every week. The receipts were computed through a punch card pinned to her negligee or special dress, which contained a zipper running down the front to hasten the act of disrobing.

In $2 syndicate houses, the sheets were not changed. A bedspread was kept in place on top of the bed. A towel was placed at the foot of the bed, to protect the coverlet; a $2 customer was asked to keep his shoes on his feet. Every time one of these johns entered the room, the maid followed him in. She took the card from the girl's dress or negligee, and punched a new hole into its perforated surface. This was a system of checks and balances that ensured that the girl's total earnings matched the number of holes in the card. At the end of every week, the girl sat down with the madam and together, they calculated her earnings. A good night's work was thought to be at least fourteen johns. Less than that was a shortfall.

The gross receipts went first to the madam, who made the deductions before paying the girl her share. Out of the gross, the madam got half. The girl, retaining 50 percent, turned over 10 percent to the booker, with an additional 10 percent for paying the bond. The sum of $3 went to the doctor, who visited every Monday morning; $2 came out for maid services; $25–$35 was deducted for the girl's rent. Therefore, at $200 a week, a prostitute's net earnings were $30–$40 a week. Although it was a decent sum in the Depression, she often lost it to gambling, drugs, and liquor. Besides her other expenses, she had to pay for her wardrobe. In the mid-1930s, one vendor sold gowns to the combination prostitutes.[7]

An itinerant merchant, who combined loan sharking with dress sales, Gustave "Cut Rate Gus" Koenig sold the glittery evening apparel the girls needed to ply their trade. His arms overflowing with boas, gowns, dresses, and lingerie, fresh from the garment district, he would display his wares during daylight hours. It was an early version of shop at home service. Gus combined dress sales with his sideline as a loan shark. With his partner, Benny Spiller, he loaned money to the prostitutes, to be paid back within a six-week period at "a dollar on every five." Gus showed his dresses on the same day the physicians visited the houses. Both arrived "early," which was usually late in the afternoon. A messenger, Cut Rate Gus knew everything that was going on. He could help a girl develop an exit strategy if she was unhappy in a house. If a madam wanted a change, he could move her away from a booker.

In spite of the transient nature of the business, figureheads remained in place during the 1920s and early 1930s. Everyone paid their weekly tithe to bondsman Jesse Jacobs. The system was a well-oiled machine.

For instance, Sally Osborne was arrested while working as a prostitute for madam Rose Cohen. Sally's bail was set at $300. Cohen's maid, Agnes Wilson, had her bail fixed at $100. Jacobs bailed them out by paying for the three women after the booker posted the money to Jacobs. Occasionally, Jacobs went on record under other names, like Joe Kent of 113 W. 110th Street. It was transparent that "Joe Kent" was giving the address of the bail bondsmen's offices across the street from Women's Court.[8]

If the bailsman was essential, the booker was even more important to the livelihood of those connected to the racket. Bookers were popular figures. Even the doctors, who visited the girls every Monday afternoon, needed to be in good standing with the bookers if they wanted to get work.

The underworld doctors formed an important link in the network as well. They saw the prostitutes as part of their regular round of patients in everyday walks of life. While operating underground, they nevertheless performed a service to society. They controlled the spread of venereal disease by administering swab tests on the genitals and throats of the prostitutes on a weekly basis. "You can identify a prostitute by her swollen genitals," one physician later testified.

The doctors showed a certain reticence to performing Wasserman tests, however, and gave them only if a woman displayed the physical signs of having contracted syphilis or gonorrhea. There was a method to keeping the doctors alert for VD. If a john caught a disease because of a doctor's negligence, that physician had to treat him free-of-charge.

Most were physicians in good standing with their families and fraternal organizations. Nonetheless, they abided by the underworld code. Some were abortionists, leading a double life. In spite of their token attempts to curb the advance of venereal disease, underworld doctors did nothing to help the prostitutes. They looked the other way, from the drug-addicted, pathetic women lying before them, to their golf course friendships and social club network.[9]

Once a syndicate prostitute became addicted, her value within the combination decreased. As her looks disintegrated, she would descend further down the ladder, into houses charging as low as $1. Her addiction was a two-sided coin. She was dependable, and needed to remain within the combination. A junkie couldn't leave the underworld that provided her with heroin. It was a darkly symbiotic relationship with no way out. She would die of an overdose. Her pimp boyfriend could murder her. She might commit suicide.

A sanitary, safe drug cure for a $2 prostitute was not an option. The safest way they found was to go "cold turkey" in jail. Called a quick reduction, it amounted to putting an addict through complete withdrawal, within the confines of a steel cell. The climax came in the fifty-sixth hour, which is when the symptoms escalated. It was common for police and district attorneys to approach the women while in the throes of quick reduction. At the point where her skin would turn blue and pucker, like that of a turkey, she'd be offered a way out of her torture. The district attorney would appear at the cell door. He would kindly offer her a sanitarium cure. At this pivotal point in withdrawal, the woman often agreed, during these crucial hours, to testify against her friends. It was another kind of death sentence.[10]

Cockeyed Louie Weiner was a booker who was wiretapped due to the revelations of informant Jennie the Factory. Even before he was indicted for compulsory prostitution in June 1935, Weiner had begun making payments to the combination. Bookers Charlie Spinach, Dave Miller (also called David Marcus), and Pete Harris, who held the biggest slice of the booking pie, would have to pay, also. As the bookers traded their independence for loyalty to a new syndicate operation, the madams were slow to comprehend the change. They still maneuvered around the bookers to their best advantage. And the bookers themselves had to be broken and reeducated to the new system before they'd be effective in disciplining recalcitrant madams.

In a change of administration that took place between 1933 and 1934, booking switched hands to a new generation. Madams, who formerly booked with Nick Montana, went over to David Marcus. His interest ended shortly after the combination drove him out of town. Many of the madams then started booking with Pete Harris, who was an illustrious bookie.

But his success would be short-lived.

Pete Harris went by two separate, but equal identities. He lived two lives, in two separate cities. While booking hundreds of prostitutes, he remained faithful to one wife. Mildred Balitzer, a madam, was an active

Peter Balitzer, aka Pete Harris, a Booker
(NYC Municipal Archives)

partner in the racket. He took piggybacked income from her business. Because of Mildred's habit, most of her earnings went into her arm. In spite of the many cures she'd attempted, Mildred Balitzer was hopelessly addicted to heroin. Harris later summed up the job description of a booker perfectly when he testified, "If the madam wanted a girl, I would send a girl. If the girl wanted work, I would see I could get her work." It was a simple statement from a booker who built his business from four madams in 1932 to the servicing of seventy-five houses by 1935.

He kept his office on 69th Street between Amsterdam and West End Avenues. A wide street with a panoramic view of the New Jersey shoreline, it was an icebox when the wind blew off the Hudson River. Freezing weather would force a streetwalker inside, to the relative security of a syndicate house. Although many would later say they preferred the streets, Pete Harris had swept them into the houses. Witness Malcolm Bailey later described how Harris recruited girls. "Pete came over to see Bonnie and explained the game to her. He said, 'Pinches you don't have to be afraid of. You got to take them, but it's a hundred percent sure thing you'll get out.'"

Pete Harris was born in Brooklyn in 1903. Pete and his brother, Edward Balitzer, had moved to Philadelphia, where they trained to work as electricians. But honest work didn't appeal to Pete. After moving to Chester, Pennsylvania, he opened a speakeasy. In Chester, he met prostitutes who told him to go to New York if he wanted to work. Taking their advice, he returned to New York in 1931. He was his own boss until August 1933, when two thugs accosted him. "A protective organization is being formed for the hookers," they told him. "All the small fry are being driven out." Harris saw it differently.

"They wanted to control the town," he later testified. "They wanted all the different bookies to pay them money." The next time Harris met the combination, it was in Williamsburg, on Marcy Avenue and Broadway. Here, thugs told him that other bookers were all paying. After that, Pete's assistant, a skinny man from Eastern Parkway named Jo Jo Weintraub, brought them a bag filled with $100 once a week. Soon it was raised to $150.

To further irritate Pete Harris, the combination sequestered him to monthly meetings held at 121 Mulberry Street. There, he listened to the loud-mouthed Jimmy Fredericks. At one meeting, Abe Wahrman accused him of holding out. Within a few months, the meetings stopped. One night, Wahrman went to Harris' apartment, where he found three men waiting for him, all holding revolvers. Forcing him into the kitchen,

Joseph "Jo Jo" Weintraub, Assistant Booker and Money Collector
(NYC Municipal Archives)

where they pushed him against the table, they wielded their .32 and .38 revolvers. They wanted $2,000 up front, and $200 a week thereafter. He promised to deliver.

On November 27, 1934, Harris married Mildred Balitzer. A big, dissipated blond, Mildred had light, steely eyes that displayed no emotion. Ignoring an underworld code that insisted that women mind their own business, Mildred seemed to know everyone. In her brash defiance of convention, she rubbed elbows with the men who did the booking. Mildred was a drug addict. She had tried all the cures, from private sanitariums to jailhouse quick reduction. With heroin so plentiful in her circles, she had found it impossible to stay clean. As Mildred Wilson, she had checked into a private sanitarium in April 1933, listing Peter Balitzer as her husband. There, she was found to be injecting heroin for an entire year.[11]

Mildred would try to check into a sanitarium if she thought she'd be swept up in an arrest. Compared with the quick-reduction, a private sanitarium was a picnic.

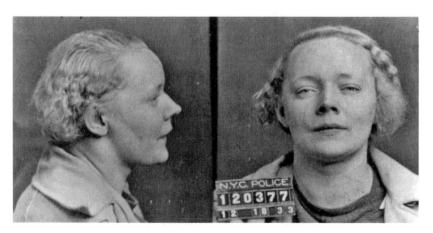

Mildred Balitzer, the wife of Booker Pete Harris
(NYC Municipal Archives)

CHAPTER 4

THE MOTT STREET GANG

The neighborhood is all Italian.
—Patrolman Dominick Ciaffone, 5th Precinct

In the early 1930s, Little Italy was a crowded bedroom metropolis. The narrow streets supported cramped tenements shielded by steel fire escapes and double-hung windows opening to the drama developing on the street below. There was little escape from the self-contained neighborhood. The geographic boundaries of the Italian section halted with a crash when Mott Street met Pell at the entrance to Chinatown. To that point, the Italians lived in the railroad room apartments, hovering over storefront restaurants and food stores. Built around 1878, the apartments often housed extended families. Charles Molino, who grew up at 78 Mulberry Street, described the layout in an interview.

"Our fourth floor apartment consisted of a narrow hallway that entered into a small kitchen area with a small toilet, called a water closet. There were two small bedrooms and a small dining room," he related. "Everything was small."

Within the tenements of Mulberry and Mott Streets, the highest-ranking members of the bonding combination lived with their family members. Their children went to the local public schools, while wives went downstairs to shop for meats and vegetables in the storefront shops along the curbs.

The drug trade controlled by Tommy the Bull Pennochio had expanded into the takeover of the prostitution bonding in the spring of 1933, yet few in the neighborhood were aware of it. Patrolman Dominick Ciaffone of the 5th Precinct, who noted that the neighborhood was "all Italian," said he "never saw any woman who looked like a prostitute, on any street in Little Italy."[1]

The bonding combination enforcers were drug runners who hung out on the twin conduits of Mulberry and Mott Streets. Flanking Mulberry Street and Kenmare, one block west on Broome Street, was the triangular corner that hosted the curbside liquor exchange of the 1920s.

The police headquarters stood like a temple at the head of the exchange. Celano's Restaurant, at 98 Kenmare Street, overlooked the curbside liquor exchange. As detectives looked the other way, Al Marinelli, the lower eastside district leader, hung out with Salvatore Lucania, known as Charlie "Lucky" Luciano, in the large, sprawling restaurant.[2] In 1933, as the Mott Street Mob moved into drug trafficking, loan sharking, and extortion, Tommy the Bull and David "Little Davie" Betillo were bankrolled by Luciano's drug money.

David "Little Davie" Betillo, Combination Boss
(NYC Municipal Archives)

Thomas "Tommy the Bull" Pennochio, Combination Boss and Treasurer
(NYC Municipal Archives)

Tommy the Bull and Little Davie had a unique strategy in the prostitution takeover. It started with the shylock racket. They approached the small-time loan sharks who preyed upon the prostitutes. They offered to bankroll them in exchange for a percentage. Cut Rate Gus, the friendly dress salesman, leant money as he worked door to door. Little Davie Betillo provided the start-up capital by funding Benny Spiller, who supervised the accounts brought in by Cut Rate Gus.

In this way, Tommy the Bull and Little Davie built the combination upon the vigs amassed by the prostitutes.[3]

Because the call houses were transient outfits, housing only one or two girls at a time, the madams made it a practice to call the bookers for fresh girls. The two head bookers, Nick Montana and Cockeyed Louie Weiner, had shared the business throughout Manhattan and Brooklyn since the 1920s. They had collected a small amount of money, and in exchange, worked with bondsmen in Women's Court to set prostitutes free after arrest. The money was exchanged every Saturday on Delancey Street and handed over to Jesse Jacobs, the chief unlicensed Women's Court bondsman.[4] As part of the takeover, Tommy the Bull and Little

Davie cut themselves into the payoffs delivered to the bondsman. They spent time every day sitting in the bail bonds' offices on W. 10th Street.

In order to steal the business from Nick Montana and Cockeyed Louie Weiner, Tommy the Bull sought political cushioning. Al Marinelli, the lower eastside district leader and mob protector brought to power by Lucky Luciano, offered his protection to the combination.[5]

Al Marinelli afforded the Mott Street gang the clout it needed to enforce the new bonding combination. Montana and Weiner would be eliminated by the legal tactic of arrest, prosecution, and conviction. Secure in the knowledge that Montana and Weiner were destined for arrest and conviction, Tommy the Bull and Little Davie Betillo hired goons Abe Wahrman and Jimmy Fredericks to act as enforcers. It would take two years, from 1933 to 1935, to bring the bookers and madams under control. When the combination was finally established, it operated like a well-oiled machine.

In its structure, the combination resembled a pyramid. Originally, only nominal bonding fees were collected by bookers, with the second tier, the bondsmen, who represented the women in court.

After the takeover by the Mott Street Mob, the bookers and bondsmen remained. With the new structure imposed on them, they had to obey several tiers of management. The highest-ranking tier was run by Little Davie Betillo and Tommy the Bull Pennochio. They worked in conjunction with the white-collar bondsmen and disbarred lawyers of Women's Court.

Betillo and Pennochio directly commanded Jimmy Fredericks and Little Abe Wahrman, the enforcers.

They controlled the bookers through four essential booking arteries. Profits were rolled back into the pockets of Little Davie Betillo and Tommy the Bull Pennochio, who recycled the money into the hands of the shylocks who loaned money to the prostitutes. The system was self-sustaining, with the highest rewards going to Tommy the Bull and Little Davie.

Both of the men who controlled the combination had come of age in Little Italy.

Tommy the Bull had grown up there, and chose to remain with his family. With his wife, Mary, he had a son who attended P.S. 23 and who played on Mott, Mulberry, and Elizabeth Streets. Pennochio kept his car in an uptown garage, out of sight of their neighbors and local beat cops. He wore clothes that positioned him as a thug. He was born on July 16, 1891 to Felomina "Fannie" and Frank Pennochio. He got his nickname as a child because, in his wife's words, "He was fat." On Elizabeth Street, Tommy the Bull would stop in a popular café every day. There, the owners served him pastries. "I ate most of what they gave me," he later told police. In the 1920s, he lived over a grocery store at 89 Mulberry Street. When he was arrested for seduction, his face was a familiar one. He was known to stand downstairs, hanging out in the doorway next to the grocery store at 89 Mulberry Street. Upstairs, on the second floor, he kept his family.

A drug trafficker and user, he shared a six-room apartment with his wife and son, his wife's parents, and her two brothers. His brothers-in-law, who had failed in their efforts to earn a living, received home relief during the Depression. Tommy the Bull's wife, Mary, had lived in poverty during the three prison terms he'd served for narcotics. While raising her son, she had depended upon the providence of her parents for the child's support. When her husband came home from prison, things didn't get better; they got worse. He caught syphilis after an extra-marital fling, during which he remained away from Mary. He never gave her spending money. People said, "Tommy the Bull wouldn't give his wife a dime." Mary was forced to borrow money from neighbors. Tommy had a local reputation as a drug dealer. When police went down to interview the shopkeepers and housewives walking on Mulberry Street, they learned that Tommy's business was drugs; that people in large sedans bearing New Jersey license plates regularly visited him, dressed in fancy clothes and driving a Buick coupe. Along with other members of the Mott Street gang, he had a financial interest in the Bol Musette, a social club at 301 W. 46th Street. His legitimate front was that he was a barber, working for William "Wild Bill" Ercolino on Mulberry Street. Ercolino, a local real estate investor, had earned his colorful name as the one-time husband of madam Peggy Wild.

Pennochio had soda concessions at the College Fountain in Ricco's

Drug Store at 230 Lafayette Street. He admitted that he performed no work there. All he did was collect money. Indeed, he was the combination treasurer. In an office at 72 Mott Street, Tommy the Bull recorded the transactions of the bookers and shylocks preying on the syndicate prostitutes.

A drug man for Luciano, he controlled the supplies that came into the country for Luciano. If Luciano wanted the prices raised, Tommy the Bull ordered the shipment withheld to raise prices. A veteran of the curbside liquor exchange, he served three separate prison sentences, including a federal prison stretch in 1928 for dealing narcotics. He was released in 1929. That same year, he was the prime suspect in the killing of mobster Solly White, who was found dead on Mott St. He took a lesser rap for narcotics rather than stand trial for Solly's murder. By 1933, he was out of prison, and known to be connected to Luciano.[6]

Like Pennochio, Little Davie Betillo was an associate of Al Marinelli, and was regularly invited to Marinelli's political beefsteak dinners.[7] Betillo shared many traits with Pennochio. While Pennochio lived in Little Italy with his family, Betillo had been born and raised there.[8] Both hung out in the triangle between Kenmare and Broome, Elizabeth, Mott, and Mulberry Streets. Both were associates of Lucky Luciano and Al Marinelli.[9]

Betillo was twenty-seven years old. A man who Luciano trusted, Little Davie was a handsome and well-dressed Dapper Dan. He wore the popular hairdo of the local mobsters, curled up in a greasy pompadour at the crown, with the sides and back shaved close to the head. He avoided eye contact. Betillo kept his eyes pointed upward, to convey a distant and arrogant impression. Such was his mystique that local detectives had heard the mistaken rumor that he was a Capone gunman. He'd been arrested only in New York and Philadelphia.

Betillo was born and raised at 63 Mott Street. He shared a piece of the social club Bol Musette, as well as some narcotics' profits, with Tommy the Bull. It was common for Betillo to withhold the bookers' profits, offering them narcotics in lieu of cash.[10]

The deadly Abraham Wahrman went by several different aliases. He was known as "Abie the Jew" and more often, as "Little Abie." He worked under the more legitimate name of Abe Heller. He ordered and supervised the combination hits. Wahrman also went door-to-door with his bombastic enforcer Jimmy Fredericks. These two were the face of the combination to the madams, as they directly confronted them in their parlors and apartments.

Jimmy Fredericks, the feared enforcer, was a career criminal. Born in Brooklyn, he grew up there at 385 South First. His first arrest, for petty larceny in July 1915, resulted in a suspended sentence. One month later, he was arrested a second time for attempted burglary, and sentenced to the Elmira Reformatory. He was released by 1921 but returned to prison shortly afterward for stealing a car. He was sentenced to five years in Sing Sing but was released on parole.

On November 23, 1925, Fredericks blew a safe at 1662 Broadway in the Warner Bros. Theater, taking $800. While being returned to Sing Sing, he escaped in Grand Central Station. He was caught, yet his lawyers established that the peaceful nature of the escape, with Fredericks simply slipping out of his handcuffs, justified a light sentence. In Dannemora until 1930, Fredericks alledgedly shot and killed John Seiaminatta during a robbery. Magistrate Healey of the Homicide Court dropped the charge. By October 1935, while riding in an automobile, police arrested him for vagrancy. By now, Fredericks had married a twenty-two-year-old woman named Lillian.

The charge of vagrancy motivated Fredericks to assume a legitimate occupation. With the cooperation of his cousin, a Brooklyn business owner, Fredericks declared his occupation as a wastepaper buyer. The "job" was a front for his real job, which was living off the proceeds of prostitutes. He alone answered to both the top echelon of the pyramid as well as to the bottom levels.[11]

When Jimmy Fredericks and Abe Wahrman visited the madams, their threats were vague until they brought in their musclemen. Santos Chappie Selafani and Ralph the Pimp Liquori pulled the guns.

Ralph Liquori was a Brooklyn thug. He packed four revolvers in his car, then drove home to Sunday dinner. He once punched his girlfriend, Nancy Presser, in the stomach, then took her to his sister's house for the standard Sunday dinner of brachiole with gravy.[12]

Within the combination, the white-collar workers populated the strip across the street from the Women's Court. They were the unlicensed bondsmen and lawyers. Once vested with civil authority, they were now disgraced and disbarred. Meyer Berkman, a bondsman who controlled the dispensation of bail in the Women's Court, kept his office on 117 West 10th Street. In 1931, Judge Samuel Seabury had given the strip the notorious title of the West 10th Street Bar.[13] There, the bondsmen earned profits by reneging on bail money to released defendants. Bondsmen also advised a girl to either skip or remain for sentencing. If the girl skipped, they said she "took a bath." Although they hung around in suits and wore white collars, the bondsmen were important links in the combination, and reported each and every arrest to Little Davie Betillo and Jimmy Fredericks.[14]

Comprising the lowest levels of management were the bookers. The bookers placed girls in their assigned houses by working on telephones. The rotation ensured fresh faces and new girls per house. The bookers were the closest link the madams and prostitutes had to the rest of the combination. Yet, they were not advocates for girls or madams. They had their own struggles to survive.

The booking operations were passed down with the imprisonment or banishment of the bookies. Like a descending staircase, the bookies took the business as the one before him failed. The bookies controlled a spiral that coiled around the prostitution ring like rattlesnakes.

On the lowest level, the booking collectors squatted at the base of the pyramid. They were the men who showed up at the houses week after week. They collected the bonding fees for the bookers. Jo Jo Weintraub insisted on taking the punch cards kept by the girls to calculate their total number of customers per night.

The pyramid supported the hierarchy. The physicians who lived a double life of respectability while performing Monday morning

Wasserman tests, kept the girls and their customers as disease-free as possible. By 1934, the pyramid had a solid foundation on the dirt floor of New York's sporting nightlife. There, domestics kept things running smoothly. They were the maids who cleaned the apartments, the doormen who took the passwords and allowed the men to enter, and the security guards taking payoffs. These house guards acted as go-betweens to the local precinct bagmen. They also worked hand in hand with the other building personnel, like the janitors who maintained the buildings.

The rotating madams and prostitutes served the customers, universally known as johns. Their prurient desires, always met, lay at the core of the syndicate.

CHAPTER 5

SCANDAL IN THE WOMEN'S COURT

Did she offer?
– Vice cops to stoolpigeon, Chile Acuna

Within the walls of the Women's Court, a flawed legal system flourished. Its venue, the Jefferson Market Courthouse, called Old Jeff, was an architectural oddity. During its tenure as the Women's Court, it stayed out of range of the spirit, if not the letter, of the guiding principles of the American criminal justice system. It housed a deadly political machine, pilfering the earnings of both innocent and guilty as charged.

The building, designed in 1876 by Frederick C. Withers and Calvert Vaux, was a Victorian-Gothic structure with stained-glass windows, a brick-walled cellar, spires, and a bell tower. It loomed like a citadel over Sixth Avenue. Until 1932, open-air produce and dry goods vendors, in the market directly south of the building, mingled with police, prisoners, and judicial workers. Within the holding cells in the basement, beneath a claustrophobic row of brick archways, prisoners waited to face the magistrates. The top floor served as a jail until the 1934 completion of the Women's House of Detention, which was built directly south as an abutment.

The courthouse jurisdiction was originally established with the 1910 Inferior Criminal Courts Act, under pressure of reformers. The Inferior Criminal jurisdiction covered felonies and misdemeanors in the Family, Traffic, Night, Women's, Homicide, and Commercial Frauds courts.[1] From its inception, it was free to flourish under the political spoils system. For fees beginning at $10,000, the Mayor placed favorites from the district political clubs on the Magistrate bench. These judges allowed corrupt bondsmen, attorneys, and magistrates to prey upon the lives of women, both innocent and guilty.

Jefferson Market was the location of the Special Magistrates Courts. This was a network that included the Homicide, Family, Commercial Frauds, Traffic, and the notorious Women's Court. Within its purview, any woman charged with sex crimes or shoplifting was hauled in for arraignment. Women's crimes came under the banner of vagrancy, which covered a range of degenerate street activity. The court exercised summary jurisdiction over all of these types of cases. If the woman couldn't make bail, she was jailed on the top floor.

In 1930, Judge Samuel Seabury, acting on the mandate by Governor Franklin D. Roosevelt, launched an investigation into the Magistrates Court system. Judge Seabury was a Victorian-era descendant of the first U.S. Episcopalian Bishop. Like Roosevelt, Seabury was an avowed enemy of Tammany Hall. The investigation was officially initiated by the entry of an Order by the Appellate Division of the Supreme Court, 1st Judicial Department, designating Hon. Samuel Seabury as Referee.

During the two-year course of the investigation, intermittently called the Hofstadter Legislative Committee, Judge Seabury was instructed to send his findings directly to the Appellate. But the semi-retired judge showed his flamboyant side by taking the shocking stories to the press. In that way, he exposed gross injustices occurring daily in the Magistrate Courts. He referred to the system as the "only branch of the judicial arm of the government with which a large part of our population ever comes in contact. . . ." His findings resulted in a reform movement that exposed horrible corruption in the Women's Court.

The 1930 scandals involving Judiciary/Criminal Magistrates Courts culminated in "The New York City Investigation." Seabury began with the charge by the Appellate to investigate attorneys "practicing in Magistrates Courts, which are obstructive or harmful to the administration of justice or unjust or corrupt, unlawful, fraudulent, or unprofessional." Seabury was appointed on August 26, 1930. On September 29, 1930, the Bar Associations of Manhattan and the Bronx held a series of public hearings. They exposed the scandals in connection with the judiciary, especially criminal courts, which culminated in the investigations of the Magistrates Courts. They continued intermittently to May 14, 1931. On March 28, 1932, Seabury filed his final report with the Appellate Division.

Isidor J. Kresel, appointed to act "as counsel," was Judge Seabury's assistant. Kresel was appointed as Chief Counsel to investigate the Magistrates Courts of the First Judicial Department, which comprised Manhattan and the Bronx. He offered a window for the eloquent Judge to view the notorious underworld characters from the shadow world of vice squads and stoolpigeons. When a stoolpigeon went to Judge Seabury, Mr. Kresel greeted him.[2]

Chile Mapocha Acuna, the worst of the lot, knocked on Kresel's door early in 1930. A Chilean immigrant who had become friendly with detectives, he sold his services as a Spanish interpreter. He would gain local notoriety as "Chile Acuna, the Human Spitoona," after he found himself double-crossed by the vice squad. His retaliation, to turn himself in to Seabury's office, was only the beginning. He became not only the most notorious witness, but also a symbol of corruption that took a heavy human toll.

Chile explained the rackets to Isidor Kresel. His job description included a false name and address. Among his duties was taking a beating in a staged "arrest." He never went to court. He denied knowing the vice squad. He was angry after the vice squad, his former organization, kicked him out of the ring of lucrative extortion. In a scheme of revenge, he told all he knew. Chile outlined a scam of blackmailing women accused of prostitution. This unlawful system was in place as far back as 1913. He revealed an organized ring involving vice squad detectives,

Chile Acuna (New York Daily News)

bail bondsmen, magistrates, and paid procurers. Samuel Seabury later summed it up in the plain language that any layman could easily understand:

"The stool pigeon or the officer framed the woman, the officer arrested her, the bondsman bailed her out at an exorbitant charge, and usually recommended a lawyer; the lawyer gouged her savings and either himself, or through the bondsman, 'fixed' the arresting officer."[3]

The ring sought out women, often widowed or otherwise vulnerable, for legally sanctioned exploitation and blackmail. One scam was called the "landlady racket." The targets were subjected to home invasions by police officers, framed for prostitution, and held in their own apartments incommunicado until being brought to the police station on charges of "exposing one's person." They would be hustled off to Jefferson Market, where they were marched through the cavernous hallways and twisting stairwells. As the gothic architecture and stained glass windows leant the feeling of medieval castles and injustice, the innocent must have experienced raw terror. Although young and possibly virgin, the women were given a rough, routine gynecological exam, an invasive procedure prison doctors randomly performed on female prisoners.

One factor determined the woman's fate—her bankbook. If she was found to have financial assets, the magistrate ordered her held, pending payment of bail. This happened with no evidence presented to back up the charges.

These conspiracies were successful due to the cooperation of the magistrates in Women's Court. In scenes reminiscent of Salem witch trials, paid procurers, called stoolpigeons by the vice squad detectives, accused innocent women of offering themselves for money. Directly across the street, in the office on 117 W. 10th Street, the bail bondsmen hung out with vice squad officers and stoolpigeons. On this block, which was called the "West 10th Street Bar," attorneys and bondsmen lurked behind the heavy, black doors dotting the street in succession. In this illicit business, the bondsmen collected the money, and later paid everyone in the conspiracy. The web started at the top with the judges, working its way down to the lowest levels held by the stoolpigeons and vice squad police.

The vice squad was a glorified term for patrolmen who worked in plainclothes. Their main occupation was to investigate narcotics, liquor, gambling, and prostitution, with the emphasis on the latter two. The squad was divided into three groups and worked throughout the city on a roving basis, investigating complaints they received from Headquarters and precincts. The conspiracies were based on the work of a paid procurer. They billed each vice squad officer $35 per month, which was paid with city taxes.

A stoolpigeon instigated the frame-up by targeting a woman. Stoolpigeons on the payroll, in addition to Chile Acuna, were Louis "the Dove" Traube, "Harry the Greek," Meyer Slutsky, and Harry Levey. Acting alone, they went to the victim's apartment or office, with vice detectives stationed outside.

Chile Acuna worked in the "landlady racket." In this lucrative scam, the stoolpigeon would rent an apartment. He would either bring a woman with him into the room, in which case she would be arrested for prostitution, or he would stay there alone. He would place some money in full view and tell the police, who had just broken into the house, that the women were prostitutes. If they could snare two women, the maneuver would pay off "double." Judge Seabury's investigations revealed that innocent women, when surprised by these accusations of prostitution, were apt to become hysterical. On more than one occasion, women were brutally beaten into submission by arresting officers.

In addition to the "landlady racket," which took place in multiple dwellings and boardinghouses, the "doctor's office racket" framed the nurse in a doctor's office while the doctor was out. Medical workers were vulnerable because after Chile entered, he would take off his shirt on the pretext of needing to see the doctor. He made sure to place the sum of $15 in cash in full view.

The vice squad police officers, with precise timing, would enter next. They would address Chile by saying, "Did she offer?"

"Yes, sir, she did."

"Did you pay?"

"Yes, sir," said Chile Acuna, pointing to $15, in bills, stacked on the table or desk. The vice detectives then placed the woman under arrest.

The other kind of racket, aimed at known prostitutes, was a variation on the "direct hit," which involved a vice detective, who would make the woman an explicit proposition. If she agreed, she was arrested. In the police station, as the woman was never arraigned in court, a fixer arrived. The fixer promised to pay off the judge. After the woman emptied her purse, and often her bank account, the fixer then absconded, leaving the woman destitute.

Judge Seabury condemned the practice of precinct arraignment, which allowed the bondsman, summoned by a phone call from Chile Acuna, to initiate a $500 bail bond, which was higher than the legally established rate. During the proceedings, the woman was held incommunicado, so none of her family members, friends, or colleagues knew where she was or what had happened.

The magistrate, who was in on the conspiracy, would free her on the $500 bond. The bondsman, by now her savior, would take her home to get her bankbook. The victim was told to write a check to the firm name of Treibitz & Steiner. Treibitz, one of the partners in the firm set up for the purpose of bilking the women, would take the check to the bank in the company of the woman. Together, they would execute an assignment of her bankbook. The woman was told this was to "fix the case."

Sometimes, the bail bondsman would find out the victim had more money than originally thought. In that case, the case went back to court where the magistrate expanded the charges, which necessitated higher bail and additional monies turned over to the court. The case went to an attorney, who took his fee. The rest was divided between the vice squad police, prosecutor, bondsman, and magistrate.

The victim was told she was not entitled to her own counsel, and that the sure way to fix the case would be through the court's attorneys. Were she free to do so, she'd only have to cross the street. Arranged in a tacky row adjacent to the Women's Court were the blackened doorways to the West 10th Street Bar—a lineup of offices for lawyers and bondsmen. The most notorious location was 117 W. 10th Street, housing Abraham "Abe" Karp. Though later disbarred, Karp would remain in the Women's Court as a "private" lawyer to madams like Peggy Wild. He got at least one-half of the cases that went through the Women's Court, sharing space with the bondsmen. The offices served as a hangout for the stool-pigeons and vice detectives, who passed the time by playing cards, while waiting for the victims to be brought in.

The payoff came in at the moment the conspirators took the woman back into court. If everyone had gotten paid, the lawyer would tell the prosecutor, "This one is okay." That was shorthand for dismissal, because the stoolpigeon wouldn't testify, and the arresting officer would develop amnesia. Everybody concurred in a hands-down agreement of innocence. The victim then left the Jefferson Market building, her money stolen by the well-oiled machinery of the Women's Court.[4]

The other scenario involved victims who didn't pay. The shortfall, whether through poverty or mere unwillingness to hand over the bank-book, resulted in a swift conviction. Seabury also uncovered the disturbing fact that innocent girls were being sentenced to the New York State Reformatory for Women at Bedford Hills, known in 1931 as the Bedford Reformatory. The Committee of 14's records showed an alarming number of girls were "duly charged with being a wayward minor, who has been willfully disobedient to the reasonable and lawful commands of her parents and in danger of becoming morally depraved in violation of Section 913-a of the Code of Criminal Procedure." Judge Seabury determined that from 1923 to 1930, a total of seventy-seven girls were committed without "competent evidence presented at a hearing." Those who were spared the ordeal of Bedford Hills, were incarcerated in the House of the Good Shepherd, a Brooklyn home for wayward girls and unwed mothers.[5]

The Committee of 14 looked the other way. They even praised the high conviction rate. But Isidor J. Kresel contradicted the Committee of 14 when he said, "What I am criticizing is the supineness of the Magistrates in the face of palpably perjurious testimony by police officers."[6]

The victimization wasn't simply male-on-female. One of the main conspirators was Magistrate Jean H. Norris, an attorney appointed on October 27, 1919 to become New York City's first female judge. She was co-leader of the Tenth Assembly District, and owed her appointment to her Democratic Party affiliations. Insiders said that her cultivated diction masked a nasal Brooklyn accent. Norris had the highest conviction and harshest sentencing rate based on uncorroborated testimony. In short, she was a hypocrite. When cornered, she ordered the transcripts changed to hide the facts. Judge Seabury established her pattern of abuses.

Norris put women on trial immediately, without a warrant or contact with the outside world. She had an astounding rate of convictions. Presiding from 1920 until she was placed on trial in June 1931, Judge Norris was convicted by the Appellate of prejudicing the rights of defendants, and exploiting her judicial position for private interests. After Norris' 1931 removal, the magistrate denied knowing that police used stoolpigeons.[7]

When Chile Acuna picked out the plainclothes cops he'd known intimately, James "Jimmie" Quinlivan's activities came to light. Quinlivan had appeared many times before Magistrate Norris, who "never thought a policeman lied." Quinlivan, like other vice cops, regularly forgot to bring the "green sheet" to court, a discretion that Jean Norris never noticed. The green sheet was a written report made by police officers promptly after an arrest, and was witnessed by the Desk Lieutenant.

When the officer took the stand, the story was supposed to match the information listed on the green sheet. While police always forgot their original entries, magistrates like Norris routinely ignored the discrepancy. Typewritten reports were never required by commanding officers. There was no paper trail.

Jean Norris acted along with Magistrates Earl Smith, H. Stanley Renaud, and Jesse Silbermann. The prosecutor had a hand in the conspiracies, also. John C. Weston was a prosecutor who for eight years, was paid from $25 to $150 by the West 10th Street Bar for each case he agreed to "lay down," or dismiss.

Weston threw out six hundred cases during his tenure. An ex-process server who became an assistant district attorney, his file revealed he'd written only one report in eight years.

Under oath, Weston named twenty-one lawyers involved in the procurement ring. Judge Seabury confiscated his bankbook and discovered between $20,000 to $40,000 in undocumented deposits.

Two police officers with the most glaring record for undocumented deposits, Officers Quinlivan and O'Connor were dismissed from the Department. Jennie the Factory Fischer, a madam who hated the vice cops, testified that they'd taken payoffs from her on a regular basis. While Jennie was a known informer who hated cops, other madams balked at the subpoenas that appeared at their nefarious doorsteps.[8]

Polly Adler, the famous parlor madam, was implicated by John Weston's revelations. Adler was a madam who enjoyed high celebrity status during the wild and roaring '20s. Born in Russia on April 16, 1900, and named simply "Pearl," she immigrated to the United States at the age of twelve. A cagey immigrant with poor English, she settled with family friends in the East New York section of Brooklyn. Unwanted and sleeping on a couch, Polly found comfort in pretty things. She loved to "walk the avenue," a local expression for shopping. She enjoyed seeing the Blake Avenue pushcarts, overflowing with things she couldn't afford to buy. Yet, she hated the Pitkin Avenue sweatshops, where she worked for pennies. Like so many young girls of the era, she wanted something more. She would board the "A" train at the Shepherd Avenue subway station, riding hopefully through Brooklyn and lower Manhattan into Times Square. By the age of seventeen, Pearl was hanging out with the playboys and racketeers of the theater district. She lived a classic double life. At night, she returned to her couch in East New York, pretending she'd spent the day in the garment sweatshop. But Polly was already arranging deals between gangsters and showgirls. As her reputation grew, Polly went out and about town in a high-profile gesture of self-promotion. She ran into problems with other madams, like Peggy Wild and Jennie the Factory Fischer, who sabotaged her with pranks. Polly never joined the network of madams, preferring to live as a mainstream figure of notoriety. Like Texas Guinan, Polly chose fame. Those madams who worked under the blanket of an underground name and persona despised her. Yet, she was unstoppable.

Polly's fame crashed with the stock market in 1929. The Depression lessened the public's zest for excess. In spite of her former glory, she was demoted by the public to a dirty commodity. The Committee of 14 made her a major object of its investigations. By 1931, she was being called a "woman with fourteen arrests" in the press. With her reputation blighted and business running underground, she received a subpoena from Judge Seabury. In disgrace, Prosecutor John Weston had told Seabury that lawyers Emmanuel Busch and Abe Karp had paid him each time Polly was arrested. Although many of her arrests had been under other names, she was found in the docket books to have been arrested at least twice under her own name.

In 1928, Adler had paid John Weston $50 for a quick release. During the trial of the disgraced Women's Court attorneys, Weston was interrogated. He was asked why he so meekly allowed the charges to "lay down."

"I was afraid of her influence," Weston said.

"Do you mean you were afraid you would be removed as prosecutor in the court?"

"More than that," Weston replied, intimating that Adler's political influence extended into Tammany Hall.

For six months in 1931, Polly played the artful dodger game by hiding in Havana. She returned in August to face the music, and surrendered to Judge Seabury in the company of a process server.

Polly was discovered to be the joint owner of stocks along with Irwin O'Leary, a suspended vice squad officer. O'Leary, a father of four children, had met Polly in a nightclub. They became friends and business associates in a symbiotic way of mutual use—each helped the other launder money. They were privy to each other's bank accounts and often made deposits and withdrawals in the other's name. Their arrangement was an illegal facsimile of power of attorney over the other's affairs. As "Maurice Adler," she purchased with O'Leary, fifteen shares of Anaconda Copper stock, the paperwork of which was found in O'Leary's "tin box."[9]

On November 29, 1930, Police Commissioner Edward Mulrooney dismantled the vice squad by demoting twenty-eight policemen. A mere slap on the wrist, he returned the men to ordinary duty. Sometimes these demotions were accompanied by a transfer to another precinct, or a lost day's wages. Charges were made against thirty-five police officers. On March 4, 1931, William O'Connor and James "Jimmie" Quinlivan were dismissed from the Department.[10] One month prior to their conviction, a vice witness was found strangled in Van Cortlandt Park in the Bronx. Vivian Gordon was found entangled in a rope that was twisted several times around her neck. When her body was found, in the early morning hours of February 26, she was clothed. Her lifeless fingers still clutched at the rope. Her body gave signs of having been dragged for several blocks.

A prostitute, she was the daughter of John Franklin, who worked as a corrections officer in the Illinois State Prison at Joliet. She had a history of arrests, one for attempted extortion. She was a three-time loser, having been incarcerated at Bedford State Reformatory for Women three times between 1923 and 1926. Her maiden name, Benita Franklin, had changed with her marriage to John Bischoff some years earlier. She gave birth to a daughter, Benita, who would go on to commit suicide two weeks after her mother's murder.

Police found Vivian's diary in her apartment. Within its pages, she listed several names, fearing that one or all of them might kill her. Vivian Gordon had been framed in 1923 by vice cop Patrolman Andrew J. McLaughlin and Sergeant William A. Haake. She was one in a legion of underground vice characters to haunt the office of Isidor Kresel. As she prepared to go before the Seabury Investigation, she was murdered. In hindsight, Judge Seabury called the two cops involved in the 1923 frame-up to go before the grand jury.

The multitude of men, and her rich history of involvement in swindles, made it difficult to connect the murder to the Seabury Investigation. The men in her diary ranged from easy dates to co-defendants and victims. One, Joseph Radlow, had been the plaintiff in the extortion charges against Gordon dating back to 1930. Others, considered casual acquaintances, were questioned and released. A Puerto Rican man named "Keno," and his pal, Harold Doman, had been out on the town with Vivian days before her murder. In her diary, she described the evening.

"We had two old-fashioned cocktails—Broadway Itch Place, 135 West 45 St.—Ye gods—nothing but gangsters there."[11]

The 1930 scandals involving the Criminal Magistrates Courts had started the "New York City Investigation." The scandals and their aftermath became wedged in the public's imagination as "Seabury," a catch phrase for the era.

Judge Samuel Seabury made changes but ultimately failed to reinvent the wheel. When the Seabury Investigation shut the door for the last time on June 1, 1932, the Women's Court was still controlled by crooked bondsmen and lawyers. But his legendary findings would dye the fabric of New York politics and pave the way for a decade of reform.

CHAPTER 6

THE LAW TAKES POLLY ADLER

I never got involved in a Mann Act case.
— Polly Adler

In the aftermath of the Seabury Investigation, the Women's Court at Jefferson Market expanded to include the new Women's House of Detention. As it started construction, the old marketplace was bulldozed. By 1934, the Women's House of "D" towered as a modern abutment to the Victorian courthouse. With the demise of the open-air market, the medieval ambiance of Jefferson Market was challenged. The new jail was an ugly, monolithic hellhole. The Sixth Avenue el, its trains screaming past the discordant buildings, showered soot onto the street already littered with disrepute.[1]

There were other, bigger changes in New York. The new fusion mayor, Republican Fiorello LaGuardia, replaced Jimmy Walker after his disastrous resignation. The dapper Beau James, popular and handsome, could not survive the scandals dredged up by Judge Seabury. Replacing Walker, LaGuardia was a workhorse with a utilitarian ethic. LaGuardia's municipal viewpoint, to rein in corruption, was compatible with Depression reform movements.[2] LaGuardia armed himself with a small army of untouchable police officials. As part of the new reforms, Fiorello LaGuardia brought Lewis J. Valentine in as the new police commissioner. An honest cop who had raided Tammany's gambling dens, he'd been kicked out to a Queens precinct in retaliation during Mayor Jimmy Walker's administration. He returned from exile triumphantly. One of the new commissioner's first moves was to transfer over two hundred vice cops out of their precincts and away from their nest eggs.[3]

LaGuardia picked up the pieces of the Seabury era. In doing so, he convinced the Board of City Magistrates to appoint a grand jury in March 1935. Through the municipal bravado, LaGuardia sensed that Judge Seabury's techniques, if repeated, would be political poison. Seabury had conducted an intrusive reign of terror. With his burrowing into cash boxes and private lives, Judge Seabury had threatened people's privacy. The tin box, a catch phrase describing hidden political spoils, hit close to home. After all, who didn't have some cash hidden under the mattress, or an extramarital dalliance to keep hidden? The Seabury investigations had threatened every man's sense of entitlement.

In the Roaring Twenties, everybody knew a butcher, a baker, and a bootlegger. The Depression that heralded in the 1930s lessened the national threshold for frivolity. The demotion of Polly Adler from parlor madam to smut queen was a case in point. LaGuardia wanted to run the madam out of town.

While Polly Adler and Peggy Wild had been equally successful as madams to the underworld, the politicians, and the show biz crowd, the Depression changed Wild's fortunes. Peggy fell into running the $2 houses. On a downward spiral, she claimed to prefer the new arrangement. Polly Adler, though, had stayed on top of her game. The former hostess to Dutch Schultz was as big as ever. Former boxing world champion Mickey Walker called her the "Queen Madam." "In my book, she is a real champ. She was a sharp businesswoman, a financial brain. You had to be somebody to go there, and you had to pay plenty, no matter who you were or how well you knew her."

Polly's troubles, which had died down after Seabury, were resurrected on March 5, 1935. She was doing business at her fashionable address on 30 E. 55th Street. On that day, District Attorney William Copeland Dodge issued a warrant for her arrest. The district attorney was a Tammany Hall Democratic, backed by district leader James Hines. With the new administration cracking down on the old order, Dodge needed to make an example—and Polly made a fine one.

Police arrested her for prostitution and tore her place apart. They found a stash of lewd films, and charged her with possession. Dodge announced that he would push Polly Adler before the grand jury. On March 14, her attorney, Samuel J. Siegel, told Assistant District Attorney Maurice Wahl that Polly would not sign a waiver of immunity. The move would cost her time in jail.[4]

While Adler's arrest was significant, a deeper stab at vice reform came with the sudden arrest of Nick Montana on May 25. Montana was the most important booker in the city. As such, the tabloids quickly christened him the "Vice Czar" of New York. Yet, the most crucial maneuver in the anti-vice crusade was coming. The arrest of Cockeyed Louie Weiner had shock wave repercussions. Weiner, the subject of wiretapping back in 1931 when he'd operated in Coney Island, was booking from 146 Rivington Street.

The sensational vice arrests cast a spotlight on the court system. Courtrooms were clogged with Tammany appointees. From the judge to the janitor, it seemed everybody had gotten their job through political connections. This included the appointment as second clerk of Municipal Court in the Second District for Nunzio "Harry" Lanza, the brother of downtown labor racketeer Joe "Socks" Lanza. The vital family connection was "Duke" Viggiano, a Tammany Hall leader, who was reputedly the brother-in-law of Socks Lanza.[5]

As Socks Lanza's family connections went public, one courtroom figure managed to remain in the shadows. Abe Karp, the covert defense attorney in the Women's Court, was disbarred and dismissed in 1934. Yet, he remained in there, working behind the scenes. In this underground position, Karp continued to supply each prostitute with an alibi to recite to the judge. The list of excuses was predictable. The woman said

Polly Adler (New York Daily News)

she was "visiting from Pennsylvania," or something similar.

While fighting the lewd possession charges, Polly Adler had to take the heat for the Justice Department's pursuit of Mann Act convictions. The Mann Act, a 1910 Act of Congress known informally as the "white slave law," was applied when minors were transported across state lines for purposes of engaging in prostitution. Yet, Adler denied she'd ever engaged in interstate trafficking.

"I never got involved in a Mann Act case. But, of course, I was always under scrutiny by the federal men," she insisted.

In March, three weeks after Adler's arrest, J. Edgar Hoover visited New York City. There, his presence added new pressures to the embattled William Dodge. Under Hoover's coercion, Dodge agreed to exchange information on local vice offenders, to augment Hoover's interstate "white slave" investigations.

Polly Adler went on trial two weeks later on charges of possessing indecent motion pictures and maintaining a disorderly house. A Special Sessions probation officer, May Mangan presented her findings. Two women arrested as prostitutes with Adler, Eve Acosta and Dorothy Walker, were convicted of vagrancy and released. On April 16, Adler entered a guilty plea to possessing a motion picture machine with lewd films in her E. 55th Street apartment. She then withdrew her plea, which meant she would stand trial on the lewd pictures charge. On May 11, under the name of Joan Martin, Adler was sentenced to a $500 fine and thirty days in the House of Detention by Justices McIneny, Murphy, and Rayfiel in Special Sessions. She served twenty-four days in jail. On her release day, a member of the Committee of 14 approached her.

"I've watched your disgusting career for years," the Committee member declared. "Is there no way to stop you from forcing young girls into a life of shame?"[6]

But Polly Adler's troubles weren't over. One week after her release, she was rearrested as a procurer on a Chicago warrant by the police of the W. 68th Street Station in New York, after trying to collect a money order for $1,250. The Internal Revenue Service made a claim the following week for $16,181 in back taxes.[7] The $1,250 that the police had seized upon her arrest was attached by the I.R.S. on the basis that she failed to pay income taxes for the years 1927 to 1930. In July, Adler was cleared of procurement charges, which prompted Commissioner Valentine to accuse Dodge of giving Adler preferential treatment.

Dodge's reinvention of himself at Adler's expense came back to haunt him. The gutsy madam released a statement that Dodge and his politician friends were in her little black book. Dodge quickly denied this accusation, saying, "There is only one name in there that I recognized or knew anything about, and he is a movie actor."

As Dodge came increasingly under fire, Samuel Marcus, counsel for the Society for the Prevention of Crime, announced that Dodge had let the vice inquiry die. Dodge panicked. Under pressure from Lehman, Dodge appointed Marcus as an assistant special prosecutor. Yet, when push came to shove, Marcus agreed that there was little to back up indictments. "As to the policy and other rackets, there is direct and positive evidence, but as yet there is lacking that legal evidence sufficient to indict and convict the 'higher-ups,'" said Marcus. "In my opinion, it will be forthcoming, but you must be patient." Within weeks after the grand jury commenced, the City Affairs Committee advised Governor Lehman that Dodge's investigation into vice and policy was a lead balloon.

St. Patrick's Day was a day traditionally put aside for hailing the Irish city officials. But no sooner was the green stripe painted down Fifth Avenue, than the Chairman of the City Affairs Committee, John Holmes, publicly criticized Dodge.

To counter, Dodge prosecuted an underworld doctor who worked as an abortionist for Nick Montana. This physician combined Wasserman tests with illegal procedures to terminate pregnancy. The doctor was sentenced to three years in prison. The conviction failed to mollify Dodge's enemies. Both The New York Bar and The New York County Lawyers Association handed him his walking papers, which came in the form of a single list, containing six names.[8] One of the men named on the list was about to take over his responsibility for supervising the grand jury.

The removal of Dodge from the grand jury caused City Hall pundits to announce another nail in the coffin of Tammany Hall.

In July 1935, Thomas E. Dewey was thirty-four years old, and, in spite of his one-year tenure in private practice at 120 Broadway, carried a name that struck fear and trepidation into the hearts of the underworld.

Special Prosecutor Thomas E. Dewey
(Author's Collection)

In short, he was despised. In his new position, he stood alone, which removed the security blanket he'd felt as assistant to Federal Prosecutor George Medalie.

Governor Lehman gave Dewey three-quarters of the fourteenth floor of the Woolworth Building, at 233 Broadway, one block south of City Hall. In what would be called a general rackets investigation, the new special prosecutor was given a budget for seventy-six employees.

Dewey brought his staff

together quickly. These men and one woman would remain with him throughout the 1930s. In hiring, Dewey borrowed the methods of J. Edgar Hoover. Dewey wanted his white-collar law enforcers to emulate the G-Man mystique that Hoover had used so evocatively in Washington, in the pursuit of the Midwestern Public Enemies John Dillinger and Baby Face Nelson. Yet, Hoover's model, transposed to a New York City setting, would undergo some radical changes, the most glaring of which was demographics. In Dewey's office, there would be graduates of the Ivy League, such as Barent Ten Eyck, Murray I. Gurfein, and William B. Herlands. Dewey would also hire applicants from New York University Law School, which attracted the self-taught, adult children of working-class, Jewish immigrants. Sol Gelb got his first law office job by going from office to office, offering to work for nothing. "I figure, if you're any good, they'll pay you." Dewey next hired NYU graduate Jacob J. Rosenblum, the son of an Orchard Street storekeeper. "Jack" Rosenblum had worked as a law clerk and knew the job from the ground up.

Bypassing race, color, or creed, the major criteria was one's total allegiance to Dewey's anti-Tammany platform. Dewey, who anticipated a prosecution of James J. Hines, sought assurance that the applicants had no allegiance to Tammany Hall. Frank Hogan once recalled his job interview in 1935, when he first applied for a position in Dewey's office. "In less than an hour, he raked me fore and aft with questions, held me up to the light, put me under a microscope, and turned me inside out," Hogan recalled.[9]

In a further departure from an elitist, white-only staff, Dewey retained Eunice Roberta Hunton Carter in August 1935. Distinguished as the first female, African American district attorney, Carter had been a Women's Court prosecutor under Dodge. Among the staff members in Dodge's soon-to-be-dismantled office, Eunice Carter was known for her honest interpretation of the law. As a young woman, she had graduated *cum laude* from Smith. She ran for the Republican Fusion Ticket for the Assembly in 1934, and was defeated by a small number of votes. Although it was a loss, it pushed her into the public eye. When a violent riot erupted in Harlem in 1935, LaGuardia appointed Carter as Secretary of a committee on conditions in Harlem. Yet Carter, perceived as an elitist, was challenged by African American groups. She was accused of being in "no position to judge the condition of the man in the street, for [she] is not hard up." This must have stung the aspiring Black activist.

From there, she joined Dodge's staff, where she was appointed to the Women's Court. In juggling her private life, which included her marriage to dentist Lisle C. Carter, she bore a son, Lisle, Jr. After her appointment to Dewey's crime-busting team, she would send her son to live safely in Barbados. Dewey's plan for Eunice Carter was to put her inside knowledge of Harlem to use in the policy investigations of Dutch Schultz.[10]

Raised in Michigan within the honeycomb of a conservative, Republican old family, Dewey had worked in 1931 as chief assistant attorney to George Medalie for the Southern District of New York.

Mrs. Eunice Carter, Assistant District Attorney
(NY Public Library)

Much of his crime-busting work before 1933 had developed out of Judge Seabury's revelations of corporate graft and payoffs. Thomas Dewey rode on the coattails of the Seabury Investigation's findings. At no time was this more apparent than in 1931, when Dewey prosecuted vice cop James J. "Jimmie" Quinlivan, on the take since 1915. Judge Seabury had uncovered Quinlivan's tin box, a safe deposit box that held thousands of dollars in cash. The tin box stood as a symbol for the era of municipal reform that heralded Dewey's debut in New York City.

Dewey's first move, once his staff was assembled, was to assemble two extraordinary grand juries. They would replace Dodge's grand jury, whose members were going to be dismissed. In spite of the initial opposition of a Tammany-based lawsuit imposed to stop municipal funds from being used for the investigation, the two extraordinary grand juries began replacing Dodge's panel.

Vice Czar Nick Montana went to trial late in 1935. He would go through two trials before being taken off the streets. Montana's trial revealed that detectives had taken stenographic notes of wiretapped conversations between Montana, madams, and underworld doctors. Witness Hugo Harris, a detective, testified that Montana's attorney, Alexander Klahr, tried to bribe him with $1,000 a month for permission to operate. Montana's first jury deliberated for twenty-one hours and on November 17, came back deadlocked.

After a second trial held the following month, Montana was convicted by the second jury to hear the evidence. He was sentenced on January 7 to twenty-five years for compulsory prostitution. A second offender, he cried hopelessly as he was led away. He needn't have bothered. Montana would win a reduced sentence on appeal. As Nick Montana was processed in Auburn prison, his bonding business was swept up by the jovial real estate agent, Jack Eller. A man with a wide smile and an easy manner, Eller had been sleeping on Montana's couch after his real estate ventures failed in the Depression. He was well liked in the prostitution business, and many of the madams felt he was too sweet for it. Jack Eller's descent into vice would cause him bitter regret.[11]

Cockeyed Louie Weiner was next sentenced to 5-10 years for compulsory prostitution. His son, Al, took over the business. His father had amassed a file of wiretapped conversations dating back to his Coney Island ventures. In 1931, Weiner sent girls to madams Jennie the Factory and Sadie the Chink. Unknown to him at the time, the two madams were acting as informers, and served the Seabury Investigation by telling what they knew.

Both women were hated by crooked vice cops, who considered them dangerous. Jennie the Factory had "put a policeman in jail before," said Seabury witness Harry Levey. He called the middle-aged Jennie "very dangerous" for refusing to let the vice cops hide behind her skirts. In 1931, Jennie acted as a state witness in the vice trial against vice cops Jimmie Quinlivan and his partner, William O'Connor. She testified that the two had taken $150 a week for protection from arrest. Levey, the taxi driver who collected the money, had initially begged the madam to deny the graft. He pleaded with the madam. "I can go to jail for twenty years."

"You been turning my place over for years," was Jennie's retort.

"If I find out you are a stoolpigeon with Jimmie, I'll fix you."

On Jennie's testimony, Quinlivan was convicted of income tax evasion and sentenced to three years in a federal prison.[12]

Convictions such as these validated the charge of income tax evasion. Encouraged by the Quinlivan victory, Dewey indicted Arthur "Dutch Schultz" Flegenheimer. The underworld grapevine insisted that Schultz wanted to kill Dewey. According to Frank Costello, Schultz felt that Dewey was going to make the big difference in bringing down the important members of the policy, gambling, and drug empires shared by the underworld bosses.[13]

Included in Dewey's groundbreaking indictments would be Irving "Waxy Gordon" Wexler and John Thomas "Legs" Diamond.

Legs Diamond, who was independent and disliked by members of organized crime, had survived many attempts to kill him. He was cornered while sleeping off a drunken celebration after an acquittal. His killers entered his room in a rooming house in Albany on December

18, 1931. They held the "clay pigeon" down to make sure his head got enough bullets to cause his death. His body was returned to his sister-in-law's house in Maspeth, Queens. In death, as in life, Diamond caused trouble. Both his family's frame home, and that of a neighbor who was also waking a relative, had large wreaths on the front doors. The bereaved neighbor, already in a poor state of mind, became hysterical when strangers came to her door, hoping to get a glimpse of the late Legs Diamond.[14]

As was typical in Dewey's pecking order, the death of one mob boss cleared the path for another specimen to go under the microscope. Waxy Gordon, known as the Beer Baron, had been indicted by the Federal Government in 1934 with a tax lien against his company, the Harrison Beverage Company, in Harrison, New Jersey. It was his "legit business" and one that he started with funding from Arnold Rothstein. The federal lien, which closed the brewery, hoped to attach the Beer Baron for the sum of $286,104.90 for the years 1927 to 1931.

Gordon's trial, in November 1933, lasted one month. He was sentenced to ten years in the Atlanta Federal Penitentiary, and fined $80,000.[15] A tragedy occurred when Wexler's son, Theodore, rushed to New York to beg for a lighter sentence for his father. Theodore was killed in a traffic accident. In a departure from policy, Dewey allowed Wexler to attend the funeral before going to Leavenworth.

With Gordon convicted, Dewey planned to pursue his nemesis, Dutch Schultz. He had tried to indict Schultz in 1933 while on Medalie's staff. According to Dewey, "He simply stayed in hiding until our group no longer occupied the United States Attorney's office."

CHAPTER 7

A "REAL" CRIME

How did you like the baby I sent you . . . did you make any money?
—Louie Weiner

Before Dutch Schultz controlled the Harlem policy rackets, they were the province of the African Americans who lived in Harlem. In the years before Prohibition, the numbers were run by an insular group of bankers, who hired their own friends to work as runners. The era was self-contained, with runners wearing a special button—in case of arrest, the button meant immunity. The bankers set the number for the day. Players wrote their bet on a slip of paper, paying bets that started at one cent. Odds were six hundred to one. To win was profitable, so bankers often staged fake raids to avoid paying. Stephanie St. Clair, an African American woman who had a role in the policy racket, told the Seabury investigators of several magistrates on her payroll. Yet, St. Clair's role was overlooked by Seabury while other bankers were discovered in the Seabury investigations to be making huge profits.[1]

Dutch Schultz forced the runners to work for African American bankers under his control. The runners would work for Schultz, unaware their boss was Caucasian. As backer of Schultz, the powerful Tammany district leader James J. Hines exploited the slums of Harlem. Hines had attended the 1932 Chicago Convention with Frank Costello and went against Tammany Hall in backing Franklin D. Roosevelt for president. Yet, he didn't grace his constituents with the promised chicken in every pot. He didn't care about the NRA, or Roosevelt's proposed New Deal. As a politician, Hines distorted the idea of liberal government. In his eyes, government meant political spoils for all groups living in his district. Yet, he backed Roosevelt, going against Mayor Jimmy Walker's favored candidate, Governor Alfred E. Smith.[2]

He partnered with Richard "Dixie" Davis, an attorney practicing in the Harlem Magistrates Court. Davis created a policy combination that put the African American policy bankers out of business. He gave bail bondsmen the power to favor Schultz's men, an act that allowed the Dutchman to control Harlem. By 1933, Schultz was collecting millions a year from the Harlem policy racket.[3] As a prosecutor working for George Medalie, Dewey went to Federal Judge John C. Knox for a warrant for Schultz and his lieutenants, Henry "Sailor" Stevens, Frank Ahearn, and George "Yarlas" Yarlasavetsky. The federal indictments were based on charges that Schultz concealed an income of more than $100,000 since 1929. George Medalie also asked for bench warrants, which would grant jurisdiction in the case of an out-of-state arrest.

Dewey managed to subpoena Abe "Bo" Weinberg, later killed on orders of Dutch Schultz. Members of the underworld attributed the death of Bo Weinberg to Schultz personally. Before his unsolved murder, Weinberg served sixty days for contempt. On November 28, 1934, Schultz surrendered in Albany. The following year, Schultz went on trial in Syracuse on charges of unreported taxable income. After a hung jury, the trial was rescheduled for Malone, a town on the Canadian border. On August 1, 1935, Schultz was acquitted. Dewey then positioned himself as the new bounty hunter who would bring Schultz to New York City in chains. Throughout the thwarted hunt for Schultz, Dewey remained solid in his vow to indict James Hines. This came to a grinding halt when Schultz was killed in a contract slaying by Charlie "the Bug" Workman at the Palace Chophouse in Newark, New Jersey, on October 23, 1935.

The death of Dutch Schultz caused a shift in priorities downtown at 233 Broadway. The Harlem policy racket squad was temporarily suspended. Dewey's investigation into the restaurant racket, a method of waiter intimidation forged by racketeers under Schultz, remained open. But the gangster's death had the effect of propelling Dewey into Luciano's orbit.

Ironically, Luciano was reputedly part of the mob that ordered the hit on Schultz. While Luciano knew that would focus Dewey on his own activities, he felt immune to prosecution. Luciano, who played golf in Hot Springs, Arkansas, sharing the golf course with Jimmy Hines and Owney Madden since the latter's recent release from prison, might have believed he was above the law.[4]

Dewey pursued high-profile criminals. In so many ways, he had modeled himself and his mission statement after the Justice Department's rising star, J. Edgar Hoover. Hoover had risen to national attention in the Dillinger campaign. Dewey, who hoped to run for a New York State political office, took a similar route.

As Hines shielded Schultz in Harlem, Luciano enjoyed the protection of Tammany Hall politician Albert Marinelli. Dewey nursed a desire to take Marinelli out of the office of District Leader, and later, Clerk of New York County, positions achieved through voter fraud and intimidation. Dewey sought to thwart Marinelli through investigations into the racketeer he aided, Lucky Luciano. It would be several years before Dewey would have the evidence he needed to accuse Marinelli of being the friend of "thugs, thieves, and big-shot racketeers."[5]

Back in 1929, during the first administration of Mayor James J. Jimmy Walker, an event in the Bronx called attention to the links between Tammany Hall politicians and organized crime figures. In the Bronx restaurant Roman Gardens, on Southern Boulevard, Magistrate Albert H. Vitale, the leader of the local Tammany organization, the Tepecano Democratic Club, held a fund-raiser attended by Ciro "Artichoke King" Terranova. One guest was ex-Magistrate Michael N. Delagi. During the course of the evening, six masked robbers held up the place and collected $2,000 in cash and another $2,500 in jewelry. During the stick-up, the bandits stole Detective Arthur C. Johnson's service revolver. Johnson was a guest at the dinner. Yet, nobody tried to notify the authorities. Vitale then made a few phone calls. All the stolen merchandise was returned to him.

Word on the grapevine said the robbery was staged because one of the guests, a Chicago gunman, was holding a murder contract, and the robbery was a ruse for retrieving it.

Formal investigations revealed that Vitale had associated with Legs Diamond when the controversial gangster had acted as bodyguard to Arnold Rothstein. Sources said that Vitale, in the company of Ciro Terranova, had met Rothstein and Diamond in the Swanee Club and Joe Ward's Uptown Club at 253 W. 125th Street.

Reports later attenuated this claim, saying Vitale wasn't there at the same time as Rothstein and Diamond. Yet, Arnold Rothstein, murdered the year before, had loaned $19,600 to Vitale. In spite of the innuendo, Police Commissioner Whalen finally cleared Vitale of having been in the Swanee Club with Legs Diamond. From then on, Vitale's activities were publicized only when he gave a break to the little guy. A gypsy fortuneteller, or a store-theft suspect, could expect to get clemency from Vitale.[6]

"Uncle" Albert Marinelli was involved in the incident that brought Vitale to citywide notoriety. Marinelli, an Italian, had burst into the Irish bastion of Tammany Hall when Luciano ordered the Irish politicians to accept Marinelli as an alderman.

A Brooklyn alderman, or district leader, Marinelli was one of the few Tammany leaders to be elected to public office along with LaGuardia. He was born on the eastside, one of seven children of Michael Marinelli, who arrived in the States as an immigrant in 1872. Young Al became a mover and shaker in the neighborhood. He did favors for the local Italian immigrants, and asked that they become naturalized and vote the Tammany ticket. His quota of votes grew, as did his stature, both in the neighborhood and at the local political club. He continued his step up the ladder to the American dream by marrying a girl from the west side. The couple had a daughter and sent her to a Catholic school. Marinelli continued to rise in stature and became a port warden in 1921, receiving a salary to examine damaged boats and make reports in New York Harbor. His first election was in 1931, when he was elected alderman from the second district for a salary of $5,000 a year.

The November 1933 election catapulted Marinelli to the post of New York County Clerk and leader of the Second Assembly District West, which covered the downtown area south of 14th Street, a post he shared with an Irishman, Christopher D. Sullivan. The area encompassed the Fulton Street Fish Market, under Socks Lanza, with three hundred people working in the political machine.

Tammany Hall hailed Marinelli's victory, garnered with 4,534 fraudulent votes. Thugs had intimidated voters with blackjacks, pipes, brass knuckles, lead pipes, bricks, stones, and hob-nailed boots. Marinelli, a known associate of Frank Costello and Luciano, maintained his office at 225 Lafayette Street. He shared the building with the Five Borough Truckmen's Association, enforced by James Plumeri, alias Jimmy Doyle, and John "Johnny Dio" Dioguardi. In its exploitation of small trucking businesses, truckers were told, "We've had a lot of complaints against us and we've beat every rap. All we got to do is call up Al Marinelli and the rap is killed. He's the man we got higher up that's protecting us."

Al Marinelli, who lived in seclusion on Lake Ronkokoma on Long Island, refused to give interviews to the press or otherwise make himself accessible to his constituents, other than those of the underworld.[7] Marinelli attended the June 1932 Democratic Convention with Luciano, along with eight delegations leaving New York, and checked into the Drake Hotel. He shared this distinction with Frank Costello and Jimmy Hines. Thomas Dewey's material witnesses would later reveal that Marinelli's Beefsteak Dinner, a 1935 affair held in New York, was attended by bonding combination bosses. They were: loan shark Benny Spiller, bondsman Jesse Jacobs, booker Jack Eller, and Little Davie Betillo.[8]

In Marinelli's district, on the corner of Mulberry and Kenmare, the liquor traders once took their orders in the curbside liquor exchange. Nearby, Meyer Lansky, with his brother Jake, hung out in Ratner's Restaurant on Delancey Street. Here, Cockeyed Louie Weiner paid $100 a week to Women's Court bondsman Jesse Jacobs. Under the eyes of the Lansky brothers, the payoffs gave Dewey one important long shot. Here was a way to connect Lansky associate Lucky Luciano to the weekly payoffs of Cockeyed Louie Weiner. As Dewey's staff evaluated the possibilities, they opined that compulsory prostitution was a real crime. It was tangible, unlike the income tax evasion charges that had proven elusive in the Schultz debacle. They decided to commandeer the wiretaps that had recorded Cockeyed Louie Weiner's old booking headquarters in Coney Island.

The wiretaps revealed great indifference to the plight of the prostitutes. In one case, Weiner suggested that one girl was an "awful dope, so give her plenty of work." In another call, he asked a madam, "How did you like the baby I sent you . . . did you make any money?" The trade was conducted in Yiddish slang and at one point, Weiner asked a madam, "Are you going to work Rosh Hashanah and Yom Kippur?" Her response was, "Give me the business and I'll work every day of the week."

The sins of the father were visited on the son. Al Weiner's phone was tapped after the arrest of his father. For five months in 1935, Acting Inspector John A. Lyons, conducting investigations with Inspector Daniel J. McAuliffe and Deputy Chief Inspector Alexander Anderson, listened to the recorded conversations. Names came up that the hardboiled detectives recognized. Some were known informants. Based on Al Weiner's inadvertent revelations on the telephone, detectives compiled a growing list of brothels, madams, and bookers.

Eunice Carter was familiar with Jesse Jacobs, who took the payoff in Ratner's every week. She'd worked in the Women's Court under the previous administration and recognized the bail bondsman instantly. The bonding racket of Abe Karp, Meyer Berkman, and Jesse Jacobs was no secret to anyone observing the Women's Court from 1929 to 1935. She agreed to aid Inspector McAuliffe in gathering evidence needed to orchestrate a massive arrest of people involved in the vice payoffs. Eunice Carter took on the task of checking the records of the Committee of 14, which were defunct and consigned to the basement of the New York Public Library.[9]

Although Eunice Carter did the legwork, Magistrate Anna Kross had declared months before that a syndicate controlled the bail bonds in Women's Court. With a hard personality and reputation for sentencing high-profile madams to certain prison terms, Kross was no lightweight. Yet, while Dodge had ignored the racket, Dewey's staff took it seriously.

Although recruited for her knowledge of the Harlem community, Carter was familiar with the local characters that paraded through Women's Court. Her new purpose, to wade through the voluminous stacks of index cards kept by the Committee of 14 from 1905 to 1931, was monotonous and seemed impossible.

Yet, Carter performed her stupefying task. The Women's Court cases were filed on dog-eared index cards listing the prisoner by name, offense, age, "nativity" (place of birth), and prosecution witness, who was often a family member, or sometimes a police officer. Categories checked included that of infectious, mentally sub-normal, or drug addict. A typical card read as follows: Mary Liquore; Witness: mother 9-28-31, Case #1872, Age: 23, 8-23-30, police checked, bail $500, probation; address 15 117th St.; Non-I (non-infectious).

Given the fact that prostitutes were rarely arrested under their real names, it was a daunting challenge for Eunice Carter. In cases where the witness was a distressed family member trying to curb a wayward girl, the name was most likely correct.[10]

Carter, with her partner Murray Gurfein, decided they had a case. Gurfein, who looked like a college student, was there to bolster the argument that Eunice Carter wanted to make. Together, they presented their case to Dewey.

Gurfein began. "Mrs. Carter has interviewed and listened to the complaints of a number of girl prostitutes. She has made reports of what she has uncovered and turned those reports in to me. There is definite evidence that the whole business of prostitution in the city is being fundamentally revised so that its control rests in the hands of a few men who are under the domination of one top-flight racketeer."

They explained that the combination madams moved from one location to another on a weekly basis. They had to keep moving. "We now have a pretty complete conception of the structure of the prostitution racket," Gurfein explained. "Until August, 1933, the bookers worked independently and were competitors. Then the combination chiseled in. Four bookers were given all of the houses. They were virtually put on a salary, the combination pocketing the rest. The bookers couldn't make any money, the combination got it all."

Under Dewey's authorization, Carter went to John A. Lyons, who headed an undercover squad of New York detectives. The detectives listened to the droning wiretap conversations. Another name was revealed. Little Jenny Fox was a powerhouse who had employed many of the prostitutes. Little Jenny did business at 214 Riverside Drive. By speaking to these informants, the investigators developed a list of names and addresses. With madams moving every week, they had to work quickly.[11]

On February 1, 1936, the skies were cloudy. The temperature hovered at 20 degrees. It was a typical frigid night in New York City—a night best spent at home, in the company of loved ones. It was Saturday night, that special purview of the wild and restless, and it beckoned in spite of the frigid temperatures.

Downtown, on Greenwich Street, Inspector Daniel J. McAuliffe's police raiders received their typed list of special instructions. Like a gift basket at Christmas, the envelope was not to be opened immediately. To prevent leaks, the procedural was to remain sealed until the radio cars sped to the addresses written on the brown manila pouches.

Commissioner Valentine dispatched the cars, each containing three police officers. The raiders left the Woolworth Building at 8:00 P.M. After leaving the corner of Broadway and Park Place, most sped uptown.

As the lights of the city blurred around them, the vice cops opened the envelopes. Each contained sheets of instructions on the taking of prisoners. Among the itemized mandates was to catch the women in the act of prostitution, that squalid maneuver called the "direct hit." Before being released to the street, men caught in the act would be forced to give their names and addresses. The raids were timed to the minute. At precisely 9:00 P.M., 165 plainclothesmen raided forty-one houses in Manhattan and Brooklyn. In one such location—261 W. 21st Street, Apt. #7—Officers DeCastro, Hunt, and Koenig broke down the door to a bedroom in the house kept by Pollack Frances Blackman. They faced the girlfriend of Ralph the Pimp Liquori—Nancy Presser—who was in the room with an unidentified partner. Police arrested both parties in a direct hit.

Those madams who had cooperated in the pre-investigation waited for the police to arrive, and participated in the arrests peacefully and willingly. Mildred Balitzer was arrested in her apartment, in a pre-determined arrest not part of the raid. But not all the prostitutes cooperated and walked easily into custody. One tried to jump out a window onto a fire escape. As she began her descent, police cornered her at the street level.[12]

The final count of eighty-eight prisoners included the bookers. Pete Harris had fled and would be arrested in Philadelphia shortly. The others were Jack Eller and Al Weiner. With the arrest of David Marcus, the four booking chains were accounted for.

The bosses were also arrested. In a dazzling display of police work, Tommy the Bull Pennochio, with Little Davie Betillo and Jimmy Fredericks, were all picked up.

The bondsmen and disbarred lawyers who controlled the Women's Court joined the bookers and captains in the long parade of vice prisoners. Arrested near their offices at 117 W. 10th Street, were bondsman Jesse Jacobs and his assistant, Meyer Berkman. Shylock Benny Spiller was also caught, along with Jo Jo Weintraub.

Mildred Balitzer, the drug-addicted wife of Pete Harris, was picked up, as was Harris' brother, Eddie. Other underlings associated with

Pete Harris' booking operation included Andrew "Co Co" Attardie, who tried to escape arrest by jumping out a window. With Co Co Attardie, was Lawrence "Red" Healey, the feared enforcer of the bonding combination.

By 10:00 that night, all 110 prisoners were assembled in the Greenwich Street Station. Taxicabs were commandeered to take the men and women in threes and fours to the Woolworth Building. They walked through the Broadway entrance, beneath the grand, domed ceiling of the lobby, and stepped into the night elevator, which went to the fourteenth floor. There, a staff of twenty stenographers took statements from the prisoners. The prostitutes, accustomed to lying their way out of night court, told their usual alibis: just visiting a sister when arrested.

At 3:00 the next morning, a red-eyed Judge McCook, appointed to handle the court cases that would arise from the arrests, showed up. Judge Philip J. McCook, who had been assigned to oversee the Supreme Court under Roosevelt's first plans for Seabury and the New York City Investigation, had sworn in LaGuardia as Mayor. Now, like a clerical warhorse, he arraigned the prisoners quickly, assigning $10,000 bail to the seventy prostitutes being remanded to the Women's House of Detention. The women left for the House of Detention in two groups going at separate times uptown to the Greenwich Village jail.

Justice McCook would develop a fatherly, protective attitude toward many of the prostitutes. Not so for the bosses of the combination, however. McCook set bail for Thomas the Bull Pennochio at $75,000; for Jimmy

Nancy Presser
(NYC Municipal Archives)

Fredericks, $40,000. Bail for Little Davie Betillo remained at $25,000; and for Benny Spiller, $10,000. All remained in custody upon transfer to the filthy Raymond Street jail.

Ralph Liquori, the enforcer and stick-up artist who backed up Jimmy Fredericks, was picked up along with the others on the night of the raids. In the Greenwich Street Station, he met his moll, Nancy Presser, a former call girl who'd been duped by Liquori. In the guise of a lover, he'd kept her supplied with heroin and morphine, two of the drugs she'd become addicted to while under his control. When her will was gone, he forced her to work for Jenny Fox, Betty Winters, and Jennie the Factory.

Nancy pinned the blame for her life's turn of events on the men who she felt put her there. She certainly blamed Liquori, who had knifed her and beaten her stomach when she'd tried to leave him. His propensity for punching her internal organs caused her chronic pain. In the early hours of the morning, as the women were hustled to elevators for the Women's House of Detention, Liguori passed by. Knowing that a scorned woman would make a vengeful, hanging witness, he made a threatening gesture. In a move to intimidate the woman, he leered at her, glowering in low tones.

"I'll kill you if you talk."[13]

Ralph "The Pimp" Liquori, Combination Enforcer
(NYC Municipal Archives)

Photo on opposite page: Luciano accompanied by New York detectives
(Author's Collection)

PART II

MATERIAL WITNESSES

CHAPTER 8

GROUNDHOG DAY

Jesus Christ! I guess I can kiss my sixteen hundred dollars goodbye.
—Abe Wahrman

In the cold February dawn, the groundhog predicted six more weeks of winter from his home in the Bronx Zoo. But the urban habitat on Southern Boulevard, with its caged apes and tethered camels, was a long way from the naked glare of the light bulbs on Greenwich Street. It's likely that many a man caught in the raids spent Sunday morning wishing he'd stayed home with his wife. Although the johns must have experienced trauma at finding themselves arrested, all were let go. They were insignificant to the investigation. In one brothel, two hundred cards, addressed to customers advising of a new location, were tossed into the wastebasket.[1]

At the end of the wild night, raids had been conducted in Manhattan and in a few isolated Brooklyn locations. Thomas Dewey, unshaven and gruff, met the press. He gave the vital statistics of his orchestrated raid: The vice racket reputably took in $12,000,000 a year. The combination was spread over 200 houses. Prostitutes were recruited from other big cities on the East Coast and throughout the Midwest. Within forty-one houses of prostitution that were invaded, eighty-eight prisoners were taken.

Dewey announced that the combination's headquarters on Mott Street, in a storefront with no telephone, was at a location that would not be disclosed to the public. 72 Mott Street was too close for comfort to police headquarters and Commissioner Valentine's offices. In a show of Department courtesy, Dewey tried to divert attention from the significance of the location's proximity to both headquarters and the 1920s-era curbside liquor exchange. Dewey countered by giving due credit to Valentine, Deputy Chief Inspector David J. McAuliffe, and Assistant John A. Lyons. Valentine interjected with a preemptive announcement. If it appeared that any madams had maintained their residences for the long term, he would root out the police and politicians who had made it possible through graft.[2] Dewey then revealed the names of the arrested gang members.

They were: bookers Peter Balitzer, alias Pete Harris, who was hiding in Philadelphia; Jack Ellenstein, alias Jack Eller, who succeeded Nick Montana; Al Weiner, son of Cockeyed Louie Weiner; and David Marcus, also called Dave Miller.

The bosses were Tommy the Bull Pennochio and Little Davie Betillo. The enforcers were Jimmy Fredericks and Ralph Liquori.

Reporters, unfamiliar with this cast of characters, preferred to focus on names their readers would recognize. They asked about the Montana-Weiner Mob, a catchphrase for Nick Montana and Cockeyed Louie Weiner. Dewey answered the reporters' questions.

"Montana and Weiner are small fry, comparatively," he said. "The men we are holding are the real head men. They are just the fellows we've been after. We've got the whole New York prostitution ring in custody now."

Dewey did not mention Luciano's name in the press conference. He didn't bog down reporters' notepads with a lot of other names, either. Binge Redman, called "Parrish," the combination's telephone operator; Edward Balitzer, Pete Harris' brother; and Benny and William Spiller, were not listed. While Dewey had named Jo Jo Weintraub, he didn't publicly name Red Healy, who worked under Weintraub. Thomas Petrovich, who was indicted but later released for having no connection, went undetected in the initial arrests.

On February 6, district attorneys Jacob Rosenblum, Murray I. Gurfein, and Eunice Carter went before the grand jury, which had been set up within the walls of the Women's House of Detention. Based on their evidence, they introduced ten indictments against all of the bookers except David Marcus. Marcus, showing symptoms of his long-term illness, and feared to be having a heart attack, was spared for the time being. The three district attorneys then introduced twenty of the prostitutes and madams, who were surprised to be held longer than they'd expected. Madams Gussie Silvers, Fay Brooks, Shirley Taylor, Betty Winters, Molly Leonard, and Little Jenny Fox were charged with "placing in houses of prostitution, and receiving money for placing."

The formative Jennie the Factory, who the papers described as a tall, buxom blond, was introduced to the grand jury as "one of the town's most frequently arrested women," and bail was set at $50,000. Prostitutes Rose Cohen, Betty Anderson, Jean Erwin, Margaret Martino, Sally Osborne, Muriel Ryan, and Lillian Gordon were charged alongside Nancy Presser with "knowingly accepting money without consideration from proceeds of prostitution." In spite of their alibis, they learned they were not getting out.[3]

Witness Sally Osborne
(Author's Collection)

For the next several months, the prostitutes' job descriptions would be that of material witnesses. In the days prior to her introduction to the grand jury, each prostitute and madam underwent a private grilling. The most popular of the young district attorneys was Barent Ten Eyck. He had a smooth way of talking that engendered trust and respect. Ten Eyck quietly told each prostitute that she faced seven years in prison. Each looked at him in disbelief as he explained this. There was another option, he said, one that would ensure that the woman would not serve a seven-year prison sentence: agree to testify against the barbarians who ran the combination. Ten Eyck told them they could expect to earn money while remanded to the new Women's House of Detention in Greenwich Village. Madams who had dealt in thousands of dollars a week were now being offered $3 per day. The State would shoulder this cost, plus an additional $2.25 per day for "board and keep" in the Women's House of Detention.

The madams, who had felt the strong arm of the enforcers in the beatings, theft, and extortion they'd endured in the takeover staged by the combination, were more pliable than the prostitutes. The working girls weren't directly involved with the combination. But the madams, who were directly victimized by the combination thugs, complied more willingly.

This was a standard procedure used to get witnesses to cooperate with prosecutors.

"That's what they had to do," said the son of Detective Abraham Belsky, who was a member of Dewey's staff during the 1930s. "The [witnesses] were either stupid or they were crooked. Everything was deals, how else could they get them to testify?"[4]

Pete Harris, the booker who had fled to Philadelphia two weeks before, was arrested on the day following the raids. Based on a tip to the police by prostitute Katherine O'Connor, two plainclothesmen tailed Pete to Philadelphia.

Murray Gurfein had to wait one week to request Harris' indictment, which would speed the booker's extradition from Philadelphia.[5] As the indictment was rushed through the system, Gurfein worked with Thomas Dewey to implement a strategy for the prosecution. Dewey wanted to ensure that the evidence against Pete Harris was so overwhelmingly in favor of a conviction, that he would turn state's evidence to avoid a long term in prison. While it appeared that more effort went into amassing evidence against Pete Harris than the others, the step was only one in a progression leading to the boss. Even Jimmy Fredericks and Tommy the Bull, both three-time losers upon whom a conviction would mean life in prison, were not investigated as thoroughly as Pete Harris.

When Abe Wahrman learned that Harris had been arrested, he turned to his cellmate, Co Co Attardie. "Jesus Christ! I guess I can kiss my sixteen hundred dollars goodbye," swore Wahrman.

"Did he owe you that much?" asked Attardie.

"Yep," was Wahrman's resigned response.

In presenting a case against Harris, Murray Gurfein outlined the roadmap for questioning the prostitutes in order to make the case against Pete Harris airtight.

Gurfein made it clear that all evidence had to be proven with verification from the wiretaps. Harris' phone at his address on the Upper West Side had been tapped since the late part of 1935. Voice identification would now play an essential role in the indictments. The arresting officers would be called upon to testify before the grand jury, and be asked to connect the voices on the wires to the voices of the witnesses. Therefore, only recent bookings, from the previous December through January, could be counted as evidence. Prostitutes needed to give details that would back up information garnered from the wiretapped conversations. Because prostitutes changed their names often, it was crucial to record the names they'd used only recently. The time and place of arrest needed to match tapes. Within the tapes, conversations had to place girls in the locations of arrest. Within these confusing guidelines, Murray Gurfein played a tough game of connecting the dots. At square one stood Harris' estranged wife, Mildred Balitzer.[6]

Mildred Balitzer
(Author's Collection)

Mildred was hardboiled from her bleached blond hair to her long, beefy legs. After police arrested Pete Harris, Murray Gurfein approached Mildred. A lot of people were talking, he said.

Her husband was facing twenty-five to fifty years. Maybe she could help him out. Mildred agreed to cooperate fully with the State's case.

Her recorded arrests had ranged from 1931 to 1933. Earlier arrests were listed in the obscure index cards kept by the Committee of 14. Originally from West Virginia, she had once been a beautiful woman. But constant heroin use had ruined her looks. She appeared sick and dissipated, with a depraved smile. She related that her history included marriage and a child, who was living safely in West Virginia. Heroin, her drug of choice, was only one of many street substances she used. Mildred craved opium and in April 1933, had checked into a rehabilitation clinic to kick it.[7] For the prosecution, she would be worth her blousy weight in gold.

Polly Adler later said, "I knew one of the star witnesses, Mildred Harris, held as a material witness against her husband, Pete, who testified that Charlie Lucky spat in her face when she appealed to him to allow Pete, her husband, to quit his racket of booking girls into houses," she wrote. "I could not accept a word of this story. What may have happened is that some new bookies muscled in on Pete Harris, and Mildred, realizing that a word from Luciano would have scared these men off, went to Charlie Lucky for help."[8]

Yet, Mildred's story was more specific to the situation than Adler described. Balitzer was supposed to be testifying against her husband, yet her statements described her desperate attempts to get him out of the combination. Mildred felt that her husband, once an independent booker, had enslaved himself to the combination by getting into debt to the loan sharks. She arranged a meeting with Tommy the Bull at the Bol Musette. "You better mind your own business," Tommy the Bull had suggested ominously.

Mildred went before the grand jury and identified a mug shot of "Charlie Lucky," which Dewey admitted an an exhibit. She testified against Lucky Luciano before the grand jury.

"David [Betillo] told me he was in the narcotics business, and that he worked for Charlie Lucky. I was introduced to Lucky down on Mulberry Street. Only Davie [Betillo] was there. Once, in my room in 1932 in the Victoria Hotel, Davie and Tommy Bull were there. They were talking about the bonding that other people had at the time, that it was very profitable."

Mildred related her husband's financial indebtedness to the combination. She asked Little Davie Betillo if Pete could be let out. "Lucky is my boss," she testified he answered. "He is behind the protection racket." She alleged she had that conversation in the latter part of 1933. On November 27, 1934, she claimed she married Pete Harris and honeymooned in Miami. In February and March of 1935, Mildred claimed she saw Charlie Lucky in the company of Little Davie Betillo and Tommy the Bull Pennochio in New York, and again at the track in Florida. One night, in a bar called the "Paddock," she claimed she approached Luciano.

"I didn't sit at a table. I met him while standing at the bar. I told him that Davie [Betillo] sent me to speak to him about Pete getting out. We talked for fifteen or twenty minutes. He didn't deny he was the boss." She related bits and pieces of their alleged conversation.

"[Luciano] said, 'I understood that he was in. That is the impression he gave me,'" Mildred testified. She claimed she met Luciano on another occasion, a few months after this, in New York's Villanova Restaurant on 46th Street.

"And [Luciano] finally said to you, that until [Harris] pays the money [he owes], he can't get out," led the prosecutor. Her response was entered into the grand jury transcript. "Right," she agreed.

When he discovered that his wife had turned against him, Harris decided that his situation was hopeless. Along with Al Weiner and David Marcus, Harris agreed to testify for the State against the other bookers and combination heads.

The next breakthrough came with the admissions of Thelma Jordan. She related that Little Davie Betillo paired off with enforcer Abe Wahrman. The duo collected receipts from shylock Benny Spiller. Thelma was running the racket for Spiller, who was "her man." Thelma claimed she'd accompanied Spiller to the Waldorf, the residence of Lucky Luciano.

"One day, [Spiller] said to me, 'I gotta see the boss.' I said, 'Who is the boss?' He told me, 'You oughta know by this time. It's Charlie.'"[9]

The arrests would continue during the first crucial week of February. Jerry Bruno, the enforcer for Jimmy Fredericks, was arrested with his wife. He was held as a material witness in the Tombs after being picked up in a poolroom at 466 8th Avenue. A more crucial arrest occurred that week when Jennie the Factory gave police the address of the joint kept by Peggy Wild. Detectives arrested Peggy Wild a few days later.[10]

Peggy Wild was born Margaret Ventimiglia in New York City. Her father had come to New York and settled in East Harlem, where Margaret had grown up. Her brothers, Nick, Joe, Dominick, Tom, and Tony, all worked in the cement business, and were members of the Cement Workers Union. They understood that she was a businesswoman, and helped her with bail when she got arrested. One brother carried the name of Jesse Jacobs in his wallet in case he got a call in the middle of the night from Women's Court.

Peggy Wild, as a young teenager, had moved out of the house at the age of sixteen to marry Louis Fischeria, a musician. By the age of seventeen, she had a baby. She and Fischeria soon divorced, and she began work in the prostitution trade. Her first place was a "call house," a flat on 95th Street and Broadway. She worked herself up the ladder in an arrangement where visitors called before coming to the house. During the Roaring '20s, Wild would rival Polly Adler as a madam to the underworld. She depended on the business of customers like Vincent Coll, Legs Diamond, Lucky Luciano, and the Ambergs, who brought their friends to her houses for an evening of cards, liquor, and women. When she was not working in New York City, she operated houses in Saratoga. Her fortunes began to ebb when she had an affair with William Wild Bill Ercolino, a Mulberry Street real estate owner and close associate of Thomas the Bull Pennochio. Ercolino, distantly related through marriage to Ralph Liquori, owned the barbershop that provided Pennochio with his cover of employment as a barber. Once she got involved with Ercolino, Peggy started setting up houses in lower income areas on the

Nassau/Queens border. Her operations covered Brooklyn's Bedford Stuyvesant section, where she kept a house at 511 Lincoln Place, operating as "Peggy Thompson." By the Depression, she was running $2 houses. She liked the fast turnover, quick buck, and lowered customer expectations. In spring, 1934, she started booking with Pete Harris and Dave Marcus.

Peggy Wild balked at the idea of becoming a witness. Yet, she had nurtured deep resentments against the combination heads, especially Jimmy Fredericks. She slowly began to talk, revealing that Chappie Selafani was one of the enforcers who traveled door-to-door with Jimmy Fredericks.[11]

A woman who opened the secret door to 72 Mott Street and its clandestine operations, Rose Lerner went before the grand jury in the parade of prostitutes. She was not a sex worker, but bore a strange distinction among the women who'd been caught up in the wheels of the combination. Rose Lerner had worked as the bookkeeper for Tommy the Bull. She claimed she never got paid for her work, which may have been a way for her to avoid complicity. After she was fired from her job as a stenographer, Tommy the Bull had felt sorry for her and offered her a job. Accepting it gratefully, she found herself sitting at a desk in his headquarters at 72 Mott Street. Her duties were to keep the books for Benny Spiller. She kept track of the money collected on the loans. After questioning her, Dewey remanded her to the Women's House of Detention, where she was held as a material witness. Lerner was outraged at her treatment and angrily wrote to Dewey, demanding extra compensation due to the low class of people she'd had to associate with in jail.[12]

A lesser-known prostitute, Irene Smith, joined the legions of women willing to testify against Pete Harris. She admitted to getting into the prostitution business by working as a waitress in Coney Island when she met Spike Green, a partner of Charlie Spinach, Harris' predecessor. She had worked in Bedroom Fannie's house on 93rd Street and Lexington Avenue. Irene would also play an important role in the case against Jack Eller.

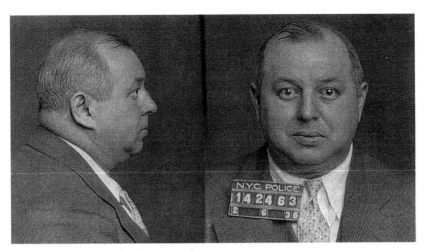

Jack Eller, a Booker (NYC Municipal Archives)

Eller had worked for Nick Montana. With Montana's arrest, Eller had taken over eight of his houses, including those run by Madam Rose Cohen. The madams and prostitutes liked him because he was less of a thug and more of a businessman, having gotten into the combination after failing as a real estate agent. He, like the other bookers, had to pay Little Davie Betillo. Eller paid his respects to his imprisoned benefactor by visiting Nick Montana in Sing Sing on January 26, 1936. As the two men sat facing each other on the long, communal benches of the visiting room, Eller agreed to help support Montana's wife.[13]

Benny Spiller, the combination loan shark, was arrested with his brother, William, who would soon be released. Benny Spiller agreed to be a witness against the most important member of the bonding combination. Little Davie Betillo would be put on the spot by many witnesses, most notably Mildred Balitzer.

Little Davie Betillo, arrested as a scion of the Mott Street Mob, was a native of New York's Little Italy. He was born to Mary and Antonio Petillo at 63 Mott Street, on March 20, 1908. The family name was Petillo, with a "P." David grew up in his family home with five brothers and sisters, including one sister, Clara, who was blind. He had gone to P.S. 144 on the corner of Oak and James Streets, but had left school at the age of twelve.

His police record indicates that between 1924 and 1925, he was arrested twice around the Staten Island Ferry slips on pickpocket charges. As Joseph Rose, he was released in 1924 but when he went before Magistrate Brodsky on June 21, 1925, he was committed to six days in the workhouse. Later that year, in Danbury, Connecticut, he was charged with vagrancy. In 1926, he was arrested on Throop and Gates Avenue in Brooklyn and charged with robbery. Magistrate Dayo discharged the case. In June 1926, he was arrested and charged with armed robbery in lower Manhattan.

The more significant arrest would occur in Pennsylvania in February 1929. There, he would be convicted and sentenced as a first offender. This charge would play significantly into the time he would later serve in prison.

More pickpocket charges followed in 1931. On December 30, 1931, Betillo was found with possession of one can of opium. For this, he was fined $25. In a second instance, in 1932, he was again charged with a "quantity of opium," but released on his own recognizance. His last arrest before the vice pickup had been in November 1935, for vagrancy. With no hard time in his record, he nevertheless had garnered a reputation for being an important tough guy along the lower eastside.[14]

With Betillo in custody, Anthony E. Mancuso of the Bureau of Criminal Identification (BCI) sent a memo to his superior.

"The undersigned, in conversations with various eastside contacts, has learned the following with regard to Dave Petillo, now under arrest in the current 'Vice Investigation.'

That Petillo is of greater importance to the current investigation than assumed. He has been classified as of lesser importance than Jimmy Federico [sic] and Tom Pinocchio but is in reality the real leader of the syndicate, making direct contact with Lucky Luciano.

That going back a number of years, at the time of Al Capone's supremacy in the Chicago racket field, Petillo was considered a pet of Capone who thought so much of him that he sent for him and brought him to Chicago. This, to other mobsters, was a high honor, conferred on Petillo by Capone, and gave him more or less of a high pedigree among the mobsters.

That when Capone went to the Federal Penitentiary, Petillo came to New York with an established reputation because of his connections with the so-called big shots.

That on the eastside from where Petillo originates, he is looked upon as a benefactor, that is, for his own type—in other words, a loan shark unable to collect his debts would refer the case to Petillo who would dispatch this information to his subordinates—Tommy Pennochio and Jimmy Federico [sic]—and they would do the necessary work in connection with the recovery of the money loaned, plus interest, etc.

That there is an organization known as the Unione Siciliana of which one Lucky Luciano is one of the main men in this city. This organization covers the world and is international in character. As a friendly gesture to Capone's former status, Petillo was taken under the wing of Luciano and since this organization has a hand in most every racket in the city, Petillo, because of this direct connection with Luciano, was the most important man in the vice racket.

Petillo's youthful appearance tends to divert police suspicion from his importance.

The reaction on the lower eastside relative to Petillo's arrest makes it obvious that his position is one of importance. There appears to be consternation among the mobsters and people in general in his district that one of his importance should have been apprehended, so easily."[15]

Yet, this colorful job description never appeared on his record. With eleven arrests and two misdemeanor convictions, all in New York, it appeared he'd never operated in Chicago.

Mario Gomes, a noted Capone researcher, notes that "Betillo and other variations [of his name] do not figure anywhere in the Capone organization. If there were any truth to it, then it's quite possible he was very low rung or insignificant and under the radar, in the gang. I have seen many instances in which New York gangsters liked to use the

Capone line for a better rep. This was also a famous line, which New York undercover cops liked to use to infiltrate gangs. They would say they were at one time part of the Capone gang back in Chicago."[16]

Betillo derived income from the Pellerano Pharmacy at 206 Canal Street. He also claimed to be a salesman for the Michael Miranda Importing Co., with a business address of 374 Broome Street.

In the early hours of Sunday morning, after his arrest, Betillo was charged with compulsory prostitution, in violation of Section 2460 of the Penal Law.

Betillo listed his address as 200 W. 16th Street, where he lived with his wife as "Mr. and Mrs. Thomas Brown." The combination bosses were married men.

David's wife moved out of her apartment at 200 W. 16th Street. Clutching her handbag, a hat box, and her brown Pekinese dog, she got into a cab bound for Canal Street before she disappeared.[17] Dewey's team spent weeks talking with doormen in New York buildings. They discovered this small human element, as seen in the sad image of a displaced woman.

The losses were accruing. But so were the gains. The next stop for Thomas Dewey's investigation team was the Waldorf Astoria Hotel.

CHAPTER 9

THE BOSS

Aw, take a day off.
– Lucky Luciano to Staten Island Patrolmen

New York doormen, those uniformed stalwarts of distinctive apartment houses and hotels, opened every door and hailed every taxi. They stood as familiar sentries to apartment dwellers accustomed to anonymity. While respecting the privacy of each occupant within their domain, no doorman ever missed a trick. In that knowledge, Dewey's investigators traveled uptown, their destination an address with an international reputation for excellence. At the Waldorf Astoria Hotel, located at Park Avenue and 50th Street, they interviewed random employees about "Charles Ross." A Waldorf permanent resident, Ross had first registered on April 7, 1935. Since then, he had been living in luxury in Suite 39D. Joseph Farrell, the Assistant Manager, spoke to members of Dewey's staff. Along with other employees interviewed, he said that Ross was only an average tipper. He was often in the company of a showgirl in her early twenties. The occupant of Suite 39D was not in residence at the time.[1]

In anticipation of Dewey's indictment, Luciano believed it would contain the language to charge him with income tax evasion. He expected a Federal indictment, like the one facing Johnny Torrio, the nationally respected Capone henchman. Reporters connected Luciano to Johnny Torrio, and linked the pair as part of a group called New York's "Big Six."

A catch phrase used by newspapers to create a group identity for mobsters who were diverse in their activities, the Big Six included a shifting assemblage comprised of almost a dozen racketeers. Due to the rapid rate of death in the rackets, names were often dropped from the roster, as new ones were included. But the most constant of the Big Six, due to the longevity of these fearsome men, were Meyer Lansky, Benjamin "Bugsy" Siegel, Ciro Terranova, Albert Anastasia, Joe Adonis, and Augie Pisano. This group also included Louis "Lepke" Buchalter, Jacob "Gurrah" Shapiro, and Abe "Longy" Zwillman. Luciano's friend and successor in the United States, Frank Costello, was a sleeper who would come to yield immense political power during the late 1930s and 1940s. Yet Costello, during the hot period of 1935 as public and police attention grew, avoided the exposure that would soon topple Luciano.[2]

A more public figure than Costello in the 1930s, Johnny Torrio originated in New York. According to Capone expert Mario Gomes, "Torrio had ties to New York, and very deep at that. Torrio originated there as a sportsman dabbling in boxing and wrestling as a manager. Besides that, he was running with the Five Points Gang."

When Torrio went to Chicago as the bodyguard of "Big Jim" Colosimo, he brought Al Capone to Chicago from Brooklyn. The two planned Colosimo's death, which occurred on May 11, 1920. Torrio left Chicago because of threats to his life, and gave the controls to Al Capone. Torrio then ran to New York to take cover under the umbrella provided by Luciano's associate, the powerful Democratic district leader, Albert Marinelli.[3]

Later, when Schultz died, speculation grew that he and Dutch Schultz had fallen out over a bonding company, which lost $220,000 of Torrio's money. Torrio fled to Miami, and may have met Luciano there for a short period of time. Snowbirds of a feather have always flocked together. But Luciano's cooling-off locale was Hot Springs, Arkansas.

Thus far, Luciano had been a survivor in the New York underworld.

Everybody said he'd been "taken for a ride," and lived. From Brooklyn kitchens to Jersey funeral parlors, people whispered that Charlie Lucky had escaped a gangster's fate. The publicity generated after the death of Dutch Schultz in 1935 lifted the drug dealer from the shadows and pushed him to the forefront as the boss to millions of New Yorkers reading the morning papers.

Thomas Dewey had copied J. Edgar Hoover's tendency to go after criminals with high-profile personas. Hoover, who ignored Luciano in the 1930s, built upon an original investigation started by the Bureau of Narcotics, and agreed in February 1935 that Luciano was the head of the underworld in New York City. Boss of the lower eastside, he had operations chiefly in narcotics, beer, and liquor.[4]

Lucky Luciano was to Dewey what Baby Face Nelson, Machine Gun Kelly, and Pretty Boy Floyd had been to Hoover. They were bad men with triumphant names, the stuff of gangbuster radio shows.

By 1935, Luciano was described in the tabloids as a boss who brought the Italians together with the Jewish and Irish factions of organized crime. He was considered to be the boss of the lower eastside extortion rackets. His associates, such as Frank Costello, made a fortune in bootlegging and later, slot machines, drug dealing, and gambling, with trucking and loan sharking growing in the 1930s. Reporters called the underworld headed by the Big Six by the title, Unione Siciliana. Yet, this tag is erroneous. There was no Unione Siciliana in New York City.[5]

Luciano's rising had its roots in the activities of Guiseppe "Joe the Boss" Masseria. In the 1920s, Masseria entrusted Frankie Uale (called Frankie Yale), an associate of Al Capone and Johnny Torrio, with enforcement and protection during the bootlegging years. When Uale was killed in 1928, Masseria was questioned but released. Replacing Frankie Uale was Augie Pisano, who, along with Joe Adonis and Frank Costello, was protected by Tammany Hall through Al Marinelli. Having first come to Dewey's attention for his associations with Marinelli, Luciano was the force behind the polling atrocities that had pushed Marinelli into power on the lower eastside.

Unlike most of the members of the Mott Street Mob who had been born and raised in the streets of New York's Little Italy, Luciano was a Sicilian immigrant. Salvatore Lucania was born to his mother, Roslyn, when the woman was thirty-one years of age. She gave birth to Salvatore, her second son, on November 24, 1897. Her husband was thirty-eight years old when Salvatore was born. Anthony Lucania was approaching middle age and the diminishing returns of remaining in Sicily. The family lived in Lercara, within Sicily's main city of Palermo. In 1902 and 1904, two daughters were born to the family, which already included Salvatore's older brother. Between 1906 and 1907, Anthony brought his wife and children to the United States. Like most European immigrants arriving in the early part of the twentieth century, he chose to live near his relatives already wise to the ways of the new world. He settled on First Avenue near 10th Street on the eastside of Manhattan. The following year, 1907, Roslyn joined him with Salvatore, along with his older brother and two sisters. The family took an apartment at 183 E. 10th Street. They would live in that apartment until the late 1920s. Even when the family later moved, it was only to go down the block. They stayed in the neighborhood, with its Italian bakeries and storefront social clubs. During that time, Salvatore attended the local public school. As he grew into adulthood, he worked occasionally as a chauffeur. Sometimes he listed his occupation as that of his brother, who was a milliner in the local garment district. Salvatore became a drug dealer while still a teenager. He was arrested for the first time on January 17, 1916 for drug possession. He was sentenced the following June to six months. Several years later he was arrested again. His second arrest occurred on December 15, 1921, in Jersey City for possession of a concealed weapon. The charges were dismissed. This started a chain reaction of dismissals and dropped charges.

Luciano befriended Frank Costello (real name Francesco Castiglia) when Frank was a gang leader to the 104th Street gang in pre-Prohibition days. In 1923, Luciano was arrested for drug possession but the charges were again dropped. In 1926, Detectives Charles Kane and Cornelius Behen found Luciano in a Marmon Coupe on First Avenue and 23rd Street. In the car were a double-barreled shotgun and a revolver. They arrested him and charged him with violation of the Sullivan Law and felonious assault. In spite of the fact that his gun was registered outside of New York City, the upstate permit cleared Salvatore of the charges. In 1928, he was again arrested for assault and robbery; and in 1929, in Richmond, Virginia, for grand larceny. In 1931, while living with his parents above a candy store at 265 E. 10th Street, he was arrested for felonious assault. By now, he had adopted the moniker of "Charles Lucania," and was known on the street as Charlie Lucky.[6]

As an associate of Frank Costello, Luciano worked in bootlegging with Lansky and Bugs Siegel. In spite of Siegel's nickname, "Benjamin was the name he used," said a resident of the neighborhood, whose mother went to school with Siegel. "If you called him anything else, he'd beat you up—he'd kill you." Siegel was one part of the terrible Bugs-Meyer Mob, an enforcement arm who offered their services to drug dealers and bootleggers Waxy Gordon and Owney Madden. Luciano, an associate of this group, made himself useful to the Italians trying to infiltrate the Irish behemoth of Tammany Hall.

Al Marinelli helped Luciano to avoid prosecution if arrested. In 1931 in Cleveland, he was held for investigation, as well as in 1932 in Chicago. In both cities, he was released. After his first dramatic arrest and conviction while still a teenager, Luciano accounted for his crimes only once.

Frank Costello
(New York Municipal Archives)

That was levied during 1930 in the form of a $1,000 fine in Miami for possession of a concealed weapon and operating a gambling game.[7]

Luciano was rising in bootlegging, while hijacking trucks in New Jersey, when Dominick Didato, alias Terry Burns, made him a partner in a chain of rackets. Once Luciano had gotten his foothold, he kicked him out, and Burns descended in the ranks. Burns would be murdered in August of 1936.[8]

On Wednesday, October 16, 1929, while still an unknown thug known as Charles Lucania, he was taken for a ride. The incident was his baptism into his new nickname. One newspaper tabloid labeled the gangster a suspected police informant. They may have gotten the tip that once, he had avoided arrest by taking the police to a location where they could find a cache of illegal street drugs.

The causes behind the "ride" have been disputed. The speculation outweighs the established facts. One theory is that Salvatore Maranzano's people lured him out of his apartment at 265 E. 10th Street, where he lived above a candy store with his father, Tony, and his mother. Some gang members met him at the corner of 15th Street and 6th Avenue, with an invitation to see a woman. They hoped to kill him, and bound and gagged him when he entered the car. A second theory is that police beat him up. A third version of the story states that he was hiding some illegal drugs, and his assailants hoped to torture him into revealing the location. Given the difficulties in navigating to Staten Island from Manhattan, it is doubtful he was kept a prisoner in the car. He must have trusted his assailants, and saw no need to put up a resistance.

Charles Lucania was found with his throat, wrists, face, and back slashed. His face was also beaten badly. It is obvious from the nature of the wounds that he was not slated for death, but for torture and punishment.

The *Herald Tribune* reported at 1:30 in the morning on October 17 that Patrolman Patrick H. Blanke of the Tottenville precinct saw a figure lying on Hylan Boulevard. The location was a deserted strip at Princess Bay, twelve miles from St. George and Tottenville. Despite his wounds, the gangster was calm.

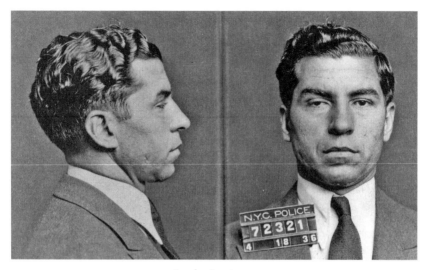

Lucky Luciano
(New York Municipal Archives)

"Get me a taxicab," he reportedly instructed the policeman. "I'll give you fifty." Blanke called for reinforcements. Detectives James Boyland and Gustave Schley asked who had attacked him.

"Aw, take a day off," Luciano reportedly replied. "I know who did it. I won't tell you. I'll settle it myself," he said. The detectives responded by putting him under the third degree lights at the precinct. Still, the gangster refused to talk.

"Get a good night's sleep and forget it," was his reported answer. The detectives arraigned him in Richmond County on suspicion of stealing an automobile. It was a trumped-up charge, instituted when the district attorney, Carl Fuchs, discovered his identity after contacting Manhattan police. Given his police record of many arrests and one conviction, for want of another reason to hold him, Fuchs ordered him held on $25,000 bail on the car-theft charge. The detectives took the opportunity to question the prisoner about the murder of two men in the Hotsy-Totsy Club at 1721 Broadway, a crime for which Legs Diamond had been indicted. Sometime after the attack, someone thought to visit Anthony Lucania, who, through an interpreter, proclaimed his son's innocence. With help from their married daughter, parents Anthony and Roslyn arranged to travel to Staten Island to see Salvatore. With the gangster handcuffed to a gurney, surgeons in the prison hospital looked at his wounds. The facial slashing had left him with a permanently lopsided expression and an eyelid that drooped on one side.

The mobster was no Dorian Gray, Oscar Wilde's fictitious character whose handsome face masked an evil nature. The signature half-closed eyes and droopy facial muscles marked Lucania as a member of the underworld. On the third day after the attack, the unknown mobster warranted a headline. The *Herald Tribune* confirmed that Lucky Lucania, who was taken for a ride, had survived.

The incident prompted the Staten Island district attorney to issue a statement. "We want it known that New York gunmen cannot dump their victims on Staten Island," declared Carl Fuchs. "We don't want them coming down here," he continued. "When they do, we intend to make it as uncomfortable as possible."9

**Gay Orlova,
Lucky's girlfriend**
(Author's collection)

During the second week in May 1929, along with Dutch Schultz, Meyer Lansky, and Frank Costello, the newly christened "Lucky" helped coordinate an amazing organized crime convention held in the open town of Atlantic City, New Jersey. It was to be conducted at the President Hotel, under the auspices of racketeer and politician Enoch "Nucky" Johnson. Luciano had already offered Nucky Johnson ten percent of all his rackets, for exclusive rights to Nucky's beach for the landing of boats containing liquor. Meyer Lansky, Bugsy Siegel, and Joe Adonis agreed to help kick in to meet the high price of access to the beach and protection along the Jersey shore. At the same time, Frank Costello was promised carte blanche on slot machines coming into Atlantic City. In the bargain was an opportunity for Luciano, Siegel, Adonis, and Lansky to highjack a truck filled with scotch. It was apparently an act of revenge as Luciano's trucks had been hijacked in that very area a few weeks before.[10]

One theory is that Luciano organized the convention as a way of bringing his reputation up a few notches after having been called an informer in the papers. The convention was attended by at least thirty major crime figures, including Al Capone, and Jake Guzik.[11]

"Who knows more about the liquor business than us?" This was the question Luciano may have posed at the meeting, according to the gangland grapevine. He hoped to solve the problem of competition and price fixing in beer.[12]

Two years later, on the morning of April 16, 1931, underworld gossip dominated the headlines. Topics of discussion included the missing Justice Force Crater. The latest scandals to surround the missing judge included his name listed as an illegal receiver in foreclosure proceedings against the condemned Libby Hotel. The attorney in the condemnation, Martin Lippman, had represented hotel owner William Moore, who was under Department of Justice investigation for involvement in a swindle in which three principals, not including Crater, had already committed suicide. A sidebar listed new allegations in the Vivian Gordon murder case. Amid the scandal, the death of Guiseppe Joe the Boss Masseria, a Harlem boss of narcotics and gambling, almost went unnoticed.[13] Police Commissioner Mulrooney, who predated the untouchable Lewis Valentine by some years, denied knowing of Masseria's activities in Harlem in bootlegging, policy, and racetrack betting. In an interview given to the *New York Sun*, the commissioner alluded only to Masseria being involved in "racetrack gambling, a dice game, and Sicilian affairs." These denials had their roots in Tammany Hall's relaxed attitude toward the associates of Frank Costello and Albert Marinelli.

In the 1930–1931 Castellammarese War, Masseria, a self-proclaimed "boss of bosses," had waged war for control of New York and New Jersey with Salvatore Maranzano. Masseria had risen to power in 1920 when he was arrested for the shooting of Salvatore Mauro on Chrystie Street. He maintained his innocence and was later blamed for the death of another gangster, Vincent Morelli, in 1922. When rival gangsters caught up with him, they fired sixty shots and several bystanders, including one little girl, were wounded in the crossfire. A second ambush was staged on the docks and although several dockworkers were shot, Masseria got away again. In November 1930, Joe the Boss was again attacked by a machinegun in the Bronx. Two bodyguards were killed.

In 1931, Masseria was out on bail of $35,000 as a material witness in the killing of two men on Pelham Parkway, Stephen Ferrigno and Alfred Mineo. Both were shot down on November 5. Usually cautious, Masseria traveled to Brooklyn on April 15 in the company of his armed henchmen, who drove him to Coney Island. He never went without his bodyguards. They included Luciano.

Gunmen killed Masseria shortly before 3:00 P.M. on April 15, 1931, in the Nuova Villa Tammaro, 2715 W. 15th Street, in Coney Island. A stucco restaurant with a green awning reminiscent of the Italian flag, it was named after the proprietor's mother-in-law, Mrs. Anna Tammaro. The restaurant cook, she had left the scene right before the killing on a mission: Her customers had asked for fish and she had none in the kitchen. They most likely told her to leave, as no first-generation Italian cook in Brooklyn would operate without a fresh supply of calamari on ice, ready for deep-frying to be served with hot sauce. Needless to say, she was sent out of the place, for reasons other than fresh fish.

Mrs. Tammaro returned as a crowd of spectators surrounded the restaurant. Masseria had been found dead with five bullets in his body. Four had entered his back and the fifth, the back of his head. This would confirm witnesses' statements that two additional men entered the restaurant after Masseria was already seated with the three who faced him. These two gunmen were said to have left the restaurant quietly after the shooting, entered their automobile, and drove away. The two newcomers, who joined the three in the restaurant, indicated that there were five men in the execution squad. There has been much speculation as to the identities of the killers. New York detectives, based on information gained from Murder, Inc. informer Abe "Kid Twist" Reles, believed that

Albert Anastasia, Joey Adonis, Vito Genovese, Bugsy Siegel, as well as Luciano, comprised the execution team.

Many gangland myths were born that afternoon in Coney Island. One, that Masseria died clutching an ace of diamonds, sprung from the fact that when Inspector Joseph Thompson and Captain John Ryan of the homicide and ballistics squad of the 10th Inspection District arrived, they found $35 strewn amid a pack of cards.

What is known is that four men's overcoats and three hats were left behind in the restaurant. Two guns were found in the alley next to the restaurant, a .32 and a .38 caliber revolver. Gone was Masseria's steel-armored motorcar, with inch-thick glass. All the police could do was charge Charles Scarpato, the proprietor, along with Mrs. Tammaro, with violating the Volstead Act after inspectors found wine on the premises. Mrs. Tammaro would not identify any of the card players, but said they had ordered coffee when they arrived.

Aside from the fabled ace in Masseria's hand, a more enduring gangland myth was born in the urban seaside restaurant that day. The myth, that Luciano strolled out of the men's room to greet the police officers, is groundless. While present at the lethal card game, Luciano left with the other owners of the coats and hats. None of the card players made their presence known to the police on that climatic afternoon. The only additional evidence found may not have belonged to the killers. A car, which fit the description of one seen leaving the scene of the crime, was found in front of 1626 W. First Street in Brooklyn. In the backseat were two .38 and one .45 caliber revolvers.[14]

Each sensational gangland slaying in 1931 prompted the tabloids to blaze stories of the wrath of Al Capone's Chicago Outfit, sure to arrive on the shores of the Hudson River bearing their signature Thompson submachine guns. But the bootleg wars waged in Chicago during the 1920s rivaled the violence that took place in New York during that same period. Joe the Boss Masseria, who controlled the curbside liquor exchange during the 1920s, reigned during a period of violence characterized by murders in which bootleggers and their molls could be bound and gagged, to be tossed alive into the Hudson and East Rivers, with or without their feet encased in cement. The mortality of low-level bootleg-gers and rumrunners was high; thousands of these soldiers were killed during Masseria's reign.

"My father was killed when I was just one year old," said the son of a murdered bootlegger during an interview. "He was the only member of the family who was making any money."

In the aftermath of Masseria's death, the proprietors of the Nuova Villa Tammaro held a banquet. Ostensibly as part of the Italian Feast held in Coney Island during the first three days in August, it was most likely the ceremony that marked the ascension of Masseria's successor, Salvatore Maranzano, as boss of the Coney Island and South Brooklyn gambling and narcotics rackets. Maranzano had been a subversive rival of Luciano since the late 1920s. On the surface, Luciano was aligned with Maranzano. However, he suspected that Maranzano had given Vincent Coll a contract to kill him along with Vito Genovese. He would act quickly—it was kill or be killed.

With the help of four of Lansky's gunmen, Luciano had Maranzano killed in his New York Central Building office on September 10, 1931. The killers left behind two revolvers and two hats with Chicago labels.

The fabled Sicilian Vespers would result in a handful of underworld deaths across the nation.[15]

The year 1931 was a very good year for Luciano.

Meyer Lansky
(New York Municipal Archives)

CHAPTER 10

THIS MAN'S SHERIFF

The legally constituted authorities were prostrate before this man.
– Thomas Dewey

The publicity surrounding the Dewey raids sent repercussions throughout the underworld. In late February, word spread that Thomas Dewey was looking for informants to help seal an indictment against Luciano. With his wide-reaching connections, it is not surprising that small fry would claim association with the powerful racketeer.

Joe Bendix, an unknown thief, was a three-time loser and facing life in prison. Feeling morose and sensing the hopelessness of his case, he agreed to make a deal.

A hotel sneak thief, Bendix appeared before Judge Nott and was sentenced for third degree burglary to fifteen-years-to-life. He'd lost his freedom for $600 worth of jewelry, which included a pair of rosary beads, in the Hotel Madison, 15 E. 58th Street. Charles Breitel, an assistant district attorney, approached Bendix, suggesting a plea deal in exchange for a future recommendation for executive clemency.

Joe Bendix agreed to testify against Jimmy Fredericks and Lucky Luciano. After his commitment, he was transferred to the New York State Prison at Ossining. He entered jail with a light step, imagining himself just months away from freedom. Like other witnesses, he soon found that prison was hell for state witnesses. His fellow prisoners called him a squealer, punctuating the harassment with spitting. For his own protection, he was forced into solitary confinement and deprived of all company for twenty-two hours a day.[1]

In Albany, Governor Lehman delivered a bill to the New York State Legislature at the same time that Bendix was talking to the district attorney. The bill was worded to permit police and prosecutors to get more racketeering convictions. The bill would amend the code of criminal procedure to permit the trial of a defendant on a series of connected or similar offenses under one indictment, making it possible to avoid separate prosecution on each count. Hiram C. Dodd, special prosecutor investigating the multiple-defendant Druckman case, joined Thomas Dewey in posturing for the passing of these anticrime laws.[2]

As soon as the bookers found themselves under indictment, they started making deals. The fate of Danny Brooks was held up as an example for them all. Brooks was a booker serving seven years upstate in Clinton Prison for compulsory prostitution. After Al Weiner became the first of the bookers to implicate the bosses, others followed suit.

The most disgruntled booker was David Marcus. Marcus was the booker with the biggest ax to grind. In the business with his wife, Ruth, David agreed to talk to the grand jury. It was part of a deal that would allow his wife to remain on the outside. After he made the deal, Ruth went home to the couple's three small boys. But Marcus suffered what may have been an anxiety attack and was hospitalized before he could talk to the grand jury.

David Marcus had started in 1929 as a dress salesman before opening a house of prostitution with his wife. Ruth knew the business and operated it herself when David developed heart trouble. In the summer of 1933, Marcus got word that he would have to join the combination. They wanted $200 a week with protection offered in exchange. The bonding combination had threatened David's simple philosophy. "It's better to be independent," he said, "because you don't get to be known."

When he ignored the threats, Ralph Liquori accosted him on the street. "We got orders to see that you get out of town or give you the business," said Liquori.

Marcus told his troubles to a male madam named Crazy Moe. Moe gave him some sound advice. "Why don't you 'get next to yourself' and do as you're told," said Moe.

Marcus next went to Abe Karp. The disbarred Women's Court attorney was a jack-of-all trades who had written Marcus' Last Will and Testament. Karp, always versatile, then arranged for police protection for Marcus. After three days of this "police protection," David was shot at while walking out of his house at 17 W. 71st Street. Although the sniper missed hitting him, it scared the daylights out of the independent booker. "When this combination started organizing, I didn't want to have anything to do with them," he told Charles Breitel.

The young assistant district attorney pressed Marcus on the details. "Did Crazy Moe tell you who this group represented or who they were?"

"Yes," replied Marcus.

"What did he say?" asked Charles Breitel.

"This is the combination from downtown," said Marcus. "The eastside and the Mulberry Street gang were getting together to form a combination, and they want you to give ten thousand dollars or else."

"He told you who the members of this mob were?" pressed Breitel.

"I didn't ask, but he didn't tell me," said Marcus.

"Did he tell you who the top was?" asked the assistant district attorney.

"No, he didn't," responded Marcus. "I think he was in on it himself."

"How did you know him?" asked Breitel.

"Sometime before, he had a place on 86th Street," said Marcus. "I used to furnish girls for him."

"[Moe] ran a house," Breitel clarified.

"Yes," agreed Marcus, "[Moe] ran a house."

"How did you happen to talk to him about this," pressed Breitel, "he being a house manager?"

"When I lived on Seventy-first Street, he came up to my home with a fellow named Charlie," said Marcus. "Who Charlie was I didn't know. As I said before, I don't bother with anyone," he continued. "He said to me, 'Dave, you know they are forming a combination downtown and they are going to ask you to join and all the books, and we want you to put us on your payroll. We want to straighten you out."

"This was Crazy Moe or Charlie?" asked Breitel.

"Crazy Moe," said Marcus. "Charlie said nothing."[3]

Marcus related that he then went to California, but returned to New York in November 1933, "after the banks closed and after the N.R.A., when Roosevelt was elected," he later said. He bought into a gasoline station on Glen Cove Road in Nassau County.

By March 1, 1935, Marcus met loan shark Benny Spiller. Spiller put Marcus in touch with Jimmy Fredericks. Together, the two went to Little Davie Betillo, who said, "We know you're broke, so for the first two weeks, you don't pay. Then, we get fifty dollars a week." With that illustrious beginning, David Marcus joined the combination. Betillo gave Marcus the business they had taken from Spike Green, a booker they had run out of town.

Little Davie Betillo then told Marcus the rules. If Marcus acquired a new prostitution house on his own, he would have to give the address to the combination so that it could be bonded. If he got arrested, he was to phone Binge Redman, who was a telephone go-between.

The next contact name came as a surprise. In early 1935, Fredericks forced Marcus to share the business with booker Danny Brooks. Brooks was a favorite of Jimmy Fredericks.

Since Fredericks couldn't operate an automobile, Brooks was his driver. Brooks pouted when he heard that David Marcus was getting the booking he thought would go to him. Fredericks, as a way to pacify Brooks, told Marcus he had a partner. Marcus was livid.

"What's the idea about including Danny?" Marcus yelled. "I don't want him as a partner," he insisted. "I don't need partners."

Danny Brooks' alliance with Marcus was short-lived and hardly sweet. Brooks was soon pinched in a Westchester raid. When prostitutes revealed that he was a booker, he was charged with compulsory prostitution. Brooks was sentenced to seven-and-a-half years, and was sent up in August 1935 to the Clinton Prison at Dannemora.

Marcus related to Charles Breitel that he was forced to attend meetings held at the combination headquarters at 72 Mott Street. They were ominous occasions during which Fredericks and Little Davie Betillo, Tommy the Bull, and his treasurer, Jerry Bruno, threatened the bookers.

Betillo would force the bookers to line up. Marcus shared a bench with Pete Harris, Jack Eller, and Al Weiner. On one occasion, Betillo ordered Pete Harris to leave town. On another, he threatened Jack Eller by telling him, "I'll kick in your big, fat stomach." Yet, Betillo ignored Al Weiner, considering him mentally inferior. Betillo directed his tirades at Marcus, Harris, and Eller.

"You're down here because you guys are holding out places on us. We're not getting collections. And the next time you hold any places out, we will kick your heads in," said Betillo. "We won't give you a chance to go to the coppers," he continued. "We will go to the coppers for you."

Jimmy Fredericks imposed heavy financial tithes on Marcus. This included an "honor" fee levied on a booker when he replaced an arrested booker. The practice was in place to force the new booker to contribute money to the support of his arrested predecessor's wife.

For example, booker Jack Eller took over the business left behind by Vice Czar Nick Montana. After Montana's imprisonment, Eller stepped in to help support Montana's wife. Jack Eller, popular and jovial, had paid his dues willingly. But Marcus, who never wanted to work with Danny Brooks in the first place, balked at the idea of supporting Mrs. Brooks after Danny's conviction.

At that point, Jimmy Fredericks muscled in and "taxed" Marcus in varying amounts, to be given to Danny Brooks' wife. Fredericks also selected Marcus to pay for Danny Brooks' defense lawyer. "During that time," Marcus confided to Charles Breitel, "I took sick and I've been sick ever since."

After he became ill, Ruth Marcus took over the booking, which was situated in Coney Island. She controlled the telephone but also ran a house of her own. This continued for ten weeks up to January 31, 1935.

During that time, she kept contacts with the underworld doctors who treated the prostitutes and madams. Ruth referred several prostitutes to a Dr. Schrage on Lexington Avenue in Manhattan. Some of the girls, who were staying in one of Ruth's houses at 2416 Neptune Avenue in Coney Island, complained about taking the subway uptown to see the doctor.[4]

While the assistant district attorneys in Dewey's office were buoyed by the admissions of David Marcus, they got nowhere when they tried to pry information out of the men at the top of the combination. Jimmy Fredericks sat under the third degree lights tight as a clam. Fredericks had a record dating back to 1915 with charges ranging from petty larceny, burglary, auto theft, safe blowing, homicide, gun possession, and one escape from a guard on the way to Sing Sing. With the exception of a short term in the Elmira Reformatory, and a five-year commitment to Sing Sing for safe blowing, Fredericks had been freed in most occasions by magistrates in Brooklyn and Manhattan criminal courts.

On February 3, in the Raymond Street jail, an assistant district attorney, Milton Schilback, interrogated Fredericks. He countered the questions by asking Schilback to validate his identity.

"Who are you? A cop . . . what?" Fredericks asked sullenly. But Milton Schilback's patience was rewarded when Fredericks leant some clues to his family background.

Jimmy Fredericks lived at 397 Manhattan Avenue, Brooklyn, with his young wife, Lillian. She endured Fredericks' philandering with paramour Florence Cokey Flo Brown.

Fredericks had a close family, with cousins lining up to vouch for him. One cousin, who owned a paper stock company, tried to provide a legitimate front for the mobster. Fredericks claimed that he worked at a paper stock company.

District attorney Schilback began the interrogation. "Ever been in a whorehouse in your life?" he asked.

"No, sir," said Fredericks with heavy sarcasm.

"Do you know any madams?" countered Schilback.

"No, sir," said Fredericks in earnest.

"Know any bookers?" asked Schilback.

"Don't know nobody," said Fredericks.

"What do you mean by that?" asked the district attorney.

"I don't know," said Fredericks. "You said do I know any madams, any bookers. What do I have to go to whorehouses for? I am married."

"How long have you been married?" pressed Schilback.

"Six years," said Fredericks.

"In a whorehouse before then?" asked the prosecutor.

"No, sir," replied Fredericks.

"Just got gonorrhea from good girls?" Schilback thought he had him.

"Do you have to get gonorrhea in a whorehouse?" was Fredericks' comeback.

After she was remanded to the Women's House of Detention, Rose Lerner, the combination's bookkeeper, fought to be released. She wrote frantic letters to family members, imploring them to try to get her out of jail. When that failed, she wrote to Thomas Dewey and his assistant district attorney, Jacob Rosenblum, asking for financial compensation for her ordeal. Dewey, believing that Rose was a valuable witness, planned to keep her in jail. She would remain in the Women's House of Detention for the next six months. Rose, a former stenographer, had worked for Thomas Pennochio as a bookkeeper at 72 Mott Street. Dewey found her to be garrulous and astute on the subject of the combination's books.

In her initial remarks to the grand jury, Lerner revealed a deeper texture to the combination than was previously believed to exist. Not only were the bosses milking the prostitutes and madams of their trade, but they were also lending them money at high vigs and demanding repayment under threats of violence. Cut Rate Gus and Benny Spiller brought the vigs back to 72 Mott Street, where Rose Lerner kept separate books for each of them.

As a result, each loan shark had different outstanding amounts, with clients who came in every week to pay Rose in person. She earned $20 a week for her services.

Her duties included rewriting cards for Tommy the Bull and keeping track of the small pieces of paper he handed her with markings and notations on them. The loan schedule was that a $25 loan would be paid over a period of six weeks, with $5 interest. The "dollar on every five" was the standard vigs in Brooklyn and Manhattan at that time. Whether she liked it or not, Rose Lerner remained inside the House of Detention with prostitutes like Nancy Presser.[5]

The prostitutes, who cooperated, named names out of personal vendettas. Nancy Presser started to talk, blaming the men responsible for her downfall.

Born Genevieve Flesher in Auburn, New York, Presser was twenty-four years old at the time of the raids. She'd lived in New York for six years, drifting into the city as a young, pretty girl in the full bloom of life.

Her story is a proverbial tale of poor choices and thwarted dreams. Before she entered into the persona of the notorious Nancy Presser, Genevieve was a young woman living in upstate New York. She wanted more than she could handle, and at a young age, traveled into Manhattan. Because she was attractive, she was able to work in the garment district as a dress model to the wholesale traders. The requirements were to be trim to size, and attractive. This work appealed to teenagers looking for glamour jobs. As a "model," Nancy took her first job at 39th Street and Fifth Avenue. Later, while modeling hats for Wilson Brothers, she began working as an independent prostitute. She claimed to have associated with mobsters Hymie Pincus, Willie Weber, and Waxy Gordon. But she couldn't survive without a pimp.

She met Ralph Liquori in 1932. Around that time, she started using drugs. Nancy's drugs were morphine and heroin. Nancy denied she'd ever used cocaine and opium during the years she abused drugs. Regardless of what she was using, she lost her looks. With Ralph's other girl, Gashouse Lil Gordon, Nancy went into a syndicate house of prostitution.

In the combination houses, she was forced to work around the clock. Nancy, who was booked by Pete Harris, was considered a problem by the bookers and madams. They said that because of her drug habits, she would get into a bed and go into a drug-induced nod. Pete Harris complained of Nancy. "She is one of those girls you have to get up," he said. "I had to get [Liquori] to wake her up."

Harris booked Nancy Presser into houses run by Little Jenny Fox and Jennie the Factory. Jo Jo Weintraub acted as Nancy's escort. For this, she nursed a grudge against him. It was the prostitute's equivalent of killing the messenger.

When she wasn't forced to work, Nancy rode with Ralph in the car, keeping his guns in her purse. In case they were caught, she would be arrested on the possession charge. Ralph gave her the opium cans to hold and brought her along on drug deals for Tommy the Bull. On one of these jaunts, Nancy accompanied Ralph to a house of prostitution where some of her friends were working. As she remained in the car, Ralph went upstairs. He held up the madam at gunpoint. Word got around in this insular world that Presser was Ralph's accomplice in the stick-up job. After that, the other prostitutes shunned her. Threatened constantly, while in her cell in the Women's House of Detention, Nancy paid dearly for those nights when she'd "kept chickie" for Liquori as his lookout. Inside the jail, Nancy was sick. She couldn't eat or sleep. She complained that something was wrong with her side. She needed a nurse.[6] But she was not the only prostitute to feel

Nancy Presser was once a small town girl
(Author's Collection)

the pressure. If they looked out the barred windows, strange men stood outside shaking fists at them. These men made menacing gestures from the train as the Sixth Avenue el roared past the barred windows.

The Women's House of Detention was built in 1934 directly behind the Women's Court at Jefferson Market. The building, called "Art Deco in design," was another kind of monstrosity. While the Women's Courthouse next door had embodied the worst of Victorian architecture, the Women's House of Detention copied architecture reminiscent of totalitarianism themes of European fascism. Some said it resembled an apartment house. Yet, the new jail contained no elements of a home-like setting.

In contrast, the Alderson Industrial Reformatory for Women had made the genuine effort to create comfort for its inmates through the building of various brick homes called "cottages." The Women's House of Detention on Sixth Avenue was progressive only in the fact that the building was new.

Like Rose Lerner, the combination's indignant bookkeeper, Nancy Presser found the Women's House of Detention to be intolerable. She was ready to do anything to get out of a place that was already called a hellhole. When it was opened in 1934, a public relations campaign was launched and members of the press were invited in to take pictures. Matrons posing in starched, white uniforms posed before comfortable beds made with hospital corners. The idea was to convey municipal efficiency. The building was a sad depository for lost women. Within the Women's House of Detention, the staff showed particular indifference to the plight of inmates committed while in the throes of narcotics addiction.

Mildred Curtis, a grand jury witness, later described the treatment of drug addicts within the Women's House of Detention.

"They give you a five day reduction and that isn't right. When these pains come up there, you have got to yell, and the matron comes at night and tells you to 'keep quiet.' You ask her to do something for you. She says, 'Oh, I can't do anything for you. Leave me alone.'"[7]

Nancy Presser had entered the House of Detention with a morphine chippie. Ralph Liquori, with drugs supplied by Betillo and Pennochio, had kept Nancy well supplied. Presser, as a pariah who was shunned by the other prostitutes because of her activities in helping Liquori with brothel stick-ups, was collapsing under the weight of her incarceration. She had a chronic pain in her side, and was found to be with venereal disease.

Nancy readily talked to the assistant district attorneys about the bad treatment levied on her by Liquori. For example, once he'd attacked her with a knife. He used to knock her on the floor and kick her stomach. As her revelations deepened, she related that she'd once accompanied Ralph to Little Italy. There, at 98 Kenmare Street, she met Tommy the Bull, Jimmy Fredericks, and Jerry Bruno. While sitting in a car outside Celano's Restaurant, she recalled seeing Jimmy Fredericks and Thomas Pennochio, and recalled hearing them discuss the combination.

Barent Ten Eyck thought Nancy would be a key witness. Based on that, Thomas Dewey made a decision to pluck Presser from the House of Detention. He assigned a police officer to guard her, and put her in an apartment in the Woodside section of Queens. From that position of comfort, Nancy provided the assistant district attorneys with new information. They sent one of her few friends in the business, prostitute Thelma Jordan, to live as her roommate.

In Woodside, the girls were accompanied out to dinner and enjoyed an occasional drink. Madams Peggy Wild, Mildred Balitzer, and Jennie the Factory would eventually join them. It was a nicer arrangement than any had known in a long time.

Nancy gave her testimony to assistant district attorney Harold Cole. She started slowly and carefully, starting with her pinch in a direct hit in the house run by Pollack Frances Blackman. Moving backwards in time, she revealed other places where she'd gone to work. Most bookings had come through Pete Harris and Jack Eller. Before that, her bookings were arranged by Ralph Liquori.[8]

The young woman, shaky and depressed, asked Harold Cole to get others to validate and provide corroboration of her story. Other witnesses began to do so.

Peggy Wild told a story that connected Ralph Liquori with downtown politician Al Marinelli. Wild said that Liquori had once had a partner named Johnny Roberts. The two had been in the extortion racket, and had taken money from Wild's partner Dora Hearns.

Peggy Wild decided to set a trap for Liquori. With the help of Deputy Inspector McDermott, she and Dora Hearns gave Liquori some marked money. Then, the 68th Street precinct detectives arrested Liquori. In the scuffle, Liquori's partner was shot. The cops beat Liquori up inside the station house.

But Peggy Wild's hopes of seeing Liquori incarcerated were dashed when Al Marinelli showed up at the arraignment and told Liquori he would "break the coppers involved." Peggy Wild's story was corroborated by Thelma Jordan, who was living with Liquori's partner, Johnny Roberts. It was then that Thelma Jordan began to give her testimony. She confirmed Presser's story that Little Davie Betillo, Jerry Bruno, and Tommy the Bull used to hang out with Al Marinelli in the Godolfo Napoli Restaurant at 380 Broome Street.

Al Marinelli was only one step away from Lucky Luciano, and soon, Nancy Presser joined the growing chorus of people who were ready to speak the name Charlie.

Nancy said she met Luciano in 1933 while hanging out in Kean's Tavern on 8th Avenue in Times Square. Presser claimed she shared a table at Kean's on several occasions with Luciano, Little Davie Betillo, Jimmy Fredericks, Abe Wahrman, Jerry Bruno, and Benny Spiller.

She heard them discuss the arson that had started the fire in Dago Jean's apartment. Nancy claimed she heard Luciano say, "Madams will have to bond and if they refuse, wreck their joints."

Presser also said she'd hung out with Luciano at the Cotton Club in Harlem. They left the table to go to a private room. While she admitted she didn't hear much conversation, Nancy corroborated the story of the shakedown of David Marcus.[9]

By March, it was clear that portions of Nancy Presser's extensive testimony were full of holes. The inconsistencies were apparent when the other parties she referred to couldn't confirm certain statements. Take the story of her involvement of the Marcus shakedown. Ruth Marcus refused to identify a photo of Ralph Liquori, as did her husband, Dave. Ruth admonished both Nancy Presser and Thelma Jordan. "Don't say anything about that certain party," she warned. Nancy and Thelma concurred that Ruth was talking about Luciano.

Other unsubstantiated statements appeared in her flawed testimony. In 1935, Nancy walked into Kean's Tavern with Liquori and ran into Luciano. According to her story, she couldn't tell Ralph Liquori that she knew Luciano. This inconsistency raised a red flag. Liquori was Nancy's pimp. Of course he would know if Nancy was acquainted with Luciano.

According to her statements, Nancy had visited Luciano in his suite in the Waldorf Astoria five or six times during the past year.

According to her account, Charlie Lucky had called Presser at the Hotel Emerson and asked her to come over to his suite. She claimed that while in her company, Luciano received a phone call from Little Davie Betillo.

"Davie was in some kind of trouble and Lucky, using a lot of profanity, told him that he couldn't depend upon Davie and it would be better if Lucky did the job himself and that he would have to get Al to fix the matter for Davie," she said. On another occasion, she contradicted herself and said that Luciano's part of the conversation had been limited to one-word answers.

Other times, Nancy claimed that combination members visited Luciano. On each occasion, Luciano sent her into the bedroom or bathroom, telling her to keep the water running so she wouldn't overhear the conversation. She listed his visitors as Little Davie Betillo, Vito (either Genovese or Lasalle), Big Frenchie, Dutch Goldberg, Jerry Bruno, Tommy the Bull Pennochio, Jimmy Fredericks, and Al Marinelli.[10]

The following month, in April, Thomas Dewey wrote a letter accompanying Governor Lehman's appeal to the State Legislature asking for consolidation of defendants to be tried under one indictment.

"A new type of criminal exists, who leaves to his hirelings and front man the actual offenses, and rarely commits an overt act himself. Seldom, if ever, does any major criminal commit any crime under circumstances in which apprehension is possible," wrote Dewey to the Legislature. "The only way in which the major criminal can be punished is by connecting to him, through various layers of subordinates, the related but separate crimes committed on his behalf," he continued. "As the law now stands, there is a procedural straitjacket which prohibits the trial of these offenses together (except in a conspiracy, which is a mere misdemeanor), though they all constitute the acts of the master through his subordinates."

In early April, Dewey's suggestions to the New York State Legislature were kicked into action when Governor Lehman signed them into law. The legislative action buoyed Dewey. He needed a psychological boost. The special prosecutor was frustrated at the Hot Springs authorities. Luciano had fled to the safe town, where gangsters like Owney Madden, Frank "Jelly" Nash, and Alvin Karpis had reaped the protection of the authorities. In nearby Little Rock, the town of Hot Springs was becoming a national embarrassment. After a Little Rock judge superceded the jurisdiction of the Hot Springs system of protection, he issued a press statement. "I am trying to demonstrate to the outside world that Arkansas is not an asylum for criminals."[11]

The judge was referring to the fact that Hot Springs had a long history of sheltering the underworld. As far back as 1883, when St. Louis gambler Dink Davis was shot by a detective there while resisting arrest, Hot Springs was a cooling off joint for criminals on the lam from more hostile cities. Along with St. Paul and Joplin, it was the place for wanted criminals to vacation safely from prosecution. According to Karpis, "All the local people asked was that you spent your money in their stores and hotels and bars and restaurants, and guys like Lucky Luciano, who was a frequent visitor, always spread around cash in bills of large denominations."[12]

Another wanted Public Enemy, Alvin Karpis, overshadowed the search for Luciano. Karpis had been spotted in Hot Springs after a November 1935 robbery of a train at Garrettsville, Ohio. When three men pulled into a cabin on the outskirts of town on April 1, a call was placed to Sheriff T.S. Fisher that one of the men looked like Karpis.

This information was forwarded to Chapmon Fletcher, SAC of the local field office of the Department of Justice, the forerunner to the FBI. The agents went to the cabin dressed like hunters and sportsmen.

While Luciano was quietly being placed under arrest on the promenade, federal agents converged upon Karpis' alleged hideout in the woods. But it was emptied of its inhabitants. They fired tear gas into the house, shattered windows, and set a bed on fire when one of the missiles landed on it.[13]

The cause of Luciano's initial arrest can be traced back to booker Al Weiner, who stated that Luciano had attempted to extort $100 from him the previous June. Based on this allegation, Dewey went to Judge Jacob Gould Schurman, Jr. to request the warrant for Luciano's arrest. The initial charge was a warrant of a city magistrate of the City of New York, for the "arrest of Charles Luciano charging extortion accompanied by threats of violence and flight from New York to avoid prosecution." Dewey announced that he would invoke Section 408e of the Federal Kidnapping Act. Passed in 1934, Section 408e made it a federal crime to move from one state to another to avoid prosecution for a felony. It also made it a federal crime to avoid giving testimony in a proceeding regarding a felony. That would allow Dewey to charge Luciano with fleeing New York State to avoid prosecution on the extortion charge.

While Luciano was being picked up in Hot Springs, the federal authorities in Little Rock prepared to intervene.

At 2:25 on the afternoon of April 1, John Brennan, a Bronx-based detective, in the company of another New York detective, Stephen Di Rosa, walked up to Luciano on the promenade of the resort city's Bathhouse Row. The two detectives quietly collared him. Luciano was walking with Chief of Detectives Herbert "Dutch" Akers. But the gangster was arrogant, believing this to be a routine arrest.[14] As he was brought to the Garland County Jail, with $500 in his pocket and Akers up his sleeve, Luciano was contemptuous. Although Dewey had forwarded the request that Luciano be held on $200,000 bail, Chancellor Sam W. Garratt, who interpreted the charge against Luciano as a morals charge, set bail at $5,000. With the bail fixed at $5,000, Herbert Akers contacted the Hot Springs officials who stepped up as Luciano's legal team. They were: the City Attorney, A.T. "Sonny" Davies; Richard M. Ryan, former president of the Hot Springs Bar Association; and James Campbell, State Assemblyman from Garland County.

The three found a judge at the Arlington Downs Race Track, and immediately put him to work. Chancellor Garratt obtained Luciano's release on a $5,000 bond by signing a writ of habeas corpus. Within the space of four hours, Luciano had been helped — it seemed — by every Hot Springs official in town. Herbert Akers handed Chancellor Garratt a signed $5,000 bail bond. The bail money was raised by Joe Jacobs, the proprietor of two popular gambling casinos, the Southern and the Belvedere. Jacobs often accompanied Luciano to the Oaklawn Race Track. After submitting the bail, Herbert Akers ushered Luciano out of the jail. He was temporarily free to await the habeas corpus proceedings.[15]

Upon hearing the news of Luciano's release, Dewey demanded an explanation. "I cannot understand how any judge could make such an order unless he was ignorant of the facts. Luciano is generally and correctly regarded as the most dangerous and important racketeer in New York City, if not the country. This case involves one of the largest rackets in New York and one of the most loathsome types of crime."[16] By telephone, the special prosecutor ordered Detective Brennan to keep tabs on Luciano and report on his whereabouts. Accompanied by Akers, Luciano had returned to his suite at the Arlington Hotel. Detective Brennan learned that Luciano had changed rooms after his release.[17]

Although events cascaded quickly, it seemed like an eternity to the staff waiting in the New York office. Dewey dispatched assistant district attorney Edward W. McLean, a young, red-haired man of Scottish descent. McLean jumped into a waiting police car parked outside the Woolworth Building on Broadway. He made it to Newark in time to catch a plane to Cleveland. But his quick action was thwarted when he became grounded at the airport in Cleveland. In frustration, McLean jumped on a railroad train bound for Hot Springs. In the meantime, Dewey began a campaign to convince Chancellor Garratt that his actions had been improper. John Brennan, joined by Detective Stephen Di Rosa from New York, rearrested Luciano.[18]

Luciano would be found with more money than he'd had during his first arrest. Detective Brennan was on hand to report that $2,900 was in his money belt, a sign that the gangster was ready to skip. Indeed, he'd been talking with Joe Jacobs, his benefactor, about signing the $5,000 bond, and discussing the idea of fleeing to Mexico.[19]

In four hours after his first arrest, Luciano had managed to find the best lawyers the county had to offer. A.T. Davies, the City Attorney of Hot Springs, had a formidable record. He'd lost only one extradition case in ten years. With this in mind, Dewey penned his anxious sentiments to Edward McLean, his assistant district attorney, who arrived on April 3 after his trip by airplane and train. McLean opened Dewey's telegram when he arrived at the Kingsway Hotel. Although the content of the telegram was discouraging, it afforded McLean a fair warning:

". . . The Mayor owns all the gambling houses, and the detectives sleep all day and dress up in tuxedos at night to guard the gamblers," wrote Dewey. "On Saturday night when they have a lot of business, they also put tuxedos on the firemen and have them guard the gamblers." Yet Dewey, so astute on most counts, made one critical error.

"There is one man in the Police Department named 'Brock,' Chief of the Bureau of Criminal Identification, who can be trusted, if you have to trust somebody."[20] Dewey's "trustworthy" Hot Springs official was none other than Lieutenant Cecil Brock. Along with Alvin Karpis, Herbert Akers, and Police Chief Joseph Wakelin, Brock would be convicted in 1938 to two years on federal harboring charges for sheltering Karpis.[21]

Next, Commissioner Lewis Valentine telegraphed Chancellor Garratt. Upon learning that Luciano would soon be charged with compulsory prostitution, Garratt apologized. He revoked the $5,000 bond and ordered Luciano retaken. Three hours later, still in the company of Herbert Akers, Luciano reentered the Garland County Jailhouse. This time, the mob boss was held without bail. In the second arrest, with

Luciano rearrested under Garratt's order, the Chancellor denied the restraining order served by Luciano's attorneys. He ordered the writ of higher court be served. "When the matter was first brought to my attention, the seriousness of the charge was not fully revealed to me," said Garratt. "I fixed what I considered to be sufficient bond, but after learning the facts in the case, I immediately ordered the bond revoked and Luciano remanded into the custody of [Chief Deputy Sheriff Roy Ermey.]"

Luciano gave a statement to the press. "I may not be the most moral or upright person in the country," he stated, "but I am the victim of the most vicious kind of politics."

On April 3, McLean's savior arrived in the person of Attorney General Carl E. Bailey, who arrived from Little Rock. Dewey had described him in his letter to Ed McLean as "a two-fisted, honest man and has everyone afraid of him." Bailey was an untouchable, one who detested the type of corruption for which Hot Springs was known.

At the time that Bailey entered the picture, two men were going to the Garland County courthouse. One, Ed McLean, represented the youth and integrity of the law. On the other hand, Lucky Luciano represented the spoils of crime. The reporters asked Luciano to stop and grant an interview. Seizing the moment, the gangster asked why the authorities waited this long to serve him with an indictment, when they knew all the time of his whereabouts. Since the death of his mother the year before, he had no reason to remain in New York. His comings and goings were no secret, as he was ready to explain. "When I left New York in the latter part of 1935, I went to Miami," he declared. "I [then] went to Hot Springs, then returned to Miami right before Christmas. After the races started in Miami, I came back to Hot Springs."

Rather than talk to reporters, McLean saved his talents for the interior of the Garland County courthouse. He explained that Luciano had been indicted by an extraordinary grand jury in New York City on charges of compulsory prostitution. McLean requested the prisoner Luciano be held on $200,000 bail, pending extradition. As though for emphasis, he produced Governor Lehman's warrant for extradition. It would be a difficult game of legal card tricks for Ed McLean, who now had to move to dismiss the original warrant, that of extortion and interstate flight to avoid prosecution, upon which Luciano was originally arrested. Luciano's attorneys, meanwhile, filed an amendment in Hot Springs Municipal Court to their original habeas corpus application. They hoped to avoid extradition to Little Rock by requesting a "Fugitive from Justice" warrant to be served on their client. Their strategy was to block the transfer of the gangster from Hot Springs to Little Rock by voiding the impending warrant for compulsory prostitution.

Dewey summed up this maneuver by saying, "Luciano had his own counsel sue out [sic] a writ for his own arrest, and, in defiance of a warrant . . . he induced the sheriff of Hot Springs to hold him in custody on the phony warrant, produced by his own counsel." Ed McLean countered by narrowing the original charge down to extortion. He produced New York City Detective Robert Goldstein, who accused Luciano of extortion accompanied by a threat of violence against Al Weiner. Luciano greeted the news with the alibi that he was in Cuba when the alleged extortion took place in New York. But Dewey had already dispatched three New York detectives, Stephen Di Rosa, James Cashmen, and John Kennedy, who would say they saw Luciano at the Jamaica Race Track, in Queens, on April 6, 1935, the day the extortion allegedly took place.

McLean scored a victory when Chancellor Garratt denied the prisoner's request for a restraining order. This paved the way for the prisoner's transfer to Little Rock. But Luciano's team convinced the court to remand Luciano to the custody of Chief Deputy Sheriff Roy Ermey of Garland County, who was part of the machinery prepared to defend the racketeer from McLean and Attorney General Bailey. Ermey refused to turn Luciano over to the custody of the New York and Little Rock authorities. As if to add insult to injury, Luciano then invited the two men into his cell to have dinner with him later that evening. Dewey would write, "The local judge . . . ordered the sheriff of Hot Springs to deliver this prisoner to the authorities from the Capitol of the State of Arkansas. Instead, right in the courtroom, the sheriff and Lucky's friends and the prisoner himself walked out and went to the local jail."

In the Garland County jail, Luciano ate his dinner of spaghetti, fried chicken, potatoes, salad, cheesecake, and coffee. The gangster smoked cigarettes for which he paid $5 a pack to the warden. The extra cigarettes were given out to all the inmates of the Garland County jail, at Luciano's request. He slept on the special sheets, pillows, and blankets, which were brought to him by Akers from his rooms in the Arlington Hotel.[22]

On April 4, twenty Arkansas State rangers invaded the Garland County jail in Hot Springs. While furnishing a warrant signed by Judge Abner McGehee of Pulaski County Circuit Court, Little Rock, they roused Roy Ermey. He didn't protest as the rangers, armed with machine guns, rifles, and pistols, removed Luciano from his custody. The gangster was sarcastic. "What's this, the National Guard?" he sneered. "Do you need all these men to take me to Little Rock?" Then he asked for permission to get clean clothes from his suite at the Arlington Hotel. But it must have occurred to him at that moment that the sweet life of Hot Springs was over.

At the same time, Carl Bailey started contempt proceedings against Sheriff Ermey and A.T. Davies, the attorney who simultaneously represented Luciano and the City of Hot Springs. Bailey charged the corrupt officials with unwarrantedly interfering with the transfer, and ordered them to appear in Circuit Court to show cause why penalties should not be levied against them.

The state rangers drove the gangster fifty-five miles over mountain roads to the Pulaski County jail in Little Rock. There, Judge Abner McGehee of the 1st Division Circuit Court set Luciano's bail at $200,000. The news was in: Governor J. Marion Futrell, as a courtesy, had honored the extradition warrant issued by Governor Lehman in New York. As good as things looked, Thomas Dewey was steering himself for the next barrage of motions from the defense. As a backup, Dewey asked U.S. Attorney Lamar Hardy to ask federal authorities in Little Rock to once again arrest Luciano on the federal charge of compulsory prostitution. This charge would stick regardless of whether Luciano's attorneys were successful in delaying or defeating extradition. "I'd rather be accused of murder," muttered Luciano. U.S. attorney Fred Dagrid said he would file a holdover warrant, which would also keep him on the federal extortion charges made by Al Weiner, in the event the state charges of fugitive-from-justice were dropped.[23]

On April 7, Attorney General Carl E. Bailey announced that an anonymous person had tried to bribe him with an offer of $50,000 for Luciano's release. Dewey would later determine that two businessmen from New York, who made this attempt to bribe Carl Bailey, also tried to get to one of Dewey's assistant district attorneys with a similar offer in exchange for throwing the trial. After all attempts to free the mobster were exhausted, his attorneys threatened to go to the U.S. Supreme Court to prevent extradition from Arkansas. Dewey balked at the actions of Federal Judge John E. Martineau in Little Rock. Served by Luciano's attorneys with a new writ of habeas corpus, Martineau granted them a stay of ten days in which to seek an appeal hearing before the U.S. Circuit Court of Appeals at Kansas City. When Dewey protested, saying that the maneuver would cost the State of New York additional taxpayer dollars, Martineau retorted, "I don't care what it is costing New York. I am determined to see that this man gets every right he is entitled to in court."

In granting the stay, Martineau imposed the condition that Luciano's attorneys complete their applications by April 17. He imposed a clause that twenty-four hours' notice must be given of the time and place of the appeal and the name of the judge who would hear it.

McLean then tried to shorten the red tape by having a court stenographer type out two complete copies of the records and testimony. He served them on the defense. Then he went into court and asked Judge Martineau for a shorter time. But in spite of McLean's efforts, Martineau refused to shorten the time for Luciano's attorneys to answer.

It seemed like nothing was going to break. Suddenly, Luciano's attorney, Dave Panich, sent a telegram to Bailey notifying him that he would apply to Martineau the following afternoon. He was still looking for an extension of the stay. Meanwhile, Panich had gone to St. Louis, Kansas City, and South Dakota in search of a Circuit Court that would allow an appeal. So far, no request for an appeal had been granted on the federal level.

Panich was still out of the city of Little Rock when McLean took note of the fact that it was the ninth and last day of the stay. "The condition on which the stay was granted was that the Attorney General would be notified of the time and place of any hearing that was granted and the name of the judge who granted it," McLean told Dewey in a telephone call. "At midnight tonight, the last chance for them to fulfill the twenty-four hour notice requirement will be gone."

Dewey concurred. He instructed McLean to "yank Luciano out of jail at one minute after midnight," if the Attorney General had not been notified of any other venue willing to give Luciano his day in court. At midnight on April 17, Attorney General Bailey went to the district attorney. They obtained the warrant for Luciano's arrest. After checking out of his hotel, Ed McLean read the train schedule, noting that the last train out of Little Rock was about to leave. Bailey made a phone call and delayed the departure. At one minute past midnight on April 18, the ten-day stay of extradition had expired. One minute later, Federal Judge John E. Martineau and Chancellor Frank M. Dodge signed orders directing Sheriff L.B. Branch of Pulaski County to surrender Luciano to the New York police.

Ed McLean, with his team of New York detectives, quickly went to the jail. They awoke Luciano's jailer, Sheriff Branch. McLean got Sheriff McGehee to explain to Sheriff Branch that the letters signed by the District Attorney and the Attorney General, along with their warrant for Luciano's arrest, were legitimate.

Governor J. Marion Futrell had signed the extradition papers. Sheriff Branch read the face sheet of the legal pleadings placed in his hands. "This requisition will be and is granted."

As the detectives hustled the handcuffed man over to the train yard, where they walked him over yards of track to the waiting train, Luciano yelled in protest.

"I'm being kidnapped."[24]

Luciano arrived at Grand Central Station in the custody of Di Rosa, Brennan, Kennedy, and McLean. Upon their arrival in New York, they went immediately over to Centre Street to have him booked. On April 19, he was arraigned before Judge Philip J. McCook. Judge McCook set

Luciano's bail at $350,000 and charged him with twenty-four counts in four indictments. Attorney Edward J. Reilly visited him in the Raymond Street jail. There, attorney Moses Polakoff also visited him. Luciano would remain in the Tombs at 101 Centre Street.

Moses Polakoff would serve as counsel in Luciano's defense. The racketeer's given name of Salvatore Lucania was purposely omitted from the pleadings, as he was no longer known by that name in the underworld, nor had he used it when checking into hotels.

For the record, he was to be known as Charles Lucky Luciano during the trial. He was charged with placing a prostitute named Betty Anderson in a house on April 22, 1935, at 1 W. 68th Street. The extraordinary grand jury stated in the indictment that she "should there live a life of prostitution."[25]

CHAPTER 11

THE SMALL FRY

That was the fur district, but I was no furrier.
—Witness Rene Gallo

With the trial four days away, a new witness appeared on the scene. A madam who'd hit upon hard times, she was arrested for soliciting an undercover vice officer. Because she was a stoned junkie, she was thrown into the Women's House of Detention for a cold turkey cure. The quick drug reduction, although hard on her body, was only one component in her many problems with the law.

On May 7, Florence Brown was arrested as Fay Marston. She hated her street name, Cokey Flo, which she claimed was "hung on her" by booker Pete Harris. Flo Brown had skipped bail three months prior to this arrest. At the time of the May arrest, she was a fugitive from three charges. She was afraid of the possibility of being fingerprinted and identified.

She'd been using narcotics since 1931, when she started with opium and morphine. She graduated to heroin in the beginning of 1936. While under the care of her own doctor, in an attempted private cure the previous February, Florence heard the news that her boyfriend, Jimmy Fredericks, was arrested in the vice sweep.[1]

"My sweetheart was in jail," Flo later wrote. "I needed him for comfort while I was sick. I needed him for money."[2] This incongruous request — to ask Jimmy Fredericks for comfort — was coupled with her business acumen. She was a tough madam and an aggressive businesswoman. If she asked Fredericks for money, she got it. Everything Flo did, she did for money.

Florence Brown was born in Pittsburgh. She was approaching the age of thirty at the time of her arrest. For roughly half her life, she'd been living in the criminal world. She'd quit school at fourteen when she ran away to Youngstown, Ohio. She had a racket with a girlfriend, selling "cheap pictures at high prices." When that dried up, she ran to Cleveland and worked in a speakeasy for three years. In 1925, she went to Chicago, where she was kept by three men. She got involved in Jack Zuta's prostitution syndicate before Zuta was killed in an underworld hit.

"Zuta was killed by some Italian mob," she related. After Zuta's death, she ran to Duluth, Minnesota. While there, she met a male madam named Joe Sussman. He brought her to New York in 1929. Soon she returned to Chicago and opened a house with Sussman's help. In her travels, she met Pete Harris, who talked her into going to New York in 1930. She worked independently from 1931 to 1933, and booked with Spike Green and Charlie Spinach. She became indebted to them after they bailed her out after a pinch. She had to pay them back at the rate of $50 a week. But her credit was good, and Flo was able to book with Nick Montana. After Montana's arrest, Flo went to Pete Harris and hung out with Harris' drug addicted wife, Mildred.

Flo got into trouble early on with the combination. She balked after hiring Gashouse Lil, Ralph Liquori's girlfriend. Upon hearing that Gashouse Lil was the girlfriend of *the* Ralph Liquori, Flo fired her. She hoped that by ridding herself of syndicate girls, she would avoid having to pay the combination thugs. But Chappie and Joe Levine found her out when they came to her door to collect. She had a plan. She wanted to meet Jimmy Fredericks.

In a quick reflection of Flo's business smarts — or sex appeal, depending on how you looked at it — Flo seduced Jimmy Fredericks. The two became a couple seen around town. They lived for a short time at the Hotel Emerson, which was a residence hotel housing Ralph Liquori and his girl, Nancy Presser.

While Flo was operating a house at 333 West End Avenue in September 1935, she became addicted to morphine.

Flo learned a bitter lesson that Christmas. While she spent $100 to give Fredericks a present, he bought her nothing. But the grapevine sent the news that Lillian Frederico, his wife, was wearing a new fur coat. In the wife verses mistress payoff, Flo had lost out. Then, she suffered a humiliating arrest. Not only was her place raided and closed, but Flo's "works" were confiscated and she was labeled, for the first time, as a drug addict. She was charged with three misdemeanors—maintaining a house of prostitution, possession of a hypodermic syringe, and possession of a cube-and-a-half of morphine.

Flo found herself in a situation similar to other madams who had bonded for her girls but not for herself. The moment of truth arrived in the Women's Court, where she found herself begging Jesse Jacobs to pay her $2,500 bail.

Jacobs did so, which put Flo in hock to the combination for the bail. At a low point, Flo tried a cure in a Central Park West sanitarium. She remained only a short time, but cleaned herself up.

On February 2, the day after the raids, she learned that Fredericks had been arrested. Her versatility rose to the rescue. Flo got a job as an editorial assistant to an author. For a short time, she had a real job. It would be the first of her two attempts to work in what she would later call, "legit business."

She wasn't able to sustain her real job for long. She went back on drugs. This time, it was heroin. After the raids broke up the combination, Flo was forced into street-walking to support her habit.

The May arrest would prove to be her worst nightmare. She went through the quick reduction, or fifty-six hours of cold turkey withdrawal. Some of the girls in the House of Detention heard of her trouble. Prostitute Grace Hall kited a letter to Flo.

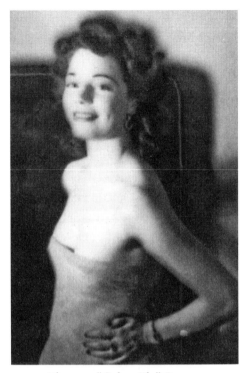

Florence "Cokey Flo" Brown
(NYC Municipal Archives)

"Please don't think we are rats," wrote Grace. "We were in a tight spot. Each one was threatened with seven-and-a-half to twenty years. We thought there was no other way to turn." Grace found a way to get in and talk to Florence. "What are you doing to yourself?" she asked her friend. "Talk to Mr. Ten Eyck. We all talk to him." She gave Florence a piece of paper and a stubby pencil. Florence soon decided to take the advice of her friends.

In wobbly script, Flo penned the first of several furtive letters to Barent Ten Eyck.

Mr. Ten-Eyck, Would like to see you to-night [sic], early, please. Not too late at night, please. Sincerely yours, Fay Marston (Flo)

Her attempts to contact Ten Eyck brought her plenty of trouble. An unsigned note was delivered to her.

Dear Flo. Jimmy does not want you to testify against Charlie, because Jimmy said it will go against him. Jimmy said he does not [sic] want you to lie about Charlie.[3]

Dewey, being an astute judge of human nature, had put Barent Ten Eyck on the job of talking to the material witnesses. The special prosecutor had learned that the prostitutes, being women, gave better testimony when approached by the handsome, accomplished men in his office. Dewey also realized that Eunice Carter would not be effective in developing a strong relationship with the prostitutes. Dewey pushed men like Ten Eyck and Sol Gelb into face-to-face relationships with the witnesses, and kept Carter in the background. Although Mrs. Carter continued to play a strong role in the development of the case, her role was downplayed from that point on.

Lucky Luciano was innocent until proven guilty. Yet, the newspapers had already convicted him. On May 12, before the trial had commenced, the *New York Daily News* labeled him the "Droopy-Eyed Czar of the Oldest Profession." Out of 200 prospective jurors, only eight were questioned the first day. One problem was the obvious risk factor for a juror. Out of the 200 who were questioned, half begged to be excused. Dewey asked each potential juror a pertinent question. "I must ask whether you are acquainted with Albert Marinelli. I ask this by reason of his relationship with one of the defendants in this case." As the wheels of justice turned at their typically slow pace, Judge McCook, setting a pattern that would continue throughout the trial, declared a night session that lasted until 11:00 [at night.] After the men were selected, the blue ribbon jury, comprised of jurors who had served before, collectively answered the prosecutor's main question.

When asked if they would believe the testimony of a woman who made her living from the streets, each juror said yes. Each claimed if the testimony was corroborated, they could believe it. Such testimony was on an equal footing with that gleaned from men making money from prostitution. The issue of credibility would not arise from the gender, or the occupation, of a corroborating witness.

In spite of the promise of the blue ribbon panel, Luciano's people would get to one of the jurors in due time. Luciano's agent, who called himself Greenhaus, would approach juror Martin Moses. It was typical of people who came to intimidate jurors and witnesses to refer to themselves as agents on Luciano's behalf. Greenhaus offered Mr. Moses a deal. There were people downtown, Greenhaus said, who were prepared to offer a job, or large sums of money, in exchange for "holding out." The sum of $2,500 would be paid for holding out in favor of Luciano for three hours. The larger sum of $10,000 to $15,000 was offered for holding out for nine hours; and $50,000 to $100,000 was being offered to disagree. Greenhaus told Mr. Moses that "there are several big shots downtown who would spare no expense to obtain an appeal." He asked Moses to "give your opinion in the courtroom proceedings and voice your dissatisfaction on certain phases of it." While Martin Moses kept this terrible secret, the tension among the other jurors was also difficult to endure. In their fear, some jurors would later claim they had tried to hold out for an acquittal.[4]

The ten defendants would be tried under the new Joinder Law, which allowed prosecutors to combine several related incidents into a single indictment. The law was being tried for the first time in a New York Supreme Court. As the trial opened on May 12, three defendants pleaded guilty. Samuel Siegel, Jimmy Frederick's lawyer, protested that they shouldn't have been allowed to switch their pleas in the presence of the other defendants. The fact remained that none were switching their pleas; they had decided long ago to cross over to the other side and testify for the State. Siegel was overruled as Pete Harris, aged 33, listed his occupation as an electrician. Harris gave his address as 54 W. 89th Street.

Al Weiner, 27, listed his domicile at 47 Sheriff Street. His occupation as a weaver had been one attempt to train the young man at a legitimate occupation. David Marcus, 45, who said he was a salesman, resided at 1480 Eastern Parkway in Brooklyn. Slumped dejectedly, the other defendants sat, each accompanied by an armed guard. With David Marcus, Pete Harris, and Al Weiner testifying for the prosecution, the remaining defendants were Luciano, Tommy the Bull Pennochio, Jimmy Fredericks, Little Davie Betillo, Benny Spiller, Abe Wahrman, Ralph Liquori, and bondsmen Jesse Jacobs with Meyer Berkman. Jack Eller was the only booker to sit with the co-defendants. The other three had agreed to testify for the State of New York.

With the courtroom jammed, spectators were kept out. The defendants and their guards occupied three rows of seats. Two parallel tables held the prosecutors and defense attorneys. For the state, Thomas Dewey sat alongside Jacob J. Rosenblum, Barent Ten Eyck, and William B. Herlands. Moses Polakoff, Samuel Siegel, Morton Levy, James D.C.

Murray, Caesar B.F. Barra, Lorenzo C. Carlino, David P. Siegel, Jacob Shientag, David Paley, and Maurice F. Cantor represented the defendants. There would be no pictures of the prostitutes displayed during the trial. Artists' renderings would substitute for photos of the material witnesses.

In Dewey's opening statement, he explained the logistics of the vice syndicate.

"Luciano will be shown not to have placed any women in houses or taken money from them. Instead, he set up his apartment at the Waldorf Astoria and was the czar of the ring. We will show that Luciano's function was to rule. All the other defendants were his servants.

"We will prove," Dewey continued, "that upon one occasion, Luciano boasted, 'We are going much further than this. We are going to put every madam in New York on a salary and then we will raise the prices.'

Luciano entered court for sentencing handcuffed to Jack Eller (foreground, far left), and Jimmy Fredericks (foreground, 2nd from left)
(Author's Collection)

"The bond was the real racket of the gang, Dewey continued. "For this bond, they guaranteed that no girl would ever go to jail."

Dewey described the office of Jesse Jacobs and Meyer Berkman, who ran the bonding agency. "Neither was licensed. Abe Karp, a disbarred lawyer, coached the girl on what to say in court."

Dewey made a comparison to the reign of Nick Montana. He stated that girls under Montana made as high as $400 a week. Under Luciano, a girl lost half her pay. In stressing the business aspect of prostitution, Dewey was able to convince the jury that he was not a prude. The inference was that these business deals were just that—commercial enterprises. This was not a social or moral problem.

In the first round of trial, Rose Cohen, 25, also called Rene Gallo, stepped up to give her address as 301 W. 57th Street, the last house in which she worked as a prostitute. Peggy Wild maintained this house. Rose was dressed neatly, in a blue silk dress, called a frock in the 1930s. The dress was trimmed in bright scarlet, and she wore a hat. She testified that in a house operated by Molly Leonard, she first met Pete Harris in summer 1933. He asked her to work for him.

"Do you know what you have to wear?" he had asked.

"Sure, I know," was her easy reply. "Evening gowns."

On the witness stand, Rose named ten madams, and said there were many others for whom she worked. She called Pete Harris every Saturday night or Sunday morning, and got the address of where she would work for the following week. Rose's first meeting with Harris came before Luciano and the mob organized the vice ring.

"Were you ever arrested?" Dewey asked her.

Rose described the usual arrangement in the event of an arrest. A girl was initially taken to the local station house, and bailed out. At that point, she was taken to the bail office on W. 10th Street. There, she would meet Jimmy Fredericks along with Max Rachlin, or one of the other bail bondsman or lawyers.

To illustrate, Rose clarified the tawdry meaning of the "direct hit."

"They told me I better show up in court, because mine was a direct case," she said.

"What do you mean by a direct case?" asked Dewey.

"Well, the cop had me in the room."

To answer the prosecutor's question, Rose Cohen continued.

"I said I worked on Twenty-Sixth Street near Third Avenue as a seamstress. But that wouldn't do because that was the fur district, but I was no furrier."

During cross-examination, Jimmy Fredericks' attorney, Samuel Siegel, attacked the character of the witness. As she was a prostitute, he had quite an advantage.

"How many men did you sleep with a night?" he demanded to know.

"I didn't sleep with them," she replied glibly.

"Well, use your own term. How many did you lie down with?"

"That depended. Sometimes fifteen or twenty."

Siegel then asked if Madam Nigger Ruth was "colored."

"She was not," Rose replied evenly. "She was Jewish."

"Did you ever stay with a colored man?" asked Siegel.

"I never did," she responded with a loud laugh.

Muriel Ryan, 24, was the second prostitute to testify. With her auburn hair and voluptuous figure, she embodied the popular fantasy of a prostitute. Under direct examination, she admitted to working for Nick Montana. She'd refused to pay bond. That lasted until Montana gave her the news of the "new combination," which meant she would have to pay. In 1934, she went over to Pete Harris.

The next day, May 13, Joan Martin came to the stand. The madam who called a conference with other madams, Joan Martin was a powerhouse. Forty-one years old and Rumanian, she wasted no time in venting her anger over the treatment she'd endured at the hands of the three defendants, Fredericks, Abe Wahrman, and Ralph Liquori. She laughed as she pointed the finger at them.

During the cross-examination, Samuel Siegel again brought up the brass tacks of prostitution.

"What did you charge in the house on Clinton Street?" he asked Joan.

"That was a three-dollar house," she replied curtly.

"Oh, I see," he countered. "Then your prices came down as you went along?"

"Yes, they did," she responded. "That was because of the Depression," she laughingly replied.

"So you think it's funny to live on the earnings of women's bodies, do you?" challenged Siegel.

"No, I don't. And neither do you. But I think you talk funny," countered Joan. "I'm laughing at you."

As much as Siegel hammered at her, she kept the atmosphere light. She described how she paid the super in her buildings. "Every tenement house superintendent in New York takes money," she explained to the jury.

Joan revealed that her relationship with Fredericks had never ended. Although she despised him, she was forced to work with him. When she suspected rival madam Nigger Ruth was "sending cops and stickup men around," she went to Fredericks.

Joan looked over at Fredericks. "You asked for it, Jimmy; you asked for it," she sneered.

She repeated the story of being forced to bond, of being beaten with the blackjack. She told of how Fredericks threatened to kill her dog. Her tough demeanor was softened.

"How did you feel?" asked Barent Ten Eyck.

"I didn't have no feeling," answered Joan Martin. "I was blood from top to toe and I was unconscious."

She identified Ralph Liquori as the stickup man. Judge McCook instructed Liquori, who was wearing glasses, to take them off.[5]

When Joan Martin returned to the Women's House of Detention, she faced Flo Brown. Flo was livid with anger at Joan for incriminating Jimmy Fredericks. Flo began screaming at Joan. Her hysteria mounted until the matrons threw her in solitary.

In solitary, she was given a piece of paper with which to pen a note to Ten Eyck. Without her realizing it, she was transferring her affections to the competent, handsome, assistant district attorney.

Dear Sir, I think it is a shame for a nervous person like June Garry (Joan Martin) to start trouble. She had me locked in solitary. I said nothing, she sure has a good imagination. Am very sick, please see what made her angry with me. Sincerely yours, (Flo) Fay Marston.[6]

The first of the bookers to testify was Al Weiner. His testimony revealed the ambivalence these underworld characters shared in their relationships. Weiner was the first of the defendants to go over to a guilty plea. On the stand, he answered Dewey's questions about being sucked into his father's illegal business. One could imagine a boy coming into the family business of a butcher or baker. But Al Weiner had started booking women from 146 Rivington Street on Saturdays and Sundays. Weiner described the day when, in September 1933, his father introduced him to Abe Wahrman.

Margaret Martino
(Author's Collection)

Al Weiner went on to implicate Jimmy Fredericks and David Betillo. In a meeting, Betillo had threatened all the bookers. He related the story of how Betillo had told Jack Eller he would kick his belly out. He'd told Al Weiner that he was lucky to be allowed in the business. Then prostitute Margaret Martino, 22, was brought in to testify that Al Weiner's father, Cockeyed Louie, had booked her in 1935. He'd instructed her to go to the combination people if she got arrested.

Weiner showed Dewey more courtesy than he would show Samuel Siegel. Siegel's aggressive tactics were more effective on the young women; in answer to Siegel's questions, Al denied everything. He denied visiting his father in prison and said he took his father's defense money and spent it. He claimed he'd never heard of income tax.[7]

The next witness was madam Dorothy Arnold. Under Ten Eyck's questioning, Dorothy explained the system of calculating earnings. The prostitute identified a card punched full of holes. "I used them to keep track of the girls' money as they earned it. When one of them got money from a man, she brought it to me and I punched it on her card." She held up the card.

Witness Mary Thomas
(Author's Collection)

"This card here shows that the girl earned two dollars from the first man, and I punched the card twice. Three dollars from the second man, four dollars from the third man, and then two dollars again for thirteen times. I kept the money and the girl kept the card. When a card was full, she would give it back to me. Every night I would write down in my books the amount a girl had taken in."

The parade of women continued. Mary Thomas, 27, a widow with two children to support, claimed she'd become a prostitute in 1933.

Betty Winters, a madam, offered some comic relief. She admitted that business had taken a dive. The recent building elevator strike had kept the customers from getting upstairs to the apartment.

With court convening on Saturday, David Marcus, the second booker to change his plea to guilty, took the stand. He was the first witness to mention Thomas Pennochio by name. He also referred to Jimmy Fredericks having mentioned Charlie Lucky.

"I asked Jimmy, 'Who's gonna take care of me?' said

Madam Betty Winters booked with Cockeyed Louie Weiner
(Author's Collection)

David Marcus. He quoted Jimmy Fredericks as saying, "Don't worry . . . Little Abie, Davie, and Charlie will take care of you."

Marcus denied ever having been charged with operating a house of prostitution in Pittsburgh, and in saying so, would make a liar of himself. The defense vowed to damage his witness credibility by showing the denials were false.

The chief defense strategy would be to discredit witnesses. It was the first instance of perjury that they could prove with evidence. The defense attorneys produced detectives from Pittsburgh who swore that Marcus had been convicted there on vice charges. To counteract the charges of perjury, Dewey claimed that Marcus had admitted to such only after giving his testimony.[8]

After the first wave of witnesses had finished their procession to the witness stand, all defendants but one had been implicated. Lucky Luciano remained unsung. As spectators anxiously awaited the forthcoming testimony of Jennie the Factory, it seemed like Lucky had still not seen his day in court.

CHAPTER 12

LIKE THE CHAIN STORES

I didn't go to church; I hate hypocrites.
—Prostitute Thelma Jordan

On May 13, the second day of the vice trial, Cokey Flo Brown was finishing her five-day reduction cure in Cell 3, Corridor A, on the fourth floor of the Women's House of Detention. With misgivings, Dr. Nisselman allowed her to speak to Barent Ten Eyck. She couldn't walk, and was placed on a cot. As she fitfully tried to recover from the ravages of the quick cure, he prepped her to testify. The woman who would never be a rat was going to join Mildred Balitzer and Nancy Presser in the job of placing Luciano within earshot of the combination bosses.

Flo Brown prepared the story she would tell the jury. "I wanted to go straight and quit all this." In spite of the simplistic overtones, Flo was not a simple woman. Her intelligence and memory were in great shape. Flo's every thought was of money and how she could make it in one scheme or another. Given a better set of circumstances, Flo could have been a woman before her time. She was smart and, financially, wanted independence. After her interview with Ten Eyck, Flo joined the convalescent ward, where she stayed until May 21.

Madam Molly Leonard was the first of the day to testify. She said she'd been a madam since 1918. The first witness to invoke the name "Lucky," she sent defense attorneys up to the bench to object. They asked Judge McCook to strike Lucky's name from the record. McCook overruled the objection.

The record would show that Molly Leonard testified that Pete Harris had told her "there was a combination with new people in it." She then asked, "Who are the people?" His answer was, "Lucky."

The news blackout was broken when photographers got a picture of the wives of some of the defendants. It was hard to imagine that men who trafficked in women's flesh, went home to their wives. Mrs. Dorothy Betillo, Mrs. Mary Pennochio, Mrs. Abe Wahrman, and Mrs. Lillian Frederico appeared in court every day to stand by their husbands. On May 19, Little Davie Betillo came into the picture, spitting and swearing.

The cause of his wrath was booker Danny Brooks, who came from Dannemora to testify. Like witness Joe Bendix, Brooks was a convicted felon. Brooks was already sentenced to serve his 7–20 year term for compulsory prostitution in the prison south of the Canadian border. Brooks' sole impetus for testifying was personal safety. Dewey promised that he would be transferred to a prison where he wouldn't be killed.

On the stand, Brooks implicated David Betillo in the combination. At the sight of the former booker, Betillo lost control of his temper. Caesar Barra, Betillo's attorney, dragged his client back after Betillo stood up, screaming accusations and profanities in the direction of Brooks. Then, Brooks joined Molly Leonard in implicating Luciano. He said he heard Fredericks say that Charlie Lucky was the head of the combination.

When Pete Harris testified, he presented himself as the walking wounded. "I was minding my own business as an independent booker until 1933."

At that time, Harris testified that he was threatened in the same manner as David Marcus: held up at gunpoint and told to leave town. That in 1933, while a successful booker, he was approached by Abe Wahrman. They pulled guns on him, he said, drove him home, and threatened to kill him if he didn't pay $250 a week for protection.

"I was afraid to leave town . . . I was afraid they were going to dump me on the road to make an example of me."

Harris claimed he'd asked Abe Wahrman a practical question. "How could they afford to bail out as many as six or seven women a day?"

Harris testified, "Little Abie says, 'Don't worry about that. Charlie Lucky is behind it.'"

As Luciano was implicated, interest extended only to the courtroom doors. The public was apathetic. To a city concerned with bread and butter issues of the Depression, the vice trial seemed hardly worth noticing. In a letter to the editor of the *New York Daily News*, one citizen had this to say:

"The Lucky Luciano trial goes to prove one thing. There's only one way to break up this revolting racket and stop these yellow rats and disgusting thugs from preying on semi-intelligent women. That way is to segregate all the prostitutes in a plainly marked and thoroughly publicized red light district, where the police can see that the dirty business is conducted as honestly as possible."[1]

Prostitute Helen Kelly returned to the stand, after making a first appearance with the words, "I am appearing in an effort to regain the self-respect lost as a prostitute." She was followed by Shirley Mason, 23. "I told Jack [Eller] I had a positive Wasserman and couldn't work in Atlantic City. Jack said, 'That's all right. I'll put you to work in New York City.'"

Jack Eller's defense counsel, Maurice Cantor, asked her who supplied her with food, rent, and clothing. She said Eller had leant her $68, and that it was a loan.[2]

Helen Kelly, Material Witness
(John Binder)

On the day that Cokey Flo Brown began her testimony, the temperature was eighty-six degrees and humid. There were thousands of people on the beach at Coney Island. Gimbels department store inserted an ad in the weekly papers. It offered shoppers a "cool bargain basement."

Flo was about to raise the heat by a few more degrees. Her legacy would be far-reaching. She attributed to Luciano the statement, "When they did get started like chain stores, the madams would be put on a salary or commission basis." By going on record with this statement, Flo branded Luciano with the logo of vice. Through the telegraph system of reporter to writer, storyteller to gangster buff, Luciano's alleged statement would evolve into the brand-specific phrase, "We'll start a chain just like the A&P."[3]

Flo was a slight, nervous brunette. She was plainly attractive, with a prominent nose, which appeared too large for her small-featured face. Because her five-day reduction had only occurred, she was feeble. Yet, she stayed on the witness stand all day, fortified by small glasses of brandy provided by Judge McCook.

Never called Cokey Flo to her face, she bore a protective attitude toward her ex-lover, Jimmy Fredericks. She debated the claims that Fredericks had committed violent acts against the madams. She claimed he was opposed to the practice, but forced himself "only when told by Luciano that madams and bookers were to be beaten into submission to the bonding combination."[4]

Flo insisted that she was a madam, a fact that may have been embellished. None of the prostitutes arrested ever mentioned having worked for her. She testified that in a Chinese restaurant uptown, Jimmy Fredericks introduced her to Charlie Lucky. Most of the conversation had been in Italian. When told to tell only the parts of the conversation that discussed prostitution, Luciano's trial attorney, George Morton Levy, objected. "Tell us the whole conversation," he said. "Luciano doesn't need any limitations."

To meet the defense attorney's challenge, Flo elaborated.

"He said, 'It was getting tough and the joints were difficult to manage and the bonding business was just a big headache now . . . Dewey's investigation coming on to make things tough. We ought to fold up.'"

Flo continued. "Charlie says a few pinches were taking the money out of the business. Little Davie Betillo then joined the conversation. 'Why don't you let it go for a while? Even if Dewey does get started, he'll probably only grab one or three bondsmen and that'll be all. We should be quiet for a while and then open up and syndicate like they did in Chicago.'

"And Charlie says, 'When they did get started like chain stores, the madams would be put on a salary or commission basis. Naturally,' he says, 'it would take time because they'd object at first but we could accomplish it. We could syndicate the places on a large scale, the same as the chain stores. We could even get the madams on a salary or commission basis.'"

Flo's testimony caused Luciano to stir around, casting constant glances at his lawyers. David Siegel accused her of being addicted to heroin.

"No, I'm not," she replied in a hurt tone. "I got the reduction treatment in the Women's House," she said, which was done a few days prior to her testimony. The defense counsel insisted on subjecting the witness to a physical examination. During the lunch break, two doctors for the defense and one for the State examined her in the Judge's chambers. They determined that Flo was no longer addicted. Her biggest vice during her days of testimony was a sip of Judge McCook's personal prescription for several shots of brandy.

Seeing that Flo had been a sympathetic witness, Samuel Siegel tried to paint her true colors. He mentioned that Flo had visited him in his office and tried to get the names of some of the girls who might testify against her boyfriend Jimmy Fredericks.

"I still have a soft spot in my heart for my sweetheart," she retorted.

Siegel wasn't fooled. "Did your arrest for offering to commit an act of prostitution with a police officer take the soft spot out of your heart?"

"No, it didn't," Flo replied.

"Well, what did?" asked the defense attorney.

"I wanted to go straight and get out of this business," she replied. As Flo stepped away from the witness stand, she walked out among the defendants. She placed her hand on the shoulders of David Betillo, Jimmy Fredericks, Abe Wahrman, and Meyer Berkman. She showed courage in facing down these tough mobsters.

The third day of cross-examination was a Saturday. Flo would have to fend off three more hours of questioning, this time by Morton Levy of Luciano's defense team. Levy focused on the fact that for two years prior to the trial, Florence had been the mistress of Jimmy Fredericks. He tried to get Flo to admit that she had sold out to Mr. Dewey for her own motives. "You wanted to get publicity to save yourself from a jail sentence, and incidentally to tell this jury how innocent your sweetheart is." By denying these and all the prior insinuations, Flo had held her ground.[5]

With three days to go before handing the trial over to the defense, Dewey would place the name of Luciano directly on the lips of two prostitutes, two convicts, and three employees of the Waldorf Astoria.

Thelma Jordan, 26, would detail another type of brutality, that of torture.

"I know what happens to people who tell on the combination. I know of girls who have had their feet and stomachs burned with cigarette and cigar butts and who had their tongues slit for talking." Off the record, Thelma revealed during grand jury testimony that a rival booker, not sanctioned by the combination, had been buried alive by men hired by Abe Wahrman.

In court, Assistant Special Prosecutor Harry Cole asked her if she knew Jack Eller and Benny Spiller. She confirmed that Spiller had told her about Lucky.

"He said Charlie Lucky was the boss, the head man. He said he wished he had the money Charlie took out of the combination every week."

"After you were arrested, did you see Ralph Liquori?" Cole inquired.

"Yes. Nancy Presser was there, also. He told Nancy that if she knew what was good for her, she would not testify against him or any of the other defendants because if she did, she would be taken care of. He said he would see that her picture was printed in her hometown so her folks would know she was a prostitute."

According to Thelma Jordan, the bathtub strangulation of Mrs. Nancy Titterton, which was making headlines in the city at the time, was held up as an example to frighten the witnesses. "[Ralph Liquori] said 'that woman was murdered and you just remember that. Just remember it won't be good for you to talk.'"[6]

Lorenzo Carlino, Liquori's attorney, asked Thelma Jordan if she was wined and dined by Dewey's staff. "Were you intoxicated and with Mr. Cole and Barent G. Ten Eyck of Mr. Dewey's staff?"

"No," she replied.

Defense Attorney David Siegel, like Samuel Siegel, asked some leading questions.

"What kind of customers did you have at 210 Avenue A?"

"Plain, honest working men," said Thelma.

"Foreigners?" asked Siegel.

"If you call Italians, Polish, and Greeks foreigners, then they were," replied Thelma.

"In that period, did you go to church?" asked the defense attorney.

"No," replied Thelma. "I hate hypocrites."

Thelma Jordan
(Author's Collection)

140

CHAPTER 13

SAMSON'S DELILAH

Reformation without Luciano's permission was impossible.
— Mildred Balitzer

While Thelma Jordan had discussed Lucky Luciano, Nancy Presser would make the biggest impression. For her shaky, unreliable testimony, she would leave the largest stain on the public record.

Her testimony was delivered with the hope that the jury would place her in the category of high-class, above-average beauty that Luciano preferred. But Nancy had lost her looks due to drug abuse. The biggest problem with Nancy Presser's testimony was the fact that she didn't keep her story consistent with the known facts about the layout of the Waldorf.

Nancy's opening statement directly contradicted information she'd given to Dewey's staff members in her opening statements to them. She had previously said that she was afraid to inform Liquori that she was acquainted with Luciano.[1] Now, she was going against her prior, recorded statement. She related that her former lover, Ralph Liquori, had introduced her to Luciano in Kean's Tavern, in the winter of 1933–1934. Then, she started visiting him, at least four or five times. She went there as a call girl.

"I told him I needed money and was going into a house of prostitution to get it. [Luciano] told me not to go into a house. If I needed money, he would let me have it. I asked him how the bonding business was going, and he said fine."

Defense attorney David P. Siegel, in a fierce cross-examination, attacked her character with references to her drug addiction, which had included morphine and heroin.

Morton Levy, Luciano's attorney, questioned her on the specifics of her love affairs and drug use. Her existence under the stubby thumb of Ralph Liquori came to light. But character assassination was hardly necessary. During her testimony, the inconsistencies were enough to damage her credibility. She had no names of anyone else who may have been around Lucky. She couldn't remember if there were twin beds or a double bed in Luciano's apartment in the Waldorf. She started to become ill on the stand when Samuel Siegel established that unannounced visitors were excluded from entering the Waldorf Towers. She didn't know whether there was a piano, or a phonograph, or a refrigerator in the suite. She couldn't describe the bedroom.

The confused woman, in avoiding the "bedroom" questions, inferred that her alleged relationship with Luciano had been platonic.

"Did he [Luciano] give you some money?" asked Samuel Siegel.

"Yes," replied Nancy.

"How much?" asked the defense attorney.

"Fifty dollars," was Nancy's reply.

"And you gave him nothing for it?" Siegel asked with a sneer. "And if he took you to dinner and a theatre—that is a high-class man—what would you charge if there was no intercourse?"

"Fifty to seventy-five dollars," Nancy responded.

"Yet, you would go to bed with a man in a house of prostitution for two dollars?" asked Siegel.

"Yes," she responded.

Perhaps knowing the poor impression she was making, Nancy begged to be allowed off the witness stand due to illness. She stepped down after inferring that Luciano had been impotent with her.

"What were you drinking?" asked Siegel.

"Champagne," she replied.

"And Charlie fell asleep and there was nothing between you?" the defense attorney asked.

"That's right."[2]

The defense attorneys countered by introducing, as evidence, floor plans of the Waldorf. George Morton Levy questioned G. David Hardy, the assistant manager of the hotel. He said that all visitors had to be announced, and that the path a Tower visitor had to take was tortuous. It was obvious that Nancy Presser had been lying.

Nancy's testimony lasted well into the evening hours. During the course of her testimony, Nancy let a dangerous fact slip from her tongue. She provided the address of her safe house in Queens. Early the next morning, the girls were covertly moved out of the Jackson Heights apartment and taken over to Brooklyn. There, they were checked into a suite in the St. George Hotel.

Cokey Flo came back into the picture after her former employer, writer Dorothy Russell Calvit, was arrested for trying to persuade Cokey Flo to change her story. The writer was the daughter of stage star Lillian Russell. Some of Luciano's people had paid a visit to Calvit's attorney, Samuel Kornbluth. They frightened the attorney into going to the Women's House of Detention to ask Florence to change her testimony. Dewey promptly had Kornbluth arrested for "a brazen attempt to wreck his case against Lucky Luciano by perjured testimony."[3]

To counter charges of featuring only low lives on the witness stand, Dewey had arranged for two model citizens who worked at the Barbizon Plaza at the time of Luciano's residency, to testify for the prosecution. A few developed cold feet. Thomas Dewey found he could depend upon one employee of the Waldorf.

A woman with the assumed name of Margarie Brown, the chambermaid, took the witness chair. She was in charge of cleaning Luciano's rooms in Suite 39-B by 2:00 in the afternoon. She identified him as Charles Ross. She also identified David Betillo, Jesse Jacobs, and Meyer Berkman as visitors to the apartment. While she couldn't find the fortitude shown by Flo Brown in walking out among the defendants, she did point to Jack Eller.

Under cross-examination by George Levy, the chambermaid clarified the layout of the suite. By doing so, she exposed Nancy Presser's lack of cognizance about the suite she claimed to visit. According to Margarie Brown, there was a large electric fireplace, disputing Nancy's claim that there had been no fireplace. Brown went on record as one of the honest people who helped the prosecution. But for the meat and potatoes of his case, Thomas Dewey would have to depend upon the testimony of the brazen and bold prostitutes.

Mildred Balitzer, the wife of booker Pete Harris, took the stand under the status of a star witness. With the vapid expression of a drug addict, she didn't look much like a celebrity. Mildred wore an expression

Mildred Balitzer
(NY Municipal Archives)

that seemed to mock everything in the room. She took the stand wearing a modest dress that was described as a "garden party frock." Yet, her jaded demeanor formed an odd mismatch for the outfit. To add to her hardened persona, Caesar Barra, a defense attorney, got her to tell the story of her past, both recent and long ago. That included an admission that she lived with a homosexual. It was a shocking revelation in the 1930s.

Under cross-examination, Mildred admitted that she had gone drinking with Sol Gelb and a police officer named George Heidt who would later take the stand as a defense witness to try to discredit Gelb.

With a razor's edge, Mildred Balitzer testified that she had pleaded with Luciano to let her husband out of the business. The testimony replicated the information she'd passed to the grand jury when she was first arrested.

Mildred repeated her story to the courtroom. This included how she had met David Betillo and Tommy Pennochio when the combination started. She was a madam, she said, who stayed in the business as the wife of booker Pete Harris. Betillo had started taking $200 a week from Harris in Fall of 1933. Seeing that Pete was getting hopelessly into debt, she asked Betillo to let Pete out of the racket. "Lucky is my boss," she testified he answered. "He is behind the protection racket."

Mildred blamed Luciano for the gangland execution of a boyfriend back in the 1920s. If revenge was a motive, she never admitted to it when she claimed to have met Luciano in Miami at the Paddock Bar & Grill. In answer to her request for an exit visa for her husband, Luciano wrote her off. She testified:

"I told him that Davie [Betillo] sent me to speak to him about Pete getting out. We talked for fifteen or twenty minutes. He didn't deny he was the boss. [Luciano] said, 'I understood that he was in. You know the racket. He owes money, and we need him. He's in and he stays in.'"

Under defense counsel George Morton Levy's cross-examination, Mildred submitted to the questions that revealed her life as a prostitute, then madam, then drug addict and practitioner of "unusual love practices." This included an arrangement by which Mildred lived with prominent homosexual Phil Ryan, a nightclub host and master of ceremonies. The defense challenged Mildred's character by suggesting that Ryan was her part-time lover.

"As a prostitute, you didn't mind undressing in front of this man, did you?" asked Levy.

"Oh, but I did [mind]. That room had two bathrooms and I undressed alone," said Mildred. She smiled innocently.

"You were angry with Lucky when he refused your request, were you not?" continued Levy.

"I certainly was," responded Mildred.

"And bitter, too?" suggested the defense attorney.

"Naturally," said Mildred. "I was bitter."

"And you are still angry and bitter, aren't you?" asked Levy.

"I am."

"You want us to understand," challenged Levy, "that when you talked with Lucky you were anxious to embark upon a career of reformation with Peter?"

"Yes, I do [want you to understand]," said Mildred.

"Then, why were you willing," asked Levy, "after Lucky turned you down, to go off to Havana on a pleasure trip with money Pete sent you . . . from the earnings of fallen women?"

"Reformation without Luciano's permission was impossible," said Mildred in conclusion.

Mildred stepped off the stand a marked woman. A former lover, Gus Franco, met her with a message. He told her that she would be killed.[4]

By the end of the week, booker Jack Eller changed his plea to guilty. Eller, 42, was the only booker the prostitutes genuinely liked. The consensus, that he was a regular guy who'd been in the real estate business before being drawn into the combination, made him the one sympathetic defendant. After Eller changed his plea to guilty, saying that he could get a break as a first offender, he went to the Tombs to await sentencing.[5]

By the fourth week of the trial, a juror got sick. Judge McCook released John McGowan and selected an alternate. By now, it was time for Ralph Liquori to testify for the defense.

Before his attorney, Lorenzo Carlino, Liquori acted as an innocent party. Liquori accused prosecutor Harry Cole of promising him immunity. "I won't commit perjury for Mr. Dewey," he said earnestly.

In spite of his dramatic flair, Liquori was an unsavory witness.

The next witness was Joe Bendix, the hotel thief. Bendix testified that Luciano had put him in the business of collecting from the houses. Pointing to Luciano, he stated they had had sixteen to eighteen conversations over the past eight years.

"Did you see Luciano and Fredericks together?" asked Dewey.

"Yes, at the Villanova," replied Bendix. "I was there with the girl who is now my wife."

According to Bendix, Luciano said, "When you are around collecting and get wise, you can make some extra money from the madams."

George Morton Levy, Luciano's attorney, brought out under cross-examination that Bendix had been offered a deal in exchange for his testimony.

Outside of the courtroom, Joe Bendix had a wife whom he dearly loved. He was passionate, crazy for her. Joy Dixon, who felt less ardor and some consternation over her husband's fate, got herself involved with Luciano's people. Some of his "agents" contacted Joy. They asked her to step up and dispute her husband's version of events. When learning that Luciano's people had approached his wife, Joe Bendix became hysterical. He wrote her a series of letters from jail. "You're being used as a tool," he wrote.

While they couldn't get Joy Dixon to discredit Joe Bendix, the defense attorneys called a surprise witness. Morris Panger, an aid of District Attorney William Dodge, testified that Bendix had previously tried to trade information on a bond robbery in exchange for a reduction in sentence.[6]

Luciano's attorneys then introduced a number of gamblers who testified that Luciano was a bettor who spent every day at the track. Max Kalik, a bookie with a thirty-year track record, said he had known Lucky for many years as a sportsman who not only made book, but also underwrote large bets for bookies. "I placed bets for the best business people," he told Dewey upon cross-examination. His associate, Henry Goldstone, said he knew Lucky as a big gambler who was the owner of the United States Hotel, a gambling establishment in Saratoga. The inference was that Luciano had no time for the prostitution syndicate; he was too busy with the gambling racket.

The defense put Luciano on the stand during the last week of the trial. During his four hours of testimony, he failed to impress the jury. His attorney, George Levy, tried to present the defendant as a gambler who had lived a wild life in his youth. That wild side included narcotics and guns. "Did you ever receive the earnings of a prostitute?"

"I gave to 'em," Luciano replied. "I never took."

Nobody laughed at the joke. The silence spoke louder than words.

Then, Dewey began his cross-examination. When pressed about his activities, Luciano answered directly.

"I don't handle dope."

Dewey tried to increase the credibility factor in the testimony of the one witness who had seemed to have an agenda, Joe Bendix. The sneak thief had met Luciano in a drugstore in New York City, when Luciano allegedly offered him a job collecting money from the prostitution houses. "You were a partner in that drugstore," Dewey yelled. Luciano merely denied the charge.

One thing he couldn't deny was his life as a stoolpigeon against other narcotics peddlers. He agreed that in 1923, he'd told police where to find a trunk full of narcotics.

According to Luciano, he couldn't have been the head of the other defendants and their vice ring, because he only knew David Betillo. He admitted to narcotics peddling and to the 1930 Florida arrest on gambling charges. As Dewey went through his history, he admitted previously possessing heroin and morphine. As for his possession of guns, he claimed he went on hunting trips. "Pheasants," Luciano insisted. Dewey then confronted him with his telephone records, which showed that Luciano had placed calls to Saline's Gardens, a West Side restaurant. This place was mentioned in previous witness testimony as where the bonding combination leaders held their meetings. Luciano admitted that he was a patron of the restaurant. He added that he used to call the restaurant when he wanted to reach his roommate, Lorenzo Bresscio (who was actually his bodyguard).

"You're a friend of Ciro Terranova, aren't you?" Dewey asked. To Luciano's denials, Dewey responded, "Then why did you call his house with his private telephone number?"

"Lots of people came to my room," Luciano answered. "I let 'em all use the phone. I don't know who made that call."

Dewey established the who's who of Luciano's contacts: Benjamin Bugsy Siegel, Max Silverman, Jacob Gurrah Shapiro, and Louis Lepke Buchalter.

Luciano testified that he first paid federal income taxes in the preceding year. Dewey charged he'd only paid federal, not state taxes, because only the federal government prosecuted gangsters.

"And why did you pay delinquent taxes for only six years in arrears?" Dewey asked. "Wasn't that because you knew the statute of limitations expires in six years?"

"I just thought that was enough," Luciano said.

The papers described the gangster with endless referrals to his droopy eye. One reporter noted that he was "a short and stocky man whose body is a trifle too long for his legs."

The only one of his co-defendants that Luciano admitted to knowing was David Betillo. Their relationship, he admitted, had spanned the past eight to ten years. The origin of their relationship, according to Luciano, had occurred when Betillo had approached him, to suggest they operate a game on a boat. As to the other co-defendants, and all of the witnesses, Luciano denied knowing them.[7]

The defense offered a last-minute allegation that Dewey and his office staff had taken some liberties in their treatment of the witnesses. The most shocking of these allegations had been those of Patrolman George Heidt, in his description of the wooing of Mildred Balitzer.

Patrolman Heidt was the notorious, star defense witness. His first blatant infraction was to talk openly to the press about the nature of his work for Dewey. Dewey then turned around and asked why George Heidt, a disreputable, veteran patrolman whose poor record of service had resulted in multiple transfers, had been assigned to work for him in the first place. That sent Commissioner Valentine to Headquarters, where he tried to determine who gave out the assignment. Heidt then answered the question, publicly, which further upset the commissioner.

"I got the job of guarding the Luciano witnesses through a phone call by an unknown person," he announced. By doing so, he directly violated Department rules by talking to the press without official permission.

Heidt would so enrage the prosecution, his activities would engender a separate investigation. Heidt had guarded Mildred Balitzer, Jennie the Factory, Peggy Wild, and Thelma Jordan in their safe houses. Heidt testified to taking the women out to restaurants until 2:30 in the morning.

Commissioner Valentine remembered George Heidt from the days of the Seabury investigations. Mildred Balitzer clued them in, saying that Heidt was a payoff man for Owney Madden during prohibition days. The commissioner told the *New York Tribune* that while serving as a deputy inspector in the Police Department, he had worked as a confidential investigator. One of his assignments had been to look into George Heidt's record.

Now the file was missing. In lieu of solid evidence, Valentine suspended the patrolman from duty at the Elizabeth Street Precinct, and relieved him of all duties pending a new investigation into his affairs.

Patrolman Heidt, a twenty-one year veteran of the force, had once been a detective, assigned to the W. 21st Street Station. Yet, his service had been unsatisfactory. He was then demoted to the uniformed force and transferred to Harlem. Three months after that, he was again transferred. His destination was the Elizabeth Street stationhouse in Chinatown. For all the outrage displayed by the top brass, they couldn't stop Heidt from having his day in court. He went on the witness stand to testify for the defense in relating the activities of Mildred Balitzer. He insisted that his job had been to bring her to Dewey's office. They allowed her to drink, believing that it would help her to relax and ease her passage to the witness stand. This came to a climax one night when George Heidt, with D.A. Sol Gelb, took Mildred Balitzer out for a night of serious drinking at Leon and Eddie's nightclub. Thomas Dewey got the policeman to admit that he'd been "bawled out" by Dewey for letting Balitzer drink too much.[8]

As the defense attorneys moved toward their summations, they tried to downplay the roles of the white-collar members of the combination:

Jesse Jacobs, Meyer Berkman, and Benny Spiller. James D.C. Murray, the lawyer for Meyer Berkman, suggested that his businesslike appearance was proof-positive that he could not be a criminal. "If Berkman went into [the Waldorf Astoria], they would have thrown him out on his nondescript looks."9

The summations would be lengthy. All but Morton Levy, attorney for Luciano, turned the jury's attention to Thomas Dewey and his controversial trial strategy. The special prosecutor sat quietly, turning the other cheek while the summations went on for hours. Caesar Barra, counsel for both David Betillo and Thomas Pennochio, delivered the most impassioned defense summation. He accused Dewey of withholding the issue of David Marcus' perjury until confronted with it by witnesses who said he'd lied. "I never would believe Mr. Dewey is as dumb as to swallow hook, line, and sinker the propositions that these procurers made to him," Barra said before embarking on his formal summation remarks.

"You're not here as a nominating committee to name Mr. Dewey, or anyone else, to the Governorship of this State. Neither is it up to you to justify the spending of a huge sum of money on this investigation. Mr. Dewey's witnesses sold him a gold brick.

"What is perjury to people like Dewey's witnesses? What is perjury, when it is sold to the prosecutor for the people of New York for holy justice's sake?"

Barra also accused Dewey of withholding the knowledge that he knew David Marcus had committed perjury when he denied ever being convicted on vice charges in Pittsburgh. "In the West Fifty-third Street prison, a diabolical conspiracy was planned by several men held as material witnesses. One of these was Marcus, a miserable scoundrel. Perjury is not a crime when it is committed for the State of New York and for the holy cause of justice."

While Barra was the most articulate, Ralph Liquori's lawyer, Lorenzo Carlino, was the most aggressive in his criticism of Dewey. Carlino called him "a boy scout" and a "David in khaki shorts," set out to "slay Goliath." He accused Dewey of legalizing prostitution by granting immunity to the witnesses.

Samuel Siegel, the attorney for Jimmy Fredericks, described the witnesses as a "parade of perjurers." He defended Abe Wahrman as being too young to have the power to "terrify bookers."

Morton Levy took three hours to sum up for the defense. He alone refrained from personally attacking Mr. Dewey.

"I'm not accusing Tom Dewey of suborning perjury. But I say his assistants, anxious for a pat on the back or a bit of glory, have collected a group of actors who have constructed a drama, which Mr. Dewey accepted as true.

"[Dewey] hopes to [convict Luciano] by prejudice, hysteria through what you have read, and by what the public had been taught to believe by this master showman. He hopes to do it by crimes Lucania committed years ago, because he was taken for a ride, because he lied to get a pistol permit. He hopes to railroad him because Lucania lied when he said he was a chauffeur in obtaining an automobile license when he was nothing but a bootlegger and gambler."

After seven months of preparation to bring Luciano to justice, Dewey now delivered his final summation. He talked for five hours. One key point was his denial that he had tampered with witnesses and evidence. He insisted that his witnesses had been terrified: Frank Brown, Manager of the Barbizon Plaza, had been threatened to the point of taking the stand and denying that the defendants had ever been in Luciano's room. Another witness they'd "gotten to" was a bellboy at the hotel. As far as the scandal involving Heidt's conduct, Dewey continued, it was under Commissioner Valentine's investigation.

"Isn't it time we convicted the boss," he suggested. "It is time to stop sacrificing the front men in a crime organization." He accused Liquori of being a "human sacrifice for his boss." Dewey then addressed defense allegations that he'd bought witnesses. "Does anyone think I'd place my reputation in the hands of criminals?"

Both sides rested on the afternoon of June 4. Judge McCook sent the jurors out to dinner. The long, monotonous charge to the jury took over two-and-a-half-hours. The jury charge is standard procedure and can, under the best of circumstances, be tiring. The jury's work was coming to a crescendo. McCook hoped to revive the men with a spirited lecture on their collective duty, which was to return with a verdict. Thinking of what this trial had cost, he knew that the State of New York could not afford a hung jury.

Judge McCook invoked the tenets of the conspiracy law to the jury. "You must establish a common desire and unity of purpose among the defendants. Even though the degree of involvement for each defendant was different, they were all implicated on the same level." McCook emphasized Luciano's role last, and with the most emphasis, calling him by the nickname, "Lucky." McCook brought bondsmen Jacobs and Berkman into this conspiracy. While the defense had said that these two were "no more guilty of crime than would be a department store sales-man who sold a bed to a prostitute on the installment plan," McCook reiterated their roles. Of the prostitution witnesses, he said, "A prostitute is at once a victim of an enticer and her life is full of lies, but I say she is not unworthy of belief merely because she is a prostitute."[10]

The twelve began deliberations. Each of the nine defendants remaining who had not changed their plea to guilty—David Betillo, Thomas Pennochio, Abe Wahrman, Jimmy Fredericks, Benny Spiller, Ralph Liquori, Jesse Jacobs, Meyer Berkman, and Charles Luciano—were charged with sixty-two counts of compulsory prostitution. Thomas the Bull Pennochio was facing life. A three-time loser, his fourth conviction would subject him to the Baumes, or "habitual offender" law.

While the wives and other family members of the defendants slept on the floor of the corridor, the jury returned quickly, after five hours of deliberation and two ballots. The first jury ballot had found Luciano guilty eleven to one. The second ballot was unanimous. All were found guilty on sixty-two counts of compulsory prostitution. It was 5:25 A.M. when the verdict was read.

CHAPTER 14

SIXTY-TWO COUNTS

I never was a crumb, and if I have to be a crumb I'd rather be dead.
— Lucky Luciano

As the foreman read the endless stream of guilty verdicts, the cries of the defendants' wives echoed through the awful room. Currents of emotion washed over the courtroom participants. The trial had ended. The repercussions were about to begin.

This had not been an airtight case for Thomas Dewey. Still reeling from the accusations that he had allowed David Marcus to perjure himself, he went on the offensive. As Mayor LaGuardia publicly lauded him, Dewey didn't take time to pull his pen out of the inkwell. He began actions to track down Women's Court attorney Abe Karp, who had been left out of the indictments due to lack of evidence. Now, Dewey claimed that Karp had been one of two lawyers to try to bribe his staff members, two of whom had been offered Supreme Court judgeships, with $250,000 offered as an alternative gift. In return, the assistant was asked to cooperate with Luciano's defense. Karp managed to get to one of the material witnesses being held in prison, although Dewey failed to divulge the man's identity.

Wives of the defendants
(John Binder)

Dewey had spent $250,000 on the State's expenses, which had begun in Arkansas. At the same time that Dewey was making pronouncements, the defense leaked statements to the tune of appeals. They wanted to attack the constitutionality of the new Joinder Law, which had resulted in all of the defendants being tried together. Dewey countered that printing the record for the Appellate would cost about $15,000 of the taxpayers' money. Luciano, on the other hand, had spent at least $50,000 for lawyers. He put up additional money at various stages of his arrest for bribery money.

Of Patrolman Heidt, Commissioner Valentine announced that he was starting an investigation into his conduct. Upon looking for some old files on the policeman, who at this point still had a clean record, they were found to be mysteriously missing from the folder at police headquarters. While the investigation remained pending, George Heidt was removed from the Elizabeth Street stationhouse and transferred to the office of Chief Inspector John Seery. Before he could be silenced, the demoted detective had started giving statements to the press, an act that didn't help his standing within the Department. By July, Heidt would find himself facing departmental discipline proceedings. The unauthorized interview was only a drop in the bucket, which contained bank deposits of more than $70,000 from 1926 through 1933. Heidt countered that he had made most of the money by gambling. All things considered, Valentine's public announcement centered only on the Luciano verdict and not the escalating investigation in Heidt's affairs. Claiming that Luciano was involved in many activities, not just vice, Valentine focused on the fact that it was "a racket prosecution," first and foremost.[1]

As part of the sentencing procedure, Judge McCook ordered psychiatric evaluations of the convicted men. Pennochio was called a dullard, an "unresponsive, uncooperative individual of rather dull mentality, the product of a broken home." Jimmy Fredericks scored even lower, as "a low and despicable character who of late has had no compunctions about living on the earnings of prostitutes." David Betillo was again cited as being an affiliate of Al Capone, and this statement, which had no basis in fact, was substantiated only by a four-year gap in his criminal record during which it was assumed he was in Chicago working for Capone. But it was Luciano to whom Drs. Walter Bromberg, Charles B. Thompson, and David Impastato delivered the most scathing profile.

"His social outlook is essentially childish, in that it is dominated by recklessness and a craving for action. His behavior patterns are essentially instinctive and primitive, his manner easy, copious, and ingratiating. His ideals of life resolved themselves into money to spend, beautiful women to enjoy, silk underclothes, and places to go in style. He was a chronic truant from school. During this phase of his life, the defendant was reared in an impoverished environment on the lower eastside, and at an early age he was beyond the control of his parents. His behavior patterns and social attitude during this formative period were largely conditioned by the influence of unwholesome associates, with the result that by the time he was eighteen years old, he acquired a definitely criminalistic pattern of conduct.

"Lucania has been arrested twenty-five times, and is reputedly the head of the Unione Siciliana, an organization for Italian gangsters, and a dominant figure in the sale of narcotics, policy slips, stolen goods, gambling houses, and the intimidation of businessmen and unions.

"He is also suspected of having a hand in the slaying of Arthur Flegenheimer (Dutch Schultz)."[2]

On the same day that Luciano was evaluated, he was sentenced in the company of his co-defendants. Luciano remained stoic as the judge sentenced him to from 30–50 years. The other sentences were meted out to David Betillo, 25–40 years; Thomas Pennochio and Jimmy

Fredericks, 25 years as habitual criminals; Abe Wahrman, 15–30 years; Ralph Liquori, 7½–15 years. Jesse Jacobs, Benny Spiller, and Meyer Berkman had promised to cooperate with Dewey in his new investigations into "industrial rackets," and their sentencing was delayed. The bookers received lighter sentences as follows: Pete Harris and Al Weiner, 2–4 years; David Marcus, 3–6 years, the extra time tacked on for having been caught in a lie on the witness stand; Jack Eller, 4–8 years. Initially, all went to Sing Sing, although they were later scattered and moved out to other facilities. The bookers remained in Sing Sing and were kept in solitary confinement. Betillo was later moved to Comstock, Fredericks to Auburn, and Luciano to Dannemora.

Judge McCook had a few choice words for the bookers. Eller, who was a popular man among the prostitutes and one not considered to be a real criminal, was not spared by McCook, who blamed his "flabbiness of body and soul," which led him to take over the business of Nick Montana. Of Pete Harris, McCook had this to say:

"The psychology of the booker is peculiar.

"He lacks what is ordinarily called a moral sense, but he seems to make some distinctions of his own.

"He does not regard it as essentially wrong to give employment to girls at what he and they call their work."

Yet, McCook felt that Harris was "not entirely devoid of human feeling." To Al Weiner, McCook alluded to his nickname, "Dumb Al."

He said "I am showing some regard for your dumbness."

As during the trial, the defendants' family members gathered for the sentencing. Among them were Mary Pennochio, who was there with Tommy's brother; Jesse Jacobs' wife and mother; and Ralph Liquori's mother and sister. David Betillo's wife, who had fled her apartment after his arrest clutching her small dog, was also there for the sentencing.

It is difficult to imagine the thoughts of the defendants' wives. They had screamed their wrath at the prostitutes during the trial. Their anger was not directed toward jealousy that their husbands had had dealings with these paid women. It was more their outrage that the prostitutes' testimony threatened to send their men to jail for a lifetime. They would have no means of support. For the wives, it meant destitution.

The sensationalism was not finished. The following July, police discovered a woman beaten in a Washington, D.C., apartment. A startling aspect of her condition was a carved set of initials, "C.L.," etched into her thigh with a nail. She was bound in an apartment filled with gas. Her rescuers found she'd also been carved on her abdomen with the numbers "3-12," which symbolized the initials "C.L."

Margaret Louise Bell, alias Jean Costella, claimed that she was paid $500 by a lawyer for Luciano. For the money, she was to say she'd been framed by Dewey. She'd agreed, then reneged, and in fear of underworld retribution, had run away. She was found when an enforcer named "Leo" invaded her room and knifed her in retribution for reneging on her part of the plan. Before she was finished with her story, the police already sensed she was a crackpot. Experts on the scene were suspicious. It didn't conform to a typical profile of mob revenge.

Detectives who flew in from New York, J. Dwyer and P. Lockwood, brought two Brooklyn thugs, Leo Marmone and Joe Silvers, along for the trip to Washington. The woman was asked to identify "Leo" in a lineup. She didn't recognize him, and within two days, she was written off as a nut. Dewey announced that "Jean Bell" was never a witness for the people. Washington's police chief declared that it was "the greatest fabrication of falsehoods I have ever been confronted with." The publicity smoked out the fact that she had rolled a guy at a party, taking $700 out of his wallet. Jean Bell, with her thighs and abdomen permanently disfigured, was charged with robbery.[3]

As the fuss died down over "C.L.," the defendants went through intake procedures at Sing Sing. All were placed in segregation. The warden felt that the trial had caused tensions that would result in serious violence if the men were to see each other. As a result, all of the defendants were consigned to solitary confinement, that they eat all meals in their cells, and that they be allowed only limited periods of exercise. For some, like Pete Harris, this arrangement lasted for at least two years.

After the short intake period in Sing Sing, the defendants were transferred to other state facilities. Luciano, Ralph Liquori, and David Betillo went to Dannemora. Thomas Pennochio and Jack Eller went to Attica. Jimmy Fredericks and Abe Wahrman went to Auburn. They were still hopeful of deliverance. But hope faded when all of the appeals, which the defense attorneys had threatened to take all the way to the Supreme Court, were denied.[4]

As the commitment papers determined the fate of the prisoners, Patrolman George Heidt was brought to trial by Commissioner Valentine. He'd been found to amass various amounts adding up to roughly $74,500 between 1926 and 1933. He defended himself by saying that some of the money had been bequeathed to him as an inheritance; the rest he'd won at the track. Heidt had angered the Department when he'd given an interview to a newspaperman. In addition to being charged with holding unsubstantiated sums of money, he was charged with the lesser offense of discussing the Department without permission from a superior officer. He retained as counsel State Senator John J. McNaboe, who called Commissioner Valentine to the witness stand. In spite of his defense, Heidt was dismissed from the Department on August 31, 1936. The dismissal would prove to be temporary. Heidt would be reinstated in 1938 and assigned to the 28th precinct.[5]

Magistrate Anna Kross delivered the truest postscript. The judge had known of the scandals in the Women's Court long before anyone in Thomas Dewey's crowd had even considered attacking the problem. Kross had been the person behind the famous names, the woman who had known of the bonding combination long before the pretrial investigation of 1935. Now, she made a statement that the problem of prostitution will never be solved by criminal proceedings "as long as the Women's Court at Jefferson Market continues to handle a social question by criminal legal procedures." Her statements kicked off a new mood of social welfare. Representatives of the League of Women Voters urged that "sympathetic social treatment" would help solve the problems of prostitution.[6]

Photo on opposite page: Lucky Luciano
(John Binder)

PART III

RECANTMENT

CHAPTER 15

INDEPENDENCE DAY

I'm too old for social service ladies.
—Jennie the Factory

The morning of June 8, 1936 washed upon the streets of lower Manhattan with the promise of New York's summer. The Battery, downtown, glistened before the wide shores of Brooklyn and New Jersey. In the morning, before the stifling heat and noise crashed down to break the calm, the city swelled with pride and promise.

In the Women's House of Detention on W. 10th Street, the morale was high. The witnesses boarded a series of dirty prison busses. As they rode from the West Village House of Detention, driving to the Centre Street courthouses, some squinted through the barred windows. As they rode downtown past Mott and Elizabeth, Kenmare and Mulberry Streets, some reflected on the trial. For most, the ride around the lower east point of Manhattan, the location of the former Five Points Gang, meant nothing more than a trip out of the jail.

Today, the witnesses would give Judge McCook some lip service, get their paychecks, and go out the door to the streets of freedom. For most of the prostitutes, this meant a revolving door return to the $2 houses.

Judge McCook suspected that Luciano's people would find some of these witnesses. He fully expected some to recant their testimony. His preemptive strategy would be to get them to swear, before leaving the bench, that they had not been coerced into testifying for the prosecution.

Under pressure from Magistrate Kross and other social service advocates, McCook had asked some women's social service groups to join him. He called them "The Committee of Ladies." Comprised of women from various agencies, most notably the Catholic Charities, Jewish philanthropies, and the Church Mission of Help, they sat in an adjoining room.

Judge Philip J. McCook had presided over the witnesses like the father many had never known. On this last day, he would address their behavior patterns like a physician examining their private body parts. All illusions were gone, punched out like the cards they'd worn, pinned to their button-front frocks. As they stood, one by one, before the bench sharing the same empty, raw expression, he knew this was the last chance he'd have to be their savior.

Barent Ten Eyck and Thomas Dewey were there when the first witness, Shirley Taylor, stepped up to the bench.

McCook addressed her with a question. He would go on to query each departing witness, in the same manner, with the same questions. "Who did you first speak to, after you were first arrested?"

"I spoke to Mr. Robertson, I think it was," said Shirley Taylor. "It was the first night that we were all arrested."

"And what did you tell him in a general way?"

"I told him a bunch of lies, I guess."

"Then whom did you see after that?" asked Judge McCook.

"Mr. Ten Eyck," replied Shirley Taylor.

"How many days or weeks [later]?"

"About one month later [after we were arrested]," said the young woman.

"What inducements did he offer you for telling the truth?" grilled McCook.

"He didn't offer anything," she said. "If we didn't tell the truth, we could be convicted."

Similar statements would be repeated by each of the witnesses who stepped before Judge McCook that day. For instance, that they had not been approached, or sexually abused by the staff in Dewey's office. They were housed, fed, clothed, and safely transported from Dewey's office to the courthouse. All had lied initially when arrested. Individual interrogations by Mr. Hogan, Ariola, and Tyng had revealed the truth. The threat of "getting time" had brought each witness to her role in the trial and the testimony she gave, either before the grand jury or in open court during the trial. One by one, each insisted she had not been abused in the process of becoming a witness.

Most claimed they were going back to work, in gardens and knitting shops, or as seamstresses and beauticians. There was a fair sprinkling of waitresses. Some held hopes of returning to a husband, a mother, a brother. They all shared stories of estrangement.

Then Judge McCook made an announcement.

"You will be interviewed by one of these district attorneys, and also by one of the ladies from these various institutions who are so much interested in what is going to happen to you when you get outside," he said. "Every one of them wants to help you."

The idea landed on these prostitutes like a lead balloon. McCook was undaunted as he continued.

"Now I know women sometimes are hard on other women, but not one of these women is. I have told them with care, so that I could be sure that they, all of them, were warm-hearted and anxious to do everything for your future.

"They are good women, they are not the kind of hard women that you and I know who have no use for a girl like you, who thinks she is damned forever. They are not that kind of people. They are going to talk to you to find out what they can do for you and after you leave here, so that you can be reasonably protected, so that you can get a job, if possible, and so that you will have enough to live on, and you will not be forced back to doing anything that you do not really want to do. Do you want to go straight?"

"Oh, yes," said former prostitute Jean Bradley. "I met a lovely woman in there, Mrs. McCarthy."

"She is one of your own, isn't she?" McCook asked.

"Oh, yes, your honor," said Bradley.

"Are you Irish?" asked McCook.

"Yes, your honor."

June O'Brien stepped up next. "You know, there are some tough, hard women that just have no use for a girl like you, that think she is dirt under their feet; you know that," said McCook.

"You have seen plenty of them, I have no doubt, in your life?" asked the judge.

"Yes, sir," replied June O'Brien.

"Are you going straight, or are you one of those that will just say, 'Oh, well, back to the woods'?"

"I'm going to take a beauty course," replied Miss O'Brien.

To Eleanor Jackson, McCook broached the subject of Jack Eller, the one booker popular among the prostitutes.

"He is a mutt, isn't he," McCook suggested. "Came back from the war with problems."

Eleanor Jackson was quick to protest. "Underneath, there is something good about him," she said. "He's not vicious, and not the sort that the others are. He was a real estate agent and lost his job, and another girl and I let him live with us and sleep on a couch. We had a suite of rooms, and Nick Montana offered him this job. He wasn't paying him very much money, probably twenty dollars a week, at first, and I don't think he realized . . ."

The judge cut her off.

"How long since you have been to Mass?"

"Ever since I've been in here," said Eleanor Jackson.

"While you were living around?" asked Judge McCook.

"No," replied the former prostitute.

"God bless you, my child," said McCook as he dismissed her.

As the judge tossed the Irish blarney, Margaret Martino, who was among the first witnesses, and Helen Hayes, a Dane, stepped up. To Martino, who was going home to Brooklyn, he said:

"You have been sexually active. Unless you get married right away, how are you going to meet that temptation? How do you think you can get along without it?"

Then, McCook addressed Marie Williams.

"And what are your plans?"

"I will go crazy if I stay here," said the tired prostitute. "That is one plan."

To Joan Martin, the 41-year-old Romanian madam, the judge alluded to her hysterical account of her troubles at the hands of the combination enforcers.

"I remember you very well on the stand. Nobody can forget you," McCook said kindly. "You had a tough time on the stand, but they did not do very much to you. Did you tell the truth?"

"I did," replied Martin. She had provided comic relief when Defense Counsel Samuel Seigel had taunted her by accusing her of operating a $1 house, a reduction she said was caused by the Depression. Now, she told McCook, she was going back to work as a waitress.

"My mother was sick with cancer, and there was no chance for me to give her the medical treatment that I had to give her for three years on twenty to twenty-two dollars per week," said Martin.

To Flo Brown, McCook became jubilant.

"May I congratulate you on looking so much better than you did in court? And I congratulate you also on the way that you seemed to be able to stand the strain of the court. Did you tell the truth?" asked McCook.

"I did," replied Flo.

"Were you plied with liquor?" asked the judge.

"No," said Flo.

"All that happened is that when you were sick once or twice," said the judge, "they gave you liquor by my directions?"

"Yes," she answered.

"I realize that your situation is quite different from that of the others here, a good many of them, most of them," said Judge McCook. "All I can say is that I believe the D.A. will continue to help you by keeping his promises to you in every way that he can. You have a brain. That is all. Next time, use it for some better purpose," said McCook to Flo Brown.

The judge then dismissed the 887 or "Prostitution" charges as he continued with the parade of witnesses. One departing prostitute who disturbed him was Jean Attardie. She was going home to marry Andy Lococo, called "Co Co" Attardie, a material witness and former assistant to Jack Eller. She had a child with him, who was currently stashed away in the Bronx with a woman caregiver. McCook suggested that she return to her father in Newark. "Co Co never booked as long as I have ever been with him," she said defensively.

"What did you think he was doing, running a church?" asked the judge.

"He used to gamble," said Jean, "and play horses."

"Please talk to Father Hickey," McCook implored. Father Hickey was the Pastor at St. Joseph's Church, and the Chaplain at the House of Detention. He'd already advised Jean Attardie to marry Co Co Attardie, as he was the father of her child.

Judge McCook elaborated. "The Catholic Church doesn't make it easy, but you have got to behave."

"Well, I know," agreed Jean Attardie. "But I was taught that once you missed your Easter duty the first time, you are really denounced from the Catholic religion."

Some, like Marie Dubin, had been held as witnesses against defendants who had never materialized. One had been "Gypsy Tom" Petrovich, whose disposition was still pending. To Marie, the judge said, "If you don't know anything about it, we won't keep you."

Another wife of a combination member, Nancy Brooks, the wife of

Danny, said she had "left Danny," who was sent back to Dannemora after testifying against David Betillo. Nancy Brooks was going to live with her family members.

One of the maids who had been detained, a Black woman named Helen Jones, presented a problem when she didn't produce a "clean bill of health." McCook seemed concerned with ancestry, or racial heritage at one point. To Helen Guidry from New Orleans, he asked, "You are of the old French stock?"

"That is right," answered the maid.

"There isn't any better," said the judge.

McCook sent the Jewish madams to the Jewish philanthropies. For example, Little Jenny Fox, who was Jewish, was sent to Miss Grossman, from the Jewish Guardians. But Jennie the Factory Fischer balked at the idea. "I'm too old for the social service ladies," she announced indignantly. "I'm fifty-seven years old."

Many of the prostitutes who had found their assumed names listed in the tabloids, said they were going home. Muriel Ryan planned a "church wedding in New York." Joan Martin said she was going to "Brooklyn with her sister." Some claimed to have children in other cities.

With respect to compensation, McCook told the departing women that they would get the full pay of $3 per day. Those who did not give full cooperation, but who had human considerations like children or parents, would get half, or $1.50 per day. Those who were not cooperative would get nothing. Some of the detained witnesses were deprived of their pay based on this standard. Helen Kessler, one housekeeper, was not paid because she had denied being a prostitute. Yet, when an arrest card from 1935 indicated that she'd been arrested for 887 (Prostitution), she was deemed an uncooperative witness and deprived of her pay.

There were others who were angry at the treatment they'd received. Mildred Curtis, who had gone before the grand jury but had not testified in court, had been one witness whose initial testimony, that she'd known Luciano, had not been used. It was considered too unreliable, even by the loose standards applied to other prostitution witnesses claiming to have known the mobster. Mildred Curtis now came before Judge McCook.

"They told me they would put me in jail with the gun they found in my vault," she tried to say. Harold Cole had threatened her with "cold turkey," she said. Curtis had been a mistress of Thomas Pennochio. She claimed he gave her "everything I wanted," so that she wouldn't "go out."

One of the last to leave was Peggy Wild. "Are you otherwise known as 'Venti'?" Judge McCook asked her.

"No. W-I-L-D," said Peggy.

Wild had stayed in the Jackson Heights apartment with Nancy Presser, Thelma Jordan, Mildred Balitzer, and Jennie the Factory Fischer. She denied exchanging stories. They had not prepared their testimonies with each other. Wild denied knowing Nancy Presser or Thelma Jordan on the outside.

"I spoke to Mildred one day, and she told me she knew Luciano from Florida. She asked if I knew him," said Peggy Wild. "I said, 'I only know him as a customer.'"

"Mildred says there was a good deal of drinking?" asked McCook.

"Yes," said Peggy.

"Did you take part in the drinking?" asked McCook.

"I don't drink. Mildred likes a little drink, because she is a very nervous type. Jennie Fischer don't drink, Thelma and Nancy. . . . "

The judge cut her off. "Did they drink heavily at all?"

"Yes," replied Peggy.

"And the officers let them drink more than they should?" asked McCook.

"You can have one drink, and you go into the second and third and you start feeling good," said Wild. "The girls were a little nervous; they wanted a little drink. That's all."

"Can you describe Officer Heidt?" asked the judge.

"He acted very, very quiet," said Wild. "He read the paper, and smoked a cigar. Sat down, and if we wanted to go to eat or to a show, he would come with us if it was his time on. He never talked to anyone else, always reading the paper."

"Are you going home?" asked the judge.

"My house was at 1703 Montgomery Avenue, in the Bronx. My father built that house," said Peggy. "But both my parents are dead. My father left the house to my sister." Peggy then told McCook she had "two daughters, and a grandchild."

"You were what I call a fashionable madam, at one time," said McCook.

"I ran the place for twelve years," said Peggy.

"I used to hear about you," said the judge. "You don't have any black-mailing on your mind?"

"No, sir," said Peggy Wild. "I received Holy Communion while I was in the House of Detention, and I'm going back to my church in the Bronx, Saint Ann."

"Do you think there's any chance of redemption for any of the defendants?" asked McCook.

Peggy Wild laughed. "All them fellows I had for customers? No, no chance."

CHAPTER 16

THIEVES IN THE NIGHT

I'm in a legit business now.
—Florence "Cokey Flo" Brown

Two weeks before Justice McCook released Nancy Presser from custody, a letter arrived in the offices of Thomas Dewey. Nancy's brother asked for information about his sister. "I have been acquainted with the fact of her arrest this afternoon by a man from New York City, an investigator on the case," he wrote. "She was a good girl, wrote home, and helped out as much as she could."[1]

Nancy, meanwhile, had made plans that did not include going home. Just as Dewey's staff prepared to release these women to the dangers of the streets, they panicked. Thelma Jordan, Nancy's roommate, was especially fearful of going out. She had heard a rumor that some remaining factions of the combination planned to "snatch Thelma." The plan was to torture her. Thelma had also revealed that the combination members had buried a rival alive in the New Jersey marshes. Jordan explained it to Harold Cole. "A squealer who talks about the torture . . . that's something that you are not supposed to say, under any conditions."[2]

There was more frightening news from the underworld grapevine.

"Nancy would be getting it, because Lucky wanted to snatch Nancy. She was going to get knocked off."

Harold Cole tried to help the panicked women. He gave them each a small sum of money, and a ticket out of the country. On July 16, armed with $154 each, Thelma Jordan and Nancy Presser shipped out to London on the *S.S. Samaria*. Disguised as "Mildred and Dot," the two stayed in the Regent Palace Hotel in Piccadilly Circus. Soon, they were wiring Cole for money.

Harold Cole received the first in a series of telegrams from the women. "Chance to rent a very good apartment—a sublet at $17 per month," they wrote from England. "Need hundred dollars in advance. Must take it by Thurs." Soon Cole made the decision to cut the women off from further financial assistance.

On October 6, the two hunted women returned to the United States. Their requests for help had resulted in diminishing returns. With their European trip fresh in their minds and imaginations, they gratefully accepted two coach tickets to Cincinnati.[3]

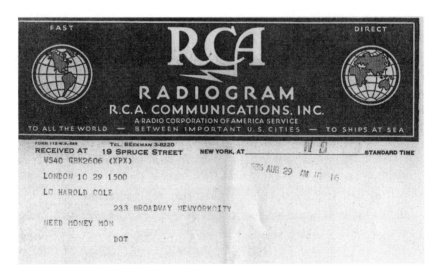

(NYC Municipal Archives)

After Flo Brown's release from the House of Detention, she moved to New Rochelle for a short time. With Mildred Balitzer, she made a deal with MacFadden Publications for a series of articles to be published in *Liberty* Magazine. Always keeping her eye on the dollar, Florence negotiated her contract with ease. She arranged that the two women should be paid $750 each, in weekly installments of $50. With this small nest egg, Mildred and Flo returned to New York City to stay in the Park Crescent Hotel. The two women were planning to go into business together in California. To celebrate the 4th of July, Mildred went home to West Virginia in the company of Bill Grant, a policeman. Florence reported to Ten Eyck that Florence was having an affair with Grant. Florence was happy about the *Liberty* Magazine articles. "I'm putting my whole heart into this writing business," she wrote.

Within the tone of the articles, Flo got some credit for "helping Mr. Dewey send Lucky Luciano to Sing Sing." Mildred's history—never before understood due to her propensity for changing it every time she spoke—was written with the poignant suggestion that she had been hoodwinked into prostitution while still a young girl. The text—that "She went immediately to see Madame A. Her eyes were opened before the first night was ended. It sickened her. . . ."—leant vindication to her life story.

The veiled hint of "white slavery" was a throwback to an earlier era. By 1936, the idea was outdated. Professionals, like police and district attorneys, scoffed at the idea that white slavery had existed at all. It was considered a newspaper expression from an era when prostitution did not appear in print.

In spite of their editorial success, there was an undercurrent to the women's happiness. On a visit to Pete in Sing Sing on October 3, Mildred heard all the news of the imprisoned men still locked up there. On August 17, Harris had been put into isolation, along with Dave Marcus and Joe Bendix. These convicts bitterly hated Thomas Dewey, who had made all kinds of promises to them. Now, even though they had testified, they were being penalized and kept in isolation.

Joe Bendix was especially disgruntled. Upon his entry into Sing Sing,

Bendix had been threatened and other convicts made a practice of spitting on him. So, for his own protection, in spite of the deal he thought he'd made, he was forced into solitary. There, he was deprived of all company save that of his fellow material witnesses. This proved to be a mistake as the politics of the trial had created enmity between the witnesses. In September 1936, Joe Bendix and Benny Spiller got into a brutal fight. Bendix managed to break Spiller's jaw before the two were ripped apart. When guards dragged Bendix away to solitary, he kicked, scratched, and bit the prison guards. He banged on the steel door for hours, threatening to harm himself or someone else.

Luciano's people had gotten to Pete Harris in Sing Sing, hoping the booker would recant his prior testimony. Harris was getting $50 a week, delivered to him through Jo Jo Weintraub. He was also getting food and cigarettes, which he shared with guys who got no packages from home. Harris had also heard that Luciano's people were searching for Mildred and Florence. They wanted to make the two women an offer, which amounted to a free supply of heroin. The only payment they wanted was recantment of their testimony. By the end of October, Mildred and Florence skipped town. In November, they sent Barent Ten Eyck a letter postmarked Hot Springs. "We left like thieves in the night," the letter said.

"Am completely without funds," wrote Flo. "Try to get money from the movie company." The *Liberty* stories had been bought by a theatrical agent and were being shopped around under the option.

While still hopeful, Mildred and Flo postmarked a letter from the Arlington Hotel in Hot Springs.

"Hot Springs is on our route," they wrote, "so we figured we would stop over for a day or two and look over the place that put up such a good battle for our friend Charlie; this was the place that was the beginning of the end for him. Ha Ha." The letter was accompanied by a gag postcard marked: "Where Lucky got his . . . Hot Springs, AK."

They reached California within the next few days. As "Norma Gordon," Flo wrote to district attorney Barent Ten Eyck. Ten Eyck received another letter a few days later. The biggest news was that the

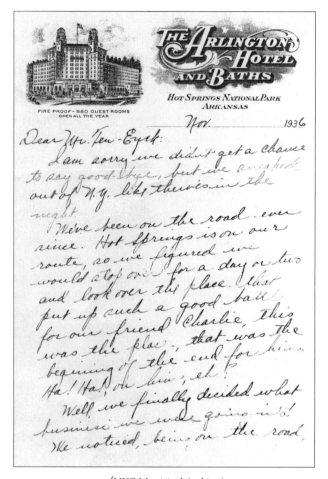

(NYC Municipal Archives)

women had been paid the last of the checks from *Liberty*. The final payment was $500 to each of the women. They were now looking for a steady source of income. "We decided what business we were going into. Mildred promised me she wasn't going to get in touch with Pete."

On November 21, the two women wrote to Ten Eyck from Phoenix. They were enjoying the weather and the wide-open spaces. It seemed, for a moment, that the two jaded women had actually found a new life for themselves. But their elation would not last.

The two were getting increasingly worried about money. They pes-

Mildred Balitzer, left; Florence "Cokey Flo" Brown, right
(NYC Municipal Archives)

tered Ten Eyck. They were anxious to hear from the "movie company." They leased a gas station, and worked changing oil and tires. "I'm in legit business now," Florence wrote with some pride. "This is Olixir Gas. We sell a lot of it. We have three pumps, one is Texaco, the Fire Chief, the Olixir, and the Wuppet. The last two are California gases. Proof enough, that we can own a station? Yours as ever, F.B."

On December 12, *Liberty* ran two installments. Success buoyed Florence's spirits. Yet, she was starting to fight with Mildred Balitzer. After Flo's ex-maid contacted her to say the mob was looking for them, she panicked. As "Norma Gordon," Balitzer wrote to Ten Eyck. "This arrangement not working out. Need money."[4]

The bottom fell out when the option was pitched to the major motion picture companies, including Paramount, Warner Bros., RKO, Universal, MGM, Columbia, and United Artists, to no avail.

Florence wrote to Ten Eyck:

> *Did you or anyone in the office send anyone out here to investigate us? Is it the office checking on us? I don't think it was you, on account of the way they are going about it. There is a leak somewhere. Somebody is busy getting a line on us. They found out where the station is, and my name from the letters I sent you. I am sure of that. Please check up on your end, and let me know if anyone in the office looks over, or can look over, the envelopes of your mail before it's laid on your desk. Anyway, they know where we are, and they must be here for no good.*
>
> *I'm going to write a letter, seal it up, and if anything happens to us, I'll leave instructions to mail it to you. In it will be the names of the people that have approached me, while I was in N.Y. From that maybe you can get some information. Well, let me know by Special Delivery, Air Mail, whether it's the office checking up on us, or whether it's **them** checking up on us. The man knew the name 'Norma Gordon,' and knew we were trying to go straight.*

As if to counter Florence's impressions, Mildred also wrote to Ten Eyck. She'd penned it on the day after Christmas.

> *I ran out of funds three weeks ago. Of course, I have worked every day since we got the station. I was so happy. It meant a new life, living right, having the respect of people. I ask nothing more. Then, the other day, Flo come down to the station and she says, I can't support you any longer . . . I am just about ready to go off the deep end. It seems the only answer. God knows I have tried. I had hoped that we could stick together. I know she is worried, too. She put nearly all her money in this place but, of course, it's a slow turnover. It takes time to build up.*

The tone of the letter, that the two were quarreling over money, was not surprising to the district attorney. The harmonious trip to the West had deteriorated into the familiar nightmares the women had suffered for years. "I am worried to death about those people, too. Flo is going out to buy a gun," wrote Mildred. "You are allowed to have a gun to protect your home and business in California."

On December 26, Barent Ten Eyck addressed their concerns in a letter addressed to Florence under her assumed name: Miss Norma Gordon, White's Auto Camp, 985 East Holt Ave., Pomona, Calif.

> *As to your belief that you have been located by the people of whom you write, I think there is no real reason to believe that any such thing has happened. You must remember that the two of you arrived in California in a car with NY plates, and that you are naturally suspicious as two women running a gasoline service station. In a small community such as the one in which you are located, the local authorities might well be doing a little checking up on their own account.*

As though to compound the panicked state of affairs, Mildred followed with another letter. "I want to live outside of rackets but know I can't." It was obvious to both women that Ten Eyck had cut them off financially. They had nowhere to turn.

On December 21, 1936, a message from Pomona, California, arrived in Ten Eyck's office. "10:08 P.M. Mildred wired Jo Jo Weintraub for the address of Mr. Dunn [an attorney] in California. Signed—J.P. McCarthy," an agent for Moses Polakoff." Jo Jo, an informant who avoided a jail sentence, had become an intermediary for Polakoff.

After reading the ominous telegram, Barent Ten Eyck dictated a memo to file: "Something vital to these two women must have happened."[5]

On Tuesday, January 26, 1937, Flo swore out an affidavit in Los Angeles, where she recanted her prior testimony. "Everything I ever said was a lie." She was being cared for now by three strangers named Joe McCarthy, "Mr. Maxwell," and "Mr. White." She went to a newsstand to pick up the last installment of her articles in *Liberty*.

Both women had gone "back to the cooker," which meant they were addicted to dope. The following month, in February 1937, both women entered a rehabilitation clinic on Central Park West. "Mr. Stern" paid the sum of $400 for the cures. But this time, it was a difficult cure. Flo still had leg cramps and was vomiting two weeks after she was admitted. While still in the throes of the speedy recovery, Flo and Mildred were removed from the rehabilitation center by "Mr. Stern," their malicious benefactor.

By May 1937, Flo and Mildred had become wards of the mysterious bounty hunters. The two men arrived just as the women had cut themselves on the shards of their dream. The movie option was a Hollywood joke. Barent Ten Eyck was to work on Dewey's investigation of the "industrial rackets," and seemed to have forgotten them. Their auto business had failed. Frightened and abandoned by the Manhattan district attorneys, they had nowhere to turn when Maxwell, White, and McCarthy gave them the old, familiar relief of the heroin needle.

Maxwell, White, and McCarthy had seduced their victims. With junk flowing through their veins, Florence and Mildred left their California gas station. As prisoners of the three men, they drove to the East Coast. In May 1937, Florence tried to send a Mother's Day card to her mother. Joe McCarthy wouldn't let her mail it. When he refused to allow the card, Flo kicked McCarthy's door down. His reaction was to slap her around the room. She escaped to the hotel lobby and sent a telegraph to Frank Hogan's office. "We are through with the carnival," she wrote.

Upon seeing the telegram, Hogan asked, "What do they mean by 'the carnival'?"

Florence later wrote, "The whole crowd of us together. We're in two cars, living like gypsies."

In the Packard, they drove through Omaha, Pittsburgh, and Boston, and into New York, where they picked up Nancy Presser. Florence and Mildred were astounded to see that Nancy was accompanied by a "relative" of Ralph Liquori. From the corner of 71st and Broadway, where they met Nancy, they went back out to the West Coast. After a short stay in the Baker Hotel in Dallas, they drove to El Paso.

Now the Packard contained the three women, stuffed into the backseat like cattle. In another postcard, Florence indicated that their moves were being controlled by McCarthy, Maxwell, and White. "We have everything but money and freedom."[6]

In a law office on the West Coast, Nancy signed an affidavit. She recanted her prior testimony against Luciano, stating that Mr. Cole had told her what to say on the witness stand. Cole's reason, she affirmed, was to get a "bonding conversation against Charlie."

"My prior affidavit, and trial testimony, had been falsified and given under duress of the District Attorney." Nancy claimed that the trip to Europe had been a payoff for the testimony. Sol Gelb countered by saying, "Nancy Presser and Thelma Jordan reported to my office after the trial that they had been threatened with murder and said that it was necessary to leave the United States for personal safety. No public funds were used for this purpose, although I would have regarded it proper so to use them." Angered by Luciano's defense attorney, Moses Polakoff's actions, Dewey accused the attorney, along with Lorenzo Carlino, attorney for Ralph Liquori, of perjury.[7] The fallout in the downtown offices of the district attorney reverberated up the Hudson River. In Sing Sing, convict Joe Bendix tried to hold Dewey to his promise. He brought a motion for a new trial, based on Dewey's pretrial statements that he would be eligible for parole within two years. His problems had escalated when his wife, Joy Dixon, threatened to divorce him. He wrote to her, saying, "When your blind eyes are opened and you have faith in the man you married, and if it will not be too late, come to me. . . ."

In desperation, Bendix insisted that Thomas Dewey had promised him a reduction to a misdemeanor plea and, also, a chance at executive clemency. None of these promises, he alleged, had been kept by Dewey's office. He was ready to stand up and charge that his testimony was induced by fraud and misrepresentation. Bendix was ready to join the legions of witnesses who had gotten less than they'd been promised.[8]

In November 1937, Florence sent Barent Ten Eyck a picture post-card. Her last, agonizing cure had been in vain. She was now in Juarez, Mexico, where the dope was cheap and plentiful. The missive, with its funny little picture and faded postmark, was the last of her letters home.

(NYC Municipal Archives)

EPILOGUE

CODE NAME "HUSKY"

It surprises me they didn't give Luciano the Navy Cross.
— J. Edgar Hoover

In spite of the recantments issued by three key witnesses, attorney Moses Polakoff failed in his attempt to free Luciano when all appeals were denied in April 1937. Resigned to his fate for the time being, Luciano served his time quietly.

The immigrant mobster would soon appear for Scene Two of his great American performance. In 1943, the nation was consumed with World War II. On the home front, Justice McCook was nearing mandatory retirement age. Thomas Dewey was now the Governor of New York State, a post he had grabbed with the help of the sensational publicity he'd garnered in the Luciano prostitution trial.

In early 1942, American isolationism had come to a full-throttled ending. During the period between the two world wars, nobody in America wanted to know about Europe. It was the old country. The interwar period of isolationism had left the United States Navy unprepared for war. When the Axis shifted its submarine warfare to the western Atlantic, the allies lost over five hundred ships. As the Navy struggled with a shortfall of manpower, ships were torpedoed from the St. Lawrence River, down to the Caribbean and Brazilian coasts, and the Gulf of Mexico.

Among numerous other sinkings, the Axis submarines had torpedoed a Norwegian oil tanker off the coast of Montauk Point on January 14, 1942. But most shocking of these statistics was the fact that many of these occurrences had happened off the coasts of Long Island and New Jersey. On April 18, 1942, the waterfront areas of Brooklyn, Queens, and Staten Island were ordered extinguished for the "duration of the war." On June 27, 1942, J. Edgar Hoover announced the arrest of eight "trained German saboteurs" in New York and Chicago, who had been hauled from Axis submarines. Four of these had been off the coast of Amagansett, Long Island.

On January 1, 1942, Frank S. Hogan, one of Thomas Dewey's assistant district attorneys, became the district attorney of New York County. His new responsibilities were shared with battle-hardened men upon whom he'd come to depend. One of the problems facing the new district attorney was the issue of waterfront sabotage. On February 11, 1942, the French luxury liner *S.S. Normandy* caught fire in New York harbor. At the time, the ship was being converted to wartime use. Commander Anthony J. Marsloe, a St. John's Law School graduate who investigated the event, never established the culpability. Some felt Nazi sympathizers had set it. Years later, Frank Costello boastingly took credit for having set the fire.

Murray I. Gurfein, who had been promoted after the Luciano trial to Assistant District Attorney in charge of the rackets bureau, joined Hogan in attending a conference with Captain Roscoe MacFall, District Intelligence Officer of the Third Naval District, Office of Naval Intelligence (ONI); and Lieutenant James O'Malley, Jr., his assistant, on March 7, 1942. Captain MacFall asked Hogan for cooperation in connection with "matters affecting the national security, which came within the jurisdiction of the District Intelligence office." MacFall shared with Hogan his thoughts that "movements and assistance in refueling of enemy submarines might be traced to criminal elements of Italian or German origin on the waterfront in the metropolitan area." He felt that "such persons might sell information, or give information to the enemy out of alien sympathy, or even that some among them, who had been rum-runners during the days of Prohibition, might find a new source of revenue from running oil supplies to the enemy submarine fleet." Frank Hogan agreed to cooperate fully by opening up his rackets files to the U.S. Navy.

As a follow-up, a second meeting was held in Hogan's office on March 25, 1942. This meeting was attended by Commander Charles Radcliffe Haffenden, who was in charge of the Investigative Section of the Third Naval District Intelligence Office under Captain MacFall. At this meeting, Frank Hogan gave Murray Gurfein permission to make contact with Joseph Guerin, a lawyer representing Joe Socks Lanza, who was under indictment on charges of conspiracy and coercion in the Court of General Sessions.

With his attorney, Mr. Guerin, in attendance, Joe Socks Lanza agreed to help. The rackets boss of the Fulton Street Fish Market concurred that the racketeers knew everything that was going on. If something happened on the waterfront, and in the waters off the eastern seaboard, the underworld would know it first. He knew his position was awkward. Facing an indictment, he feared that his association with authorities would brand him as a rat. "Get Luciano involved," he said. Luciano at the time was serving his term in the outback of Dannemora. An association with the boss would sidestep underworld rumors that Lanza had become an informant behind closed doors.

Luciano was still respected in the East Coast rackets. The suggestion, at first thought to be outrageous, was soon taken seriously. Lanza needed more clout if he was going to broaden his influence outside the Fulton Street Fish Market. Luciano would bring Joe Adonis and Frank Costello into the picture. Between April 15 and April 30, the decision to get Luciano involved was finalized. "The word of Charlie may give me the right of way," said Lanza.

On April 29, 1942, Frank Hogan authorized Murray Gurfein to

obtain permission for Lanza to visit Luciano in jail. Lanza was given a code number. The labor racketeer used his knowledge of the Fulton Street Fish Market—which included connections among the ship captains—to start vigilance along the waters along the eastern seaboard. He also obtained union cards for Naval Intelligence officers, which enabled waterfront spying of the waterfront.

The justification for involving the underworld was hardly needed. Many Americans at the time felt that intelligence duty was "somewhat akin to spying, and therefore, in time of peace an undignified and unworthy occupation," according to Rear Admiral W.S. Pye in an address to a Naval Training School in 1944. In his address, he listed the reasons why he felt the Navy had not developed a reliable system of intelligence.

"Real naval development began with World War I, but that war was in no respect a naval war. Our fleet, as a fleet, did not conduct a single war operation . . . the only type of naval intelligence that was required was information as to enemy submarine activities, a duty which was performed, for the most part, in the British Admiralty.

"With the possible exception of Japan, we did not anticipate a possible war, and in the case of Japan we permitted ourselves to be barred from the areas within which we might have obtained some information, which today would be most valuable.

"In the Atlantic, especially in North Africa and in Italy, we found that we lacked much information required for the most effective planning. We should not be too critical because of the unavailability of such latter information, for up to three years ago or less, no one could have foreseen our need for information of the coasts of North Africa and Italy."

Murray Gurfein contacted Moses Polakoff. The attorney told Gurfein that he'd written the Luciano case off. He claimed he hadn't spoken to Luciano since 1939. Luciano's new lawyer was George Wolf, who applied for a sentence modification before Justice Philip McCook. Polakoff then joined Mr. Wolf in acting as Luciano's counsel.

Before delivering his decision, McCook interviewed Commander Haffenden and Murray Gurfein, then a captain in the Army. Judge

McCook, in a decision, denied the application. Yet, the decision that was written on February 10, 1943[1] contained ambiguous language that "Executive clemency may become appropriate at some future date."

"That he has given affirmative indication of a repentant spirit, has been cooperative in the War effort and has demonstrated his ability to redeem himself," wrote McCook, adding, ". . . These considerations, taken together, do not form a proper basis for judicial relief." McCook invoked the fate of Thomas the Bull Pennochio, saying, "Justice requires that the cases of all sentenced for this conspiracy should be considered together on any request for clemency or relief resembling clemency."

Commander Charles Radcliffe Haffenden, who had joined Murray Gurfein in requesting a modification of Luciano's sentence, was an Officer in Charge of the District Intelligence Office, Third Naval District. In the latter part of 1942, Haffenden began working with a group that was known in the District Intelligence Office as the "Target" Section. Prior to that, he had served in the "B-3" Investigations Section of the District Intelligence Office. While Luciano served his sentence, his friend and successor, Frank Costello, had become a fixture among Democratic Party politicians in New York City. Costello was an associate of Mayor William O'Dwyer, named by President Roosevelt to head the economic section of the Allied Control Commission in Italy during the war. O'Dwyer had to answer charges that his 1945 mayoralty campaign was engineered by Frank Costello, Joe Adonis, and Irving Sherman, an intimate of Bugsy Siegel.[2] Costello's air of respectability moved Commander Charles Haffenden to play tennis and golf with the gangster in Flushing.[3]

Haffenden appealed to Moses Polakoff. He asked for mob intervention to avert a threatened strike on the waterfront. Polakoff and Gurfein, who was now Colonial Gurfein, met Meyer Lansky at Longchamps Restaurant. Lansky, who hated the Nazi party, offered his assistance with great enthusiasm. "But we have to be careful in making any moves because Mussolini is popular with some Italians in New York," Lansky added. They left Longchamps and went over to the Astor Hotel. In this opulent setting, they had a meeting with Commander Haffenden.

On May 12, 1942, Luciano was transferred from Dannemora, where he'd been institutionalized since July 2, 1936. His new institution, in spite of its pastoral name, was another maximum-security prison in the New York State penal system. Great Meadow, called "Comstock" by its inmates, was closer to the city than Dannemora. Officially, the transfer was arranged when Polakoff and Naval officials balked at the long trip to Dannemora. But Luciano, in professing his absolute hatred of the institution that was the U.S. equivalent of Siberia, may have demanded a transfer as a bargaining chip.

If the convicted racketeer could save one American life, it would be well worth obtaining his help. In that spirit, the Naval Intelligence officers went up to Comstock to visit Luciano. Moses Polakoff, Meyer Lansky, Joe Lanza, Mike Lascari, Frank Costello, Willie Moretti, Mike Mirandi, and Joe Adonis also visited.[4]

On July 10, 1943, the invasion of Sicily began. The code name for the Allied invasion of Sicily was "HUSKY." Commander Joachim Titolo was a practicing attorney serving in the District Intelligence Office, Third Naval District, from March 1942 until May 15, 1943, when he received orders for active overseas duty. He landed with the first assault wave on the beachhead of Licata in Sicily. He then participated in the invasion of the Italian mainland and served as the commanding officer of the joint British, American, and Italian counterespionage group that went up the western coast of Italy. Commander Paul Alfieri also participated in the invasion of Sicily. Both of these naval commanders later testified for the Herlands Report.

After a few days in Palermo, the local mafia, led by Don Calo, an avowed antifascist, embraced the Americans. A Palermo city editor wrote, "When [the Americans] met formidable resistance, and then after only a very few days, they arrived in Palermo. The Americans wanted to win the war, and they found a group within the country that counted." The invasion ended on August 17.[5]

At home, Haffenden was pressured into explaining a few key aspects of his role in the parole. On May 17, 1945, he wrote a letter to

Charles Breitel, Dewey's former assistant district attorney, who was now appointed as Counsel to Governor Dewey.

"Through the cooperation of Major Murray Gurfein, now of the OSS, who was formerly an Assistant District Attorney in Manhattan, contacts were made with Mr. Moses Polakoff, who was an attorney for the subject Charles Luciano. This contact was made for the purpose of reaching Sicilian-born Italians who could give pertinent information regarding the conditions in Sicily that would be helpful to our Armed Forces preparing the intelligence for the campaign, which eventually developed in the aforementioned country. Large numbers of informants were constantly sent to my office, then located at 50 Church Street, and were interviewed by agents under my command. I am confident that the greater part of the intelligence developed in the Sicilian campaign was directly responsible to the number of Sicilians that emanated from the Charlie "Lucky" contact. Additional assistance on various subjects came from this same informant, which can be explained to you in detail at a later date."

On December 3, 1945, the New York State Board of Parole recommended commutation of Luciano's life sentence. On January 3, 1946, then Governor Thomas E. Dewey, of New York State, granted Luciano a commutation. It is difficult to believe that Dewey relished the task of unleashing his old nemesis. Dewey had no choice but to adhere to due process in granting the parole.

Commissioner Moran was appointed to the State Board of Parole in 1938. He wrote the decision that attempted to remove blame for the parole on Thomas Dewey. "Governor Dewey has never granted an application except after independent investigation and unanimous favorable recommendation by the Board of Parole," he wrote. "The Board's investigation showed conclusively that Luciano's minimum term should be commuted so he could be deported as an undesirable alien in accordance with the customary practice of the State. Governor Dewey followed the Board's recommendation."[6]

On January 1, 1946, Mayor William O'Dwyer appointed Haffenden to the post of Commissioner of Maritime and Aviation. This was an important post, one that had been sponsored by Haffenden's neighbor, Congressman Jim Roe, Democratic leader of Kings County (Brooklyn). The post granted control of the docks of the City of New York, as well as La Guardia and Idlewild Airports. Idlewild, in particular, was considered ripe with the possibilities of graft due to the tremendous number of concessions to be leased. But Haffenden's friendship with Frank Costello caused the general feeling that Costello had control in the City Administration. Haffenden would lose his position a few short months later when, on May 31, 1946, O'Dwyer would force his resignation. Haffenden resigned amid allegations that he had formed a corporation with two congressmen from Brooklyn, for the purpose of getting a monopoly on all the concessions at Idlewild on the basis of subleases. Distrust of the entire affair went public when Walter Winchell reported the rumor of "talk around the city" that $250,000 had, or would shortly, be paid to various political circles for Luciano's parole. A few years later, Estes Kefauver unsuccessfully tried to obtain information on the incidents leading up to Luciano's parole in his hearings of the committee to the Senate in 1951.

After his parole, Luciano was released to U.S. authorities for deportation. He moved from Comstock to Sing Sing, where INS officials claimed him on February 2, 1946. The day before, the office of Deportation and Parole, INS, authorized the Chief of Detention and Deportation to issue passes to Ellis Island for Luciano's lawyer and three "family members": Meyer Lansky, Albert Anastasia, and Frank Costello. As Luciano arrived at Ellis Island, the group visited him at 1:20 P.M., carrying parcels of clothing. Costello gifted Luciano with $400 in cash and $2,500 in unsigned travelers checks. A freighter to the Liberty Ship *Laura Keene* then transported Luciano on February 8. It was docked at the Bush Terminal in Brooklyn where, on February 9, Luciano held court.

Guards posted on the ship refused entry to reporters. When asked why he wouldn't talk to reporters, Luciano simply answered: "The press has not been too nice to me in the past." The frustrated reporters, barred from both Ellis Island and the *Laura Keene*, took creative measures to get a story. A few of them hired a barge that would follow the *Laura Keene* through the Narrows before it opened throttle for the open seas.

The *Laura Keene* was held an extra day, to February 10, due to apprehension over the heavy rains destroying a cargo of flour.

On February 28, 1946, Luciano arrived in Naples, Italy.[7] He crossed the Atlantic in 1947 and operated gambling operations in Havana at the Jockey Club and National Casino with Meyer Lansky and Bugsy Siegel. The visa was issued in the name of Salvatore Lucania, and granted by the Cuban charge d' affaires. Under pressure from the U.S. government, the Cuban government revoked Luciano's visa. He was forced to return to Italy, where he was barred from the United States for the rest of his life. After his death in Italy of a heart attack in the Capodicino Airport in Naples on January 26, 1962, his family brought the body back to New York. He was buried on February 7, 1962, in St. Johns Cemetery, Queens, New York.

Luciano Leaving Cuba
(Author's Collection)

Appendix

The Sixth Avenue elevated train that ran in front of The Women's House of Detention was taken down in 1938–39. The Women's House of Detention, behind Jefferson Market Courthouse, was razed in 1974. A community garden was built in its place. The Courthouse—which was saved in the 1960s by community activists who rallied to preserve the threatened building—is currently in use as a branch of the New York Public Library. Even today, the old aura of the Courthouse surrounds the building. The bell tower clangs in the early afternoon, alerting library patrons to the opening of the doors on Sixth Avenue.[1]

After the 1936 vice crusade officially ended, the woman behind the scenes, Magistrate Anna M. Kross, continued her hard line against prostitution. In 1937, Kross ordered Wasserman tests on sixteen johns arrested in a house of prostitution in East Harlem. The johns were part of the new influx of Puerto Ricans changing the face of the Italian neighborhood. "The wealthy are as likely to become infected with disease as the people of Harlem," she declared. "Nearly all of Polly Adler's 'expensive girls' were found to have been diseased."

Polly Adler's troubles with the law didn't end with the March Grand Jury of 1935. In 1938, the Federal Government filed an income tax lien against her for the years 1927 through 1930. In 1939, Polly paid her outstanding tax debt. The sum was $12,425. On January 16, 1943, Polly was arrested for the seventeenth time, for maintaining a house of prostitution. Sick with pleurisy, the madam was put into the prison ward of Bellevue Hospital in New York. Two weeks later, back inside the Women's Court at Jefferson Market, Polly was freed on the grounds that police had not established a case. But the experience, one in a long chain of public arrests, threatened her with notoriety. She redeemed herself, however, with the payment of her tax debt. Always good at public relations, she began work on a memoir. Adler was not a native English speaker, a sore point that forced her to seek out Virginia Faulkner, a novelist, who ghostwrote the memoir. In 1953, *A House is Not a Home*, published by Rinehart & Company, Inc., remained a bestseller for two years. The *New York Herald Tribune* Book Reviewer, Stanley Walker, said, "There has never been anything quite like it written by an American. The world of beautiful letters must welcome her now." On September 2, 1954, the Popular Library paperback was released, at a list price of thirty-five cents.

Polly Adler
(New York Daily News)

Adler moved out to California, where she lived until her death. On June 10, 1962, Polly Adler died of cancer in Cedars of Lebanon Hospital in Hollywood at the age of 62. In 2004, Polly was implicated in the cold case of Judge Joseph Force Crater, who disappeared on August 6, 1930. Author Richard Tofel, in his book *Vanishing Point: The Disappearance of Judge Crater and the New York He Left Behind,* advanced a theory that Crater had died in the act of illicit relations with one of Adler's prostitutes on August 6, 1930, the night he disappeared. Adler then called one of her underworld associates, possibly a Dutch Schultz emissary, to remove the body from her establishment.[2]

Mildred Balitzer and Florence Brown were not paid a movie option on their life stories as published in *Liberty.* In 1937, a film starring Humphrey Bogart and Bette Davis was released. *Marked Woman* was loosely based on the Luciano trial.

The prostitutes and madams from the early 1930s' Seabury and Dewey investigations went back into the trade or dropped out of sight. After the recantment statements were complete, the three witnesses issuing them—Florence Brown, Mildred Balitzer, and Nancy Presser—disappeared. Thomas Dewey issued a statement during the appeals process. He indicated that the witnesses would never again be found.

Ninety Times Guilty, Hickman Powell's book on the Luciano trial, was published on April 13, 1939 by Harcourt, Brace & Co. for an original list price of $2.50. In the staid era of the 1930s, the subject matter was considered shocking. A pre-publication advertisement offered a mail-in coupon for a free sample chapter to be mailed to the reader's home, one presumes, in a plain brown envelope. This classic has undergone several reprint editions.

While in Sing Sing, Peter Balitzer, aka Pete Harris, had issued orders to Jo Jo Weintraub to pay for the withdrawal treatment for both Mildred Balitzer and Florence Brown. At the time, both were patients in Town's Hospital, 293 Central Park West. The price Jo Jo had paid was $400 to cover treatment for both women before they were removed by Joe McCarthy, Polakoff's agent. Harris served four years on the Luciano conviction. After his release, he resumed booking with Jo Jo Weintraub.

1941 Raid on Pete Balitzer's Vice Ring
(New York Daily News)

On March 4, 1941, Dewey's racket squad staged another series of raids in an attempt to preempt Harris and Weintraub from proliferating. They arrested sixty johns and twenty-four prostitutes in the raids. Following their 1936 strategy, they released the johns and held the prostitutes as material witnesses. By the end of the month, both of the seemingly incorrigible bookers were back in jail. General Sessions Judge John J. Sullivan sentenced Harris to 10–20 years, and Weintraub to 4–8 years. "There is no sense in lecturing you," said the judge. "It would make no impression on you."[3]

Suspects Entering Dewey's Office in 1941 Raids
(New York Daily News)

Jesse Jacobs, Benny Spiller, and Meyer Berkman cooperated with the office of Thomas Dewey in the latter's investigation of the restaurant racket. The suspect who never went on trial, Thomas Petrovich, was finally judged not to have been a part of the prostitution bonding combination at that time. Berkman was finally brought before the court on May 25, 1937, almost one year after his conviction as a co-defendant in the Luciano case. Because of his coop-eration with other investigations, Berkman received a suspended sen-tence from Justice McCook, who explained that Berkman was "essentially not a vicious person." Spiller and Jacobs had been sentenced on May 3, 1938. Spiller received 5–10 years, and Jacobs received 10–20 years in prison. Frank Hogan suspended their sentences based on time served and the fact that both had cooperated in subsequent rackets investigations.[4]

Jerry Bruno was convicted along with Louis Liquori, a relative of the incarcerated Ralph Liquori, on narcotics conspiracy charges in June 1938. Bruno had gotten the nickname "Jerry the Lug" after his arrest during the February 1936 vice raids.

Moses "Moe" Ducore, a combination hanger-on, was convicted of receiving stolen goods in 1939 and sentenced to 4–10 years.[5]

Al Marinelli died on April 24, 1948 of a heart attack. Thomas Dewey accused Marinelli in October 1937, via a radio address on station WJZ, of being a "political ally of thieves and big-shot racketeers." By December, Dewey reopened an old case that charged Marinelli with harboring Federal fugitive Charles Falci, Marinelli's chauffeur. Marinelli went on trial in Federal court in Brooklyn in spring 1938. In 1939, Governor Lehman ordered his removal. John Salvio replaced him as district leader. At the time of his death, he still lived downtown at 246 Lafayette Street, across the street from his political club at 225 Lafayette.

Marinelli's associate, "Uncle" Al Vitale, was disbarred by the Appellate after an examination of his bank records revealed his tin box, which held $165,000 in undocumented income. In a surprising deci-sion, the Appellate issued a decision on December 17, 1937 with regard to the defense witness who had so rocked the boat in the Luciano trial. The decision ordered Patrolman George Heidt reinstated to the Police Department on February 2, 1938, with $4,300 in back pay ordered refunded to him. The decision maintained that there was nothing to show that the bank deposits or withdrawals were not legitimate.[6]

Joe Bendix was never given the clemency he was promised by Thomas Dewey. He spent his prison time designing miniature oil paintings on linen surfaces. Altogether, he made two thousand designs and distributed them as holiday cards. In 1937, he made an application for executive clemency. When that failed, he suffered a nervous breakdown and landed in the Bellevue prison psych ward. As a desperate way of getting out of jail, he began "aiding other investigations," a misnomer for his pattern of giving false testimony in exchange for a sentence reduction. His later applications for commutation of sentence were denied in August 1938, and again in November 1939. Joy Dixon, Bendix's wife, applied for an annulment. Later, as "Miss Schultz," she expressed a burning desire to reunite with him and flee to South America. In 1941, Bendix filed an affidavit saying he had cooperated with prosecuting attorneys in return for "certain promises and assurances," such as recommending a misdemeanor plea and seeking executive clemency from the Governor of New York State. The Governor denied his application for commutation of sentence both in August 1938 and again in November 1939. He filed a third application on November 12, 1941.[7]

Nick Montana went through a series of retrials in order to win his freedom. He was sent to Auburn in January 1936 and served his sentence with fellow con Jimmy Fredericks. Montana, not an American citizen, was facing deportation if released. The I.N.S. had lodged a warrant to deport him. In November-December 1937, Montana's term was cut on the technicality that Judge Collins had erred in accepting some evidence, and in not allowing other evidence. Montana was given a reduced sentence of three years on appeal, when it was acknowledged that important witnesses in the case had disappeared and were no longer available. Montana, through two unsuccessful writs, tried again in 1939 to gain his freedom.[8]

In 1950, Luciano's co-defendants Pennochio, Betillo, and Fredericks were still in prison. Thomas the Bull Pennochio gained his parole between that year and 1955. He was investigated for a parole violation in 1957.

Jimmy Fredericks was transferred from Sing Sing to Auburn on July

2, 1936. He wrote a letter to the parole board in 1942. From his cell in Auburn, he wrote, "Please excuse the pencil but we are a nation at war."

After the imprisonment of the combination bosses, their wives came to the surface as having had alleged involvement with the drug trades. Mary LaBella Pennochio, the wife of Thomas the Bull, was investigated in November 1937, along with Vito Pennochio, Tommy's brother, for involvement with the Hip Sing Tong, a huge narcotics racket having its headquarters in a Chinese organization. Mrs. Pennochio was arrested and held on $15,000 bail. Vito Pennochio was held on $5,000 bail.

The wife of Jimmy Fredericks, Mrs. Lillian Frederico, was convicted on October 20, 1938 for sending her husband a package of opium while he was incarcerated in Auburn. She was sentenced to serve three years in the Federal Industrial Home for Women at Alderson, West Virginia.

David Little Davie Betillo served time with Luciano in Dannemora until he was transferred to Great Meadow (Comstock). Betillo applied for a parole on April 21, 1952. Through attorney Irving Novis, he made an application based on an interpretation of his first conviction in Philadelphia in 1927 for "conspiracy to enter and steal." The application challenged the status under which he was convicted. The compulsory prostitution conviction and commitment to prison was issued to Betillo as a first offender. The application for parole alleged that he was, in fact, a second offender, which was based on a 1927 Philadelphia conviction. The parole board received letters written by his sister, Florence, who said that he was the only member of the family who had ever gotten in trouble. The family had known its share of tragedies. One of David's sisters was in an institution for the blind. His brother, a veteran with the Italian Armed Forces, was missing in action behind the Iron Curtain. Petillo was paroled in June 1952. He died in New York City in December 1983.[9]

Luciano's appeals began on August 12, 1936. In the venue of Clinton County Court, the location of Luciano's incarceration at Dannemora, attorney James M. Noonan, an Albany lawyer who had defended Dutch Schultz, filed a petition for a writ of habeas corpus. It challenged the Joinder Law under which Luciano was tried, along with the co-defendants. Dewey countered by sending Jacob Rosenblum to the State

Department of Taxation and Finance. There, he compared Luciano's statements at his trial regarding his income tax to what the racketeer actually paid. He drew up warrants on six counts of New York State income tax evasion for 1934 and 1935.

In one short month, Luciano's appearance had undergone a change. The *New York Times* reported that the warden, Thomas Murphy, "does not let convicts go in for dapper daintiness. Luciano was in prison apparel – gray cap, white shirt, black tie, gray sweater, gray trousers, black shoes, gray socks." Luciano lost the plea when Judge Croake dismissed the writ the following month. By November 1936, Noonan requested that the Appellate grant a reversal on the grounds that the Joinder Law had been enacted after the offenses were allegedly committed. Dewey again challenged the application. The following year, in April 1937, Luciano retained Moses Polakoff to represent him. In a brief, co-written with Ralph Liquori's attorney, Lorenzo Carlino, Polakoff accused Dewey of perjury. Dewey then revealed that he was aware of Mildred Balitzer's status as a ward of Polakoff's agents, and her re-addiction to heroin and treatment. He also related that two Church Mission of Health workers had told him that Nancy Presser and Thelma Jordan had feared death and torture. Polakoff retorted that he'd put the women under his command to save them from Thomas Dewey, who they now feared. Dewey argued back that "Mildred Balitzer was desperate for money for her drugs, and money alone was the issue." The Appellate upheld Luciano's conviction on April 12, 1937. The following year, a reargument motion was filed. Moses Polakoff charged that the defense had been unable to question Peggy Wild. He charged that the trial court had failed to require the prosecution to permit defense attorneys to question the witness before placing her on the stand. This was not done in the case of Peggy Wild and constituted a violation of due process. On June 3, 1938, Luciano lost the reargument motion when the court once again affirmed his conviction.

Harry J. Anslinger, Commissioner, U.S. Federal Bureau of Narcotics, would later accuse Luciano of being the mastermind behind new shipments of narcotics arriving on American shores from Europe. Luciano

Gay Orlova, Luciano's girlfriend
(Author's Collection)

had arrived in Italy after his deportation on February 28, 1946. His associate from the United States, Vito Genovese, had gone back to Italy in the 1930s to escape the prospect of being investigated by Thomas Dewey. One month after Luciano arrived in Italy, a Mexican newspaper published a photo of Luciano's girlfriend, Gay Orlova, in New York. The tone of the article—that Luciano was planning to get to Mexico City and reestablish himself—missed the mark by a few hundred miles. Cuba was the racketeer's actual destination.

In February 1947, after living in Naples for one year, Luciano traveled to pre-Castro Havana. When the U.S. found out that he was living in Cuba, they threatened the Cuban government with an embargo of prescription medications. The implementation of the embargo motivated Cuban authorities to arrest Luciano, and they placed him in an immigration camp on February 22, 1947. The following month, on March 19, 1947, the Cuban secret police escorted Luciano, looking haggard and wearing dark sunglasses, to the Steam Ship *Bakir*, in Havana, before the start of his voyage to Genoa, Italy. By 1948, he had settled in Rome. On June 11, 1948, Luciano called a news conference in Rome's Excelsior Hotel, where he told AP writer Johnny McKnight that he would "set the record straight." Yet, between February 1947 and January 1949, several seizures of narcotics in the United States caused the Federal Bureau of Narcotics to cast the blame on Luciano. In July 1949, Italian police questioned him in connection with drug smuggling. He was banned from Rome, where he'd been living in an apartment. He went to Naples in 1949, where he maintained a legitimate business in machinery during the

1950s. At this time, the convicted vice czar fell in love with an Italian ballerina, named Igea Lissoni. She was his companion for nine years. Tragedy struck when the beautiful Igea died in Naples on September 27, 1958. Luciano attended her funeral in Milan. Yet, grief did not preclude his status as a suspect in international drug traffic. A few months later, on the doorstep of a courthouse in Naples on December 13, 1958, he waved an obscene gesture to photographers. Back in the U.S., in 1951, Luciano had been linked to narcotics traffic by the Kefauver Committee, which deduced that Luciano was the head of an Italian narcotics ring. The investigations into his parole came to a head in 1954, when the details of the involvement of Frank Costello, Meyer Lansky, Socks Lanza, and others, were made public.

Frank Costello, who took over for Luciano after his U.S. deportation to Italy, was forced into retirement after being hit by sniper fire in New York City. Vito Genovese, who had tried to eliminate Costello, was removed from the narcotics trade upon a 1959 conviction, which resulted in a fifteen year commitment. Although Luciano remained an international drug suspect until his death, no formal charges were ever made to stick. On January 26, 1962, Luciano died of a massive heart attack at Capodichino Airport in Naples. He was 65.[10]

Detective Stephen Di Rosa, the police officer who assisted in Luciano's arrest in Hot Springs, reappeared in March 1937. The detective accompanying John Brennan at the time of Luciano's first and second arrest in Hot Springs, Di Rosa was implicated in the restaurant rackets when John Brennan, of the Bronx district attorney's office, claimed he'd heard Di Rosa conferring with Luciano in Italian.[11]

Judge Samuel Seabury died on May 7, 1958 in East Hampton at the age of 85.

Igea Lissoni
(Author's Collection)

The distinguished statesman, whose name was permanently linked to fighting municipal corruption, was buried in the Trinity Churchyard at Amsterdam Avenue and 153rd Street.

In March 1939, Thomas Dewey won the conviction of Tammany Hall leader James J. Hines for acting as protector of the Dutch Schultz policy gang. Dewey then made his formal transition to politics. He ran for the governorship of New York State in 1938. His first attempt was unsuccessful. But the Republican candidate tried again and was elected governor in 1942. Dewey's long career also included two unsuccessful runs for the presidency. In 1944, he lost the presidential election to Franklin Delano Roosevelt, yet was reelected in 1946 to the governor's office of New York. He lost to Harry S. Truman in 1948 on his second bid for the presidency. After the narrow defeat to Harry Truman, Dewey answered allegations that a payoff had been involved in the Luciano commutation. Rumors had circulated since the war years, and had come to a crescendo when Dewey refused to reveal information to Estes Kefauver, Chairman of the Senate Crime Investigating Committee (May 10, 1950 to May 1, 1951).

Shortly after the Kefauver investigation, Charles Breitel, an assistant district attorney during the time of the Luciano trial, went on television to defend Dewey, who decided to break his own silence on the events that had led to Luciano's deportation. William B. Herlands began his investigation into the role of the U.S. Navy. The Herlands Report was released in 1954.

Thomas Dewey died on March 16, 1971 of a heart attack at the age of 68. Frank Hogan was one of the pallbearers.

Irving Hest, Thomas Dewey's accountant, died in February 1984. Mr. Hest served Thomas Dewey through the investigations into Louis Buchalter and Jacob Gurrah Shapiro.

Harold Mercer Cole went on to serve in World War II as a lieutenant in the United States Naval Reserve. He remained active in business and Republican politics. He was named special counsel to the chairman of the National Republican Committee until 1948. He was treasurer of the New York County Republican Committee from 1949 to 1953. He died on January 18, 1972. He is buried in Mount Hebron Cemetery, Upper Montclair, New Jersey.

Jacob J. Rosenblum went on to effect twenty-two first-degree murder convictions until he went into private practice in 1942. He remained active in Jewish philanthropies all his life, including acting as honorary president of the YMHA and YWHA in the East Bronx. He died on January 23, 1971 in New York City.

Sol Gelb died on October 22, 1972 in New York. He went from prosecution in the Hines, Lanza, Luciano, Fay, and Kuhn (of the German-American Bund) cases to defense, which he took up as a private attorney in 1945. He defended James R. Jimmy Hoffa and said, "Criminal work is probably the most interesting work there is in the law."

Barent Ten Eyck died of a heart attack at the age of 66 on January 23, 1969. One of Dewey's four top assistants, he went with Dewey to the office of the District Attorney as head of the Frauds Bureau. He left this post in 1939 to track false insurance claims. In 1945, he directed the mayoral campaign of Newbold Morris, who ran unsuccessfully against William O'Dwyer. The versatile attorney was a jazz band pianist who read Norwegian novels.

William Herlands became known as the official who conducted an investigation into the U.S. Navy's role in the Luciano deportation. He worked between 1936–1938 in the prosecution of successors to Dutch Schultz's restaurant racket, the Metropolitan Restaurant and Cafeteria Association. In 1938, he became the Commissioner of Investigation and was instrumental in investigating the German-American Bund. He went into private practice after working in the New York Court of Domestic Relations. He worked in the early 1950s to take part in the investigation of waterfront crime on Staten Island. He died on August 28, 1969 in New York City.

Abraham Belsky, a first-grade detective who arrested John "Johnny Dio" Dioguardi, died on July 8, 1958. When interviewed, Detective Belsky's son said, "My nephew saw my father's shoulder holster from the 71st Precinct and asked, 'Was grandpa a cowboy?' I'd like people to know my father was more than a cowboy."

Eunice Hunton Carter was appointed by Dewey as Chief of the Special Sessions Bureau, a position she held until 1945. Throughout her life, she met many challenges. A woman before her time in the 1930s when she broke the barriers of race and gender to join Thomas Dewey's rackets squad, she continued to work for improved race relations in the latter part of the twentieth century. Mrs. Carter worked with biracial organizations to further the position of African American women in society. She made her home with her husband, Lisle C. Carter, at 409 Edgecombe Avenue for most of the 1940s. She attended the founding conference of the U.N. with her friend, Mary McLeod Bethune, and was named a consultant to the U.N. Economic and Social Council for the International Council of Women and chair of its Committee of Laws in 1947.

Mrs. Carter remained with the Special Sessions Bureau until 1945, when she decided to return to private practice and become involved in civic and social organizations. She became chairperson and trustee of the National Council of Negro Women. She retired in 1952 from legal practice, but continued to chair organizations as an activist until her death from cancer on January 25, 1970. Her son, Lisle Carter, Jr., worked as Assistant Secretary of the Department of Health, Education and Welfare in Washington, D.C.; Vice President of the Urban Coalition; and Vice President and Professor of Public Administration at Cornell University. Her husband died in 1963, leaving her to grieve with her son, Lisle, Jr., and five grandchildren. Following her death, she was given a distinguished funeral mass in St. Martin's Episcopal Church on Lenox Avenue in Harlem. She is buried in Cypress Hills Cemetery, on the border of Brooklyn and Queens.[12]

Chapter Notes

Legend

NYCMA   New York City Municipal Archives, RG Manhattan
D.A.'s Papers; Rec. Sub-Group: Lucky Luciano Trial
Series Title: Indexes; Location: Box; Inclusive Dates:
will vary; Arrangement: by subject.

C of 14 NYPL   Committee of 14 (NY NY 1905) Records, 1905–
1932, Records of a citizens' association dedicated
to the abolition of commercialized vice (especially
prostitution) in New York City. New York Public
Library, Reference, Div. of Manuscripts & Archives

FBI   Federal Bureau of Investigation, RG 39
"Charles Lucania, with aliases."

FRSS, REF NYPL   Final Report of Samuel Seabury, Referee, New York,
March 29, 1932, Magistrates' courts.
Title: In the matter of the investigation of the
departments of the government of the City of New
York, etc., pursuant to joint resolution adopted by the
Legislature of the State of New York, March 23, 1931,
intermediate report to Hon. Samuel H. Hofstader,
chairman of the committee appointed pursuant to said
joint resolution/by Samuel Seabury, counsel to the
Legislative Committee.

RBSC, U. Rochester	Commutation of Sentence of Charles Luciano
	Dept. of Rare Books and Special Collections
	Rush Rees Library
	Thomas Dewey File
	The Herlands Investigation
	University of Rochester
	Rochester, New York 14627–0055
AD	Arkansas Democrat (1936)
AG	Arkansas Gazette (1936)
BE	The Brooklyn Eagle
NYAN	New York Amsterdam News
NYDN	New York Daily News
NYHT	New York Herald Tribune (1926–1956)
NYJA	New York Journal & American (1937–1966)
NYM	New York Mirror
NYP	New York Post
NYS	New York Sun
NYT	The New York Times
NYTG	New York Telegram (1924–1931)
NYWT	New York World-Telegram (1931–1966)

Author's Preface

1   Hickman Powell, "Lucky Luciano," 34.
2. NYCMA, Box 60.
3. NYCMA, Box 38.
4. NYCMA, Box 2.
5. NYCMA, Box 38.

PART I – THE 1933 PROSTITUTION BONDING COMBINATION

Chapter 1 – The Individualists
1. NYCMA, Affidavit of Florence Brown, Box 16.
2. Joan Martin 's testimony corroborated in "Affidavit of Nancy Presser," Box 25; *NY Daily News*, 16 May 1936, p. 1.
3. C. of 14 NYPL.
4. Powell, 114.
5. MYCMA, Police Reports, Box 2.

Chapter 2 – Dance Halls and Bed Houses
1. Committee of 15 Report, "The Social Evil with Special Reference to Conditions Existing in the City of New York," dated 1902.
2. C of 14 NYPL, Statement of Purpose.
3. C of 15 NYPL.
4. Report of George S. Myers, Dancehall Inspector, Cleveland, Ohio, January, 1914; Investigation of New York Society for the Suppression of Vice, Founded 1872; C of 14 NYPL, "Hostess File," Box 37.
5. C of 14 NYPL, Box 37.
6. C of 14 NYPL, "Women's Court," Box 75.

Chapter 3 – The Doctor Called on Monday
1. NYCMA, Wiretaps, Box 2.
2. Robert J. Schoenberg, "Mr. Capone: The Real and Complete Story of Al Capone," p. 45
3. Vivian Gordon: Allen, 244; NYT 27 Feb. 1931; 4 Mar. 1931; NY Telegram, 26 Feb. 1931.
4. NYCMA, Court Transcript, Box 60.
5. Schoenberg, 45.
6. Anne Seagraves, "Soiled Doves,"135.
7. NYCMA, History & Indictments, Box 2.
8. NYCMA, Co-Def. Jesse Jacobs, Box 27.
9. NYCMA, "Physicians," Box 16.
10. NYCMA, Grand Jury Testimony of Florence Brown, Box 3, 16, 25
11. NYCMA, "Co-Defendant Peter Balitzer," Box 21–26.

Chapter 4 – The Mott Street Gang
1. Affidavit of Patrolman Dominick Ciaffone, NYCMA, "Co-Def. Pennochio," Box 34; Robert Lacey, "Little Man," p. 51–52; Tong Linked, NYT 21 Nov. 1937.

2. Thompson and Raymond, 367–369.

3. NYCMA, "Co-Def. Pennochio" Box 34.

4. NYCMA, Al Weiner Wiretap, Box 2; Al Weiner Grand Jury Testimony, Box 40.

5. NYCMA, Cokey Flo Grand Jury Testimony, Box 3,16.

6. NYCMA,"Statement of Thomas Pennochio"; "Statement of Mary Pennochio," Box 34.

7. Thompson and Raymond.

8. NYCMA, Box 41.

9. NYCMA, "Tommy Bull–Defendant," Notes in "Co-Def. Pennochio," Box 34.

10. Ibid.

11. NYCMA, "Co-Def. James Frederico," Box 30–31; Fredericks Escape: NYT 4 Jan. 1928; Lillian, NYT 20 Oct. 1938.

12. NYCMA, "Co-Def. Pennochio," Box 34; NYT Police Question Friends of Masella, 1 Nov. 1929.

13. Abe Karp was one of a group of attorneys who, on May 29, 1931, was scrutinized by Judge Samuel Seabury in an Intermediate Report. They were: John C. Weston, Abraham Karp, Mark Alter, Emanuel A. Busch, Philip Rusgo, Joseph Aronstein, Joseph A. Butler, James J. Mayer, Kevie Frankel, Robert J. Fitzsimmons, Samuel Goldstein, William J. McAuliffe, George Hirsch, Joseph Weber, Albert B. Kurtz, and Alexander Lang, deceased. After filing the report, only one, John C. Weston, consented that his name be stricken from the roll of attorneys. The Bar Association of the City of New York then brought disciplinary proceedings against these attorneys. The trial of the issues raised was referred to Hon. Clarence J. Shearn, as Referee. Judge Shearn recommended disbarment of only one attorney: William J. McAuliffe. He would recommend censure of Mark Alter. Of the other attorneys, including Abe Karp, the charges were dismissed. Abe Karp was later disbarred by the Appellate. Source: NYPL, Final Report of Samuel Seabury, Referee, New York, March 29, 1932, Magistrates' courts, p. 11–12; in an article, NYT, 25 Nov. 1930, listed the Women's Court lawyers and their locations as: Abraham Karp, 117 W. Tenth Street, Mark Alter, 101 West Tenth Street; Emanuel Busch, 109 W. Tenth Street, Philip Ruego and Joseph Aronstein, 109 W. Tenth Street, and Joseph Butler, uptown at 312 W. 54 Street. Alexander Lang, died before Judge Seabury could question him; William B. Northrup and John B. Northrup, "The Insolence of Office: The Story of the Seabury Investigations," p. 23. NYCMA, "Co-Def. Peter Balitzer," Box 21–26; Karp disbarred on March 16, 1934 (App. Div.1st D.) Christopher "Binge" Redmond, who ran messages for Karp, would refuse to testify against him when asked by Thomas Dewey. "Binge," a hanger-on and messenger, had worked for Karp before going over to Jesse Jacobs.

14. NYCMA, "Co-Def. Pennochio," Box 34.

Chapter 5 – Scandal in the Women's Court

1. Note: Readers of Judge Seabury's essays in Northrup will notice that references to the marketplace disappear from most recorded references written after 1931. The market disappeared in 1932 to make way for the Women's House of Detention. The marketplace, which housed a farmers' market and general stores, stretched south on Sixth Avenue directly south of the Courthouse, pointing downtown. Before this, the Jefferson open marketplace was the center of a bustling commercial area of lower Manhattan. In that pre-House of Detention period, the courthouse housed the jail. It appears to have been located in the top floors of the building, according to blueprints on file in the Jefferson Market Courthouse building, now a branch of the New York Public Library. The Sixth Avenue el came down in 1939. The building stopped operating as a courthouse in 1946. Source: Pamphlet, NYPL, Jefferson Market Branch, "The History of the Jefferson Market Library."

2. Note: Judge Seabury would later become Commissioner, then Counsel to Legislative Committee appointed pursuant to the Joint Resolution of the Senate and Assembly. The Seabury Investigations into other areas of corrupt city government continued before the Legislative Committee until June 1932. Altogether, 299 witnesses were examined. The transcript covers 4,596 pages. William B. Northrup and John B. Northrup, 3–16; 109; Herbert Mitgang, "The Man Who Rode the Tiger," 159–309; FRSS REF, NYPL, 12–20.

3. Chile Acuna & Vice Frameups: Northrup, p. 25–30; C of 14, NYPL, Box 75; NYDN, 3 Dec. 1930; NY Telegram, 12 Jan. 1930; 25–26 Nov. 1930; 3 Dec. 1930, 17 Jan. 1931.

4. Landlady racket: Northrup, 47–51; FRSS REF., NYPL, 21–23, 83–85; Bondsman Northrup, 23; FRSS REF., NYPL 11, 21–24, 103–108, ; NYCMA, Co-Def. Jesse Jacobs, Box 27.

5. Girls released from Bedford Hills: NYT, 14 Jan. 1931; 15 Jan. 1931; 20 Jan. 1931; FRSS REF., NYPL, 132–135.

6. Mitgang, 189.

7. Jean Norris: Allen, 243; FRSS REF., NYPL, 11, 44, 132; Northrup 81, 109.

8. Quinlivan, O'Connor, NYT, 29 Nov. 1930; NYT, 30 Nov. 1930; Thomas E. Dewey, "Twenty Against the Underworld," 91; John C. Weston FRSS REF., NYPL 78–81; NYT 30 May 1931; Reforms: FRSS REF., NYPL 147, 202–216.

9. Polly Adler, "A House is Not a Home," p. 16; NYT 7, 24 May; 17 Jun. 1931; 14, 23–24 Jul. 1931; 6, 8 Aug. 1931.

10. NYT, 4 Mar. 1931.

11. Vivian Gordon: NYT 27 Feb. 1931; 4 Mar. 1931; NY Telegram, 26 Feb. 1931; NYT 1 Sept. 1933.

Chapter 6 – The Law Takes Polly Adler

1.   Built in 1932, the Women's House of Detention in Greenwich Village razed in 1974 when the Women's House of Detention on Rikers Island, in East Elmhurst, Queens, was utilized. Source: Pamphlet, "The History of the Jefferson Market Library."
2.   Allen, 254.
3.   Ibid, 256.
4.   Mickey Walker, "Mickey Walker: The Toy Bulldog and His Times," 112; NYT, 6 Mar. 1935; 8 Mar. 1935.
5.   NYT, 8 Feb. 1934.
6.   J. Edgar Hoover's NYC visit: NYT, 26 Mar. 1935; Adler's Conviction & Commitment: NYT, 20–21, 28 Mar.1935; 16, 27 Apr.1935; 7, 11, 12 May, 1935. Quoted from Adler, 212.
7.   NYT, 11–15, 17–18, 25 Jul. 1935. Note: Adler would pay her outstanding taxes, negotiated to $12,425.72, in 1939. NYT, 25 Feb. 1939.
8.   March Grand Jury: NYT, 6–10, 17, 23 Mar. 1935; 3, 22, 26 May, 1935.
9.   NYT, 2 Jul. 1935; NYT, 18 Mar., 1971; Suit to stop rackets inquiry: NYT, 13 Jul. 1935.
10.   NYAN, Obituary, Eunice Carter, 31 Jan. 1970, p. 2; Susan C. Pruyear, "Women in the Legal Profession: Eunice Roberta Hunton Carter, 1899–1979."
11.   NYCMA, "Co-Def. Jack Ellenstein," Box 28, 29; 25 May 1935; NYT, 13, 17 Nov. 1935; 6 Dec. 1935; 7 Jan. 1936; NYJA, 17 Nov. 1937; On 7 Dec 1937, Nick Montana was given a reduced sentence of 3 years on appeal. NYT, 7 Dec. 1937; 22 Apr. 1939, 6 May, 1939.
12.   NYT, 28 May 1928; Jennie Fischer: NYCMA, "Al Weiner Wiretap," Box 2.
13.   George Wolf with Joseph DiMona, "Frank Costello," 105.
14.   Legs Diamond Death: NYT, 19 Dec. 1931; Wake: NYT, 21 Dec. 1931.
15.   NYT, 14 Mar. 1934.

Chapter 7 – A "Real" Crime

1.   FRSS REF., NYPL 135–138.
2.   Craig Thompson and Allen Raymond, "Gang Rule in New York," 365; NYT, 26 Jun. 1932; NYWT, 23 Mar. 1939.
3.   NYT, 10 Oct. 1931.
4.   Patrick Downey, "Gangster City," 116.
5.   NYT, 25 Oct; 26 Nov. 1937.
6.   Vitale: NYT, 7–9, 12 Jan. 1930.
7.   NYT, 6 May, 1933; 28 Nov. 1933; 17 Jan. 1934.
8.   NYCMA, Florence Brown, Box 3, 16, 25.
9.   NYCMA, Weiner, Box 2.
10.   C of 14 NYPL, Box 75.

11. NYCMA, Co-Def. Ellenstein, Box 28, 29; Fred Allhoff, "Tracking New York's Crime Barons," <u>Liberty</u> Magazine, 1936.
12. NYCMA, "Police Papers–Raid," Box 2.
13. NYT, 2 Feb. 1936; NYM, 2 Feb. 1936; NYCMA, "Arraignment Materials for Witnesses," Box 25; Karp disbarred on Mar. 16, 1934 (App.Div.1st D.).

PART II – MATERIAL WITNESSES

Chapter 8 – Groundhog Day

1. NYHT, 4–5 Feb. 1936; NYT 3–4 Feb. 1936.
2. NYHT, 4 Feb. 1936.
3. NYHT, 6–7 Feb. 1936; Fischer bail, NYCMA, Box 31; Petrovich, NYCMA, Box 34.
4. Telephone interview with author.
5. NYHT, 4–7 Feb. 1936.
6. NYCMA, "Co-Defendant Peter Balitzer," Box 21–26, 31.
7. NYCMA, Box 25.
8. Adler, 226.
9. NYCMA, Box 2, "Indictments."
10. Arrest of Jerry Bruno, NYCMA, Box 30; Arrest of Peggy Wild, HT 5 Feb. 1936.
11. NYCMA, Box 2, 25.
12. NYCMA, "Co-Defendant Thomas Pennochio," Box 34.
13. NYCMA, Box 31.
14. Certificate of Birth, "Davide Silvio Petillo," NYC Dept. of Health, NYCMA, Box 27, "Co-Defendant David Betillo"; Betillo's two out-of-state offenses had been in Connecticut and Pennsylvania. This Pennsylvania conviction, on 7 Feb. 1929, for breaking and entering, would, years later, be treated as a landmark case during one of the felon's unsuccessful applications for a parole.
15. NYCMA, Box 33, 17 Feb. 1936, Anthony Mancuso, BCI, to Lieutenant Dowd.
16. Mario Gomes to author, 9 Jan. 2006.
17. NYCMA, 27.

Chapter 9 – The Boss

1. Waldorf employees, NYCMA, Box 15.
2. Torrio, Chicago Times, 27 Oct. 1935; Mafia with Unione Siciliane, Burton Turkus, "Murder, Inc.," p. 75; Big Six, NYT 26 Oct., 1935; Chicago Times 27–28 Oct. 1935.
3. Torrio with Marinelli, Chicago Times, 28 Oct. 1935; NYCMA, Box 13; Researcher Mario Gomes to author, 11 Jan. 2006.
4. Chicago Times, 28 Oct. 1935; NYP, 26 Oct. 1935; FBI, "Lucky Luciano," 39–2141.

5. No Unione Siciliana in NY: Consensus by experts .

6. Luciano addresses: U.S. Federal Census; Record: NYCMA, "Defendant Luciano," Box 13; Biographical: NYHT, 5 Apr. 1936.

7. Costello: George Walsh, "Public Enemies"; NYCMA, Box 13.

8. NYT, 28 Oct. 1935; Chicago Times, 7 Aug. 1936.

9. NYHT, 17, 19 Oct. 1929; NYDN 18 Oct. 1929.

10. Jonathan Van Meter, "The Last Good Time," 51.

11. Rick Porrello, "The Rise and Fall of the Cleveland Mafia," 132.

12. Ibid, 133.

13. Chicago Tribune, 19 May, 1940; NYT, 16 Apr. 1931; NYDN, 16 Apr. 1931.

14. BE, 16 Apr., 1931; NYS, 16 Apr., 1931.

15. Interview, son of bootlegger, conducted on condition of anonymity; Feast: NYS, 11 Sept. 1931; NYWT, 11 Sept. 1931; NYT, 12 Sept. 1931; Chicago Tribune, 19 May 1940; Kill or be killed: expert opinion of Allan May; The Sicilian Vespers resulted in one-tenth of the original estimate of forty deaths: expert consensus.

Chapter 10 – This Man's Sheriff

1. Bendix was convicted of stealing 1 pair diamond crystal cuff links, 4 diamond crystal vest buttons, 2 diamond crystal studs, 2 ruby studs, 1 pocket watch, 1 diamond pin, 1 metal watch chain, 1 pair Rosary beads, 1 pair Buckskin gloves. NYCMA, "Joe Bendix," Box 13.

2. Dewey's statements on the anti-crime bills were made to the NYHT, 5 Mar., 1936. These included reference to the murder of Samuel Druckman, a case with multiple defendants. This case prompted a similar extraordinary grand jury investigation by Governor Lehman. The two cases were cited together to make a case for the anti-crime bill, which would allow defendants charged in the same crimes to be tried together.

3. Statements taken by Charles D. Breitel, 10, 18 Mar. 1936, NYCMA, Box 28.

4. NYCMA, "David Marcus," Box 27; NYHT, 17 May, 1936.

5. NYCMA, "Co-Defendant James Frederico," Box 30–31.

6. NYCMA, Nancy Presser, Box 25.

7. NYCMA, Box 60.

8. NYCMA, Presser, 25.

9. NYCMA, "Summary of Witness Testimony," Box 2–4

10. Ibid. NYCMA, Nancy Presser, Box 25.

11. NYHT, 5 Mar. Arkansas Gazette, 4 Apr. NYHT, 9 Apr. 1936.

12. Davis: NYT, 28 Aug. 1883; Trent and Karpis, 100.

13. J. Edgar Hoover, "Persons in Hiding," p. 68–69; Arkansas Democrat, 1 Apr. 1936.

14. The role of Herbert "Dutch" Akers: NYHT, 19 Apr. 1936; The role of "Dutch" Akers is evidenced in Dewey's memo to file found in NYCMA, "Luciano

Extradition," Box 13: "When arrested, Luciano was in the company of the chief of detectives when arrested by Detective Brennen on April 1st." The initial charge of extortion and interstate flight to avoid arrest was issued pursuant to section 408E Title 18, U.S. Code. Lamar Hardy, the U.S. Attorney, sent this explanation of the warrant by telegram to Fred Isgrig, the U.S. District attorney of Little Rock, NYCMA, 13.

15. AG, 2 Apr.; AD, 2 Apr.; NYT, 2 Apr.; AD, 4 Apr. 1936.
16. HT, 1–2 Apr. 1936.
17. NYCMA, 13.
18. AD, 2 Apr. 1936; Fred Allhoff, "Tracking New York's Crime Barons," Part 5.
19. NYCMA, 13; Allhoff, p. 5.
20. Ibid.
21. William Helmer and Rick Mattix, "Public Enemies," 236.
22. Luciano newspaper interview, AG, 2 Apr. 1936; Detectives Di Rosa, Cashmen and Kennedy: AG, 4 Apr. 1936; Jamaica (Queens, NY) Race Track was located in South Jamaica: Queens Historical Society; AD 2–4 Apr. AG, 4 Apr. 1936; Luciano's quotes, with Dewey's remarks, NYCMA, 13.
23. AD, 4 Apr.; NYT, 5 Apr.; AD, 5–7, 1936
24. NYT, 7–11 Apr.; AD, 7 Apr., NYHT, 7, 8, 10 Apr. 1936; Bribery: NYT, 9 Jun. 1936; Allhoff, p. 5; NYT, 12, 18, 19, 23 Apr.; NYHT, 18, 21 Apr. 1936.
25. On Apr. 15, Luciano's associate and national crime boss Johnny Torrio, who was the Chicago gang chief during Prohibition, was arrested in White Plains, north of New York City. He was held on a warrant for income tax evasion; NYCMA, 13.

Chapter 11 – The Small Fry

1. Letters of Florence Brown to Barent Ten Eyck: NYCMA, "Affidavit of Florence Brown," Box 16; Brown's treatment in House of Detention: NYCMA, Box 38.
2. Edward Doherty, with Brown and Balitzer, "Underworld Nights," *Liberty*, Pt. 1–3, 1936.
3. NYCMA, 16.
4. NYHT, 12 May 1936; NYDN, 11–14 May; NYT, 5–13 May, 1936. The selected jurors were: Foreman Edwin Aderer, Edward Blake, Theodore Isert, Paul Mahler, Hewitt Morgan, Norbert Gagnon, Charles Jones, Robert Center, Lincoln Weld, Stephen Smith, John McGowan, Martin Moses; and Henry Sturges and Talbot Squier, alternates.
5. NYDN, 15–19 May 1936; NYT, 16 May 1936.
6. NYCMA, 16.
7. NYT, 15 May, 1936.
8. Marcus/Brooks testimony: NYHT, 20 May, 1936; Marcus perjury: NYT 5 Jun, 1936.

Chapter 12 – Like the Chain Stores

1. NYDN, 20 May 1936; NYT, 17–18, 20 May 1936; NYHT, 17–20 May 1936.
2. NYDN, 22 May 1936.
3. The phrase "just like the A&P" never appeared in any of the trial transcripts or newspaper accounts that recorded Florence Brown's testimony verbatim. The "A&P" brand was added later by writers as a paraphrased summation of Luciano's alleged original statement as per Florence Brown's testimony.
4. NYCMA, "Florence Brown," 16.
5. Testimony of Florence Brown, Edward Doherty, "The Witness Chair," *Liberty* Magazine, 1936 NYDN, 23 May 1936; NYHT, 22, 23 May 1936.
6. Note on Mrs. Titterton's murder: This was an isolated crime committed by a sex offender and bore no relation to a gangland slaying. Its effectiveness as a method of intimidation rested in its use by the tabloids as a front page, sensational murder case. Thelma Jordan, NYDN, 26 May 1936.

Chapter 13 – Samson's Delilah

1. NYCMA, "Nancy Presser," Box 25.
2. Presser's testimony: NYDN, 26–27 May 1936; NYT, 27 May 1936.
3. Bribery of Kornbluth: NYDN, 27 May 1936; NYT 28 May 1936; NYHT, 27 May 1936.
4. Balitzer's testimony: NYDN, 27–28 May 1936; NYT, 30 May 1936 (Mildred claimed she had a 15 year old daughter/other times she said she had a "little boy.") Gus Franco threat: NYHT, 29, 30 May 1936; Phil Ryan's background: Hickman Powell, "Lucky Luciano, His Amazing Trial and Wild Witnesses," p. 186.
5. NYHT, 2 Jun. 1936; NYT, 2 Jun. 1936; NYDN, 2 Jun. 1936; NYCMA, "Co-Defendant Ellenstein," Box 28–29.
6. NYT, 22 May 1936; NYDN, 3 Jun. 1936; NYCMA, "Joe Bendix," Box 12–14.
7. Luciano's testimony: NYT, 31 May; 4 Jun. 1936; NYDN, 4–6 Jun. 1936.
8. Det. Heidt: NYT, 28 Nov. 1935; Reinstatement to NY Police Dept.: 18 Dec. 1937; Assigned to 28th Pct.: 1 Feb. 1938; Role in trial: NYT, 21 Jun. 1936; 3, 11 Jul. 1936.
9. Thomas Petrovitch, a combination hanger-on who had pled guilty to compulsory prostitution separately, had his sentence postponed. NYT, 2 Jul. 1936.
10. Summations: NYT, 5–6 Jun. 1936; NYHT, 7 Jun. 1936.

Chapter 14 – Sixty Two Counts

1. Heidt: NYT, 9 Jun. 1935; NYHT, 8 Jun. 1936; NYT, 21 Jun. 1936; 14 Jul. 1936.
2. Report of Chief Probation Officer Halpern, Court of General Sessions, NYT, 13, 19–21 Jun. 1936.

3. NYT, 13–14, 17 Jul. 1936.
4. NYT, 19 Jun. 1936.
5. Heidt: NYHT, 8 Jun.; NYT, 11 Jun. 3, 1936; 11, 14 Jul. 1936; Dismissal, NYT, 1 Sep. 1936; Reinstatement, NYT, 18 Dec. 1937; NYT, 3 Feb. 1938.
6. Kross: NYT, 17 Jun. 1936.

Part III – Recantment

Chapter 15 – Independence Day

The exchange between Judge McCook and the witnesses is taken verbatim from the transcript taken on June 8–9, 1936, by Nathan Behrin, the official stenographer to Judge McCook. NYCMA, Box 60.

Chapter 16 – Thieves in the Night

1. E. Flesher to T. Dewey, 15 May 1936, NYCMA, 25.
2. Ibid.
3. Ibid.
4. Edward Doherty, "Underworld Nights," *Liberty Magazine*, Nov.–Dec. 1936; NYCMA, "Joe Bendix," Box 12; Boxes 38, 39.
5. Jo Jo Weintraub's intervention in Town's Hospital, 293 Central Park W.: NYT, 21 Apr. 1937.
6. NYT, 21 Apr. 1937; NYCMA, Box 38.
7. NYT, 12 Mar. 1937; NYT, 21, 24 Apr. 1937; 17 Jul. 1937.
8. NYCMA, "Joe Bendix," Box 12.

Epilogue – Code Name HUSKY

1. Affidavit of Frank Hogan, 9 Sept. 1954; RBSC, U. Rochester; Peter Kross, "Lucky Strikes a Deal," *World War II;* RA W.S. Pye, Pres., Naval War College, Naval Operating Base, Newport, RI, at Graduation exercises of the Naval Training School, New York, 16 Mar. 1944; RBSC, U. Rochester; Hoover: FBI, 39–2141, Luciano, Memo, Hoover to Tamm, 17 May 1946.
2. George Walsh, "Public Enemies."
3. FBI.
4. RBSC, U. Rochester; Dorothy Gallagher, "The Project."
5. John Tagliabue, "How Don Calo (and Patton) Won the War in Sicily," NYT, 24 May 1994; RBSC, U. Rochester.
6. Letter, Charles R. Haffenden to Hon. Charles Breitel, 17 May 1945, FBI 39–2141–10; RBSC, U. Rochester.
7. FBI. Recommended Reading: Rodney Campbell, "The Luciano Project."

Appendix

1. Pamphlet, NYPL, "The History of The Jefferson Market Library."
2. Polly Adler's death: NYT, 10 Jun. 1962; Richard J. Tofel, "Vanishing Point," 153, 155.
3. Weintraub & Harris convictions: NYT, 5, 14, 19, 29 Mar. 1941.
4. Berkman: NYT, 25 May 1937; Spiller & Jacobs: NYT, 3 May 1938.
5. Moe Ducore: 22 Apr. 1939; Jerry Bruno: 3 Jun. 1938.
6. Marinelli: NYT, 25 Oct. 1937; 3, 29 Dec. 1937; 19, 20 May, 1938. Heidt: NYT, 2 Feb. 1938.
7. Joe Bendix: NYCMA, Box 12
8. Nick Montana: NYT, 7 Dec. 1937; 22 Apr. 1939; 6 May 1939. It was granted after it was revealed that he was convicted for the crime of placing one Beverly Reynolds into a house of prostitution. She had skipped, and by the time the case was on the calendar, she went under the status of "missing witness." The relevance of this was challenged.
9. Petillo: SS death index; NYCMA, "Appeal" Box 20; NYS Archives, "David Petillo," Inmate Series 14610–88, Great Meadow; Fredericks: NYS Archives, "James Frederico," Ref. #1430, Series B0067, Vol. 5, Auburn; Mrs. Fredericks: NYT, 20 Oct. 1938; Mrs. Pennochio: NYT, 21 Nov. 1937.
10. Luciano's 1st appeal: NYT, 12, 25 Aug.; 15 Sep. 1936; Case to Appellate, 18 Nov. 1936; NYT, 21 Apr. 1937; 24 Apr. 1937; 4 Jun. 1938; Tax evasion charges: NYT, 21 Aug. 1936. Jill Jonnes, "Hep-Cats, Narcs, and Pipe Dreams," 147; May, Allen, "Luciano's Short Return to Cuba"; Planned trip to Mexico City, FBI; 39–2141–59; Costello and Genovese, Selwyn Raab, "Five Families," 124.
11. Di Rosa: NYT, 27 Mar. 1937.
12. Seabury, Cole, Rosenblum, Gelb, Ten Eyck, Herlands and Belsky Obituaries: NYT; Richard N. Smith, "Thomas Dewey and His Times"; The Herlands Investigation, U. of Rochester; Eunice Carter: Records of St. Martins Episcopal Church, Lenox Ave., NYC; Records of Cypress Hills Cemetery, Brooklyn, New York. Obituary, NYAN, 31 Jan. 1970.

Selected Bibliography

Books

Adler, Polly. *A House is Not a Home.* Reprint Ed., New York: Popular Library, 1959. (Originally published by Rhinehardt, 1953).

Allen, Oliver E. *The Tiger: The Rise and Fall of Tammany Hall.* New York: Addison-Wesley, 1993.

Anonymous. *I Am A Marked Woman: What a Call Girl Suffered from the Vice Syndicate* (Formerly *I Worked for Lucky Luciano).* Reprint Ed., New York: Avon Publications, Inc., 1954.

Asbury, Herbert. *The Gangs of New York: An Informal History of the New York Underworld.* New York: Alfred A. Knopf, Inc., 1927, 1928.

Binder, John J. *The Chicago Outfit.* Chicago: Arcadia Publishing, 2003.

Brennan, Bill. *The Frank Costello Story.* Derby, CT: Monarch Books, 1962.

Burrough, Bryan. *Public Enemies: America's Greatest Crime Wave and the Birth of the FBI, 1933–1934.* New York: The Penquin Press, 2004.

Campbell, Rodney. *The Luciano Project: The Secret Wartime Collaboration of the Mafia & the U.S. Navy.* New York: McGraw-Hill, 1977.

Charyn, Jerome. *Gangsters & Gold Diggers: Old New York, the Jazz Age, and the Birth of Broadway.* New York: Four Walls Eight Windows, 2003.

Cooper, Courtney Ryley. *Ten Thousand Public Enemies.* Boston: Little, Brown and Company, 1935.

Crapsey, Edward. *The Nether Side of New York, Or, the Vice, Crime and Poverty of the Great Metropolis*. New York: Sheldon & Co., 1872. Digital Ed. <http://www.hti.umich.edu/>

Dewey, Thomas E. *Twenty Against the Underworld*. New York: Doubleday and Company, Inc., 1974.

Downey, Patrick. *Gangster City: The History of the New York Underworld 1900–1935*. Fort Lee: Barricade Books, 2004.

Feder, Sid and Joachim Joesten. *The Luciano Story*. Reprint Ed., New York: Da Capo Press, 1994.

Gilfoyle, Timothy J. *City of Eros: New York City, Prostitution, and the Commercialization of Sex, 1790–1920*. New York: W.W. Norton & Co., 1992.

Gosch, Martin A. and Richard Hammer. *The Last Testament of Lucky Luciano*. Boston: Little, Brown and Company, 1974, 1975.

Hamilton, Charles. *Men of the Underworld*. New York: Macmillan & Co., 1952.

Harris, Sara. *Hellhole: The Shocking Story of the Inmates and Life in the New York City House of Detention for Women*. New York: E.P. Dutton, 1967.

Helmer, William J. and Arthur J. Bilek. *The St. Valentine's Day Massacre*. Nashville: Cumberland, 2004.

_____ with Rick Mattix. *Public Enemies: America's Criminal Past, 1919–1940*. New York: Facts on File, 1998.

_____ and Rick Mattix. *The Complete Public Enemies Almanac: New Facts and Features on the People, Places, and Events of the Gangster and Outlaw Era, 1920-1940*. Cumberland House, 2007.

Hoover, J. Edgar. *Persons in Hiding*. Boston: Little, Brown and Company, 1938.

Jonnes, Jill. *Hep-Cats, Narcs, and Pipe Dreams: A History of America's Romance with Illegal Drugs*. New York: Scribner, 1996.

Katcher, Leo. *The Big Bankroll: The Life and Times of Arnold Rothstein*. Reprint Ed., New York: DaCapo, 1994.

Katz, Leonard. *Uncle Frank: The Biography of Frank Costello*. New York: Drake Publishers, Inc., 1973.

Kavieff, Paul R. *The Life and Times of Lepke Buchalter: America's Most Ruthless Labor Racketeer*. Fort Lee: Barricade, 2006.

Keefe, Rose. *The Man Who Got Away: The Bugs Moran Story*. Nashville: Cumberland House, 2005.

Kefauver, Estes. *Crime in America*. New York: Doubleday & Co., Inc., 1951.

Lacey, Robert. *Little Man: Meyer Lansky and the Gangster Life*. Boston: Little, Brown and Company, 1991.

Mass, Peter. *The Valachi Papers*. New York: Harper Collins, 1968.

Mitgang, Herbert. *The Man Who Rode the Tiger: The Life of Judge Samuel Seabury and the Story of the Greatest Investigation of City Corruption in This Century*. New York: W.W. Norton & Co., 1963.

Northrop, William B. and John Northrop. *The Insolence of Office: The Story of the Seabury Investigations*. New York: G.P. Putman's Sons, 1932.

Porrello, Rick. *The Rise and Fall of the Cleveland Mafia*. Fort Lee: Barricade, 1995.

Powell, Hickman. *Lucky Luciano, The Man Who Organized Crime in America*. (formerly *90 Times Guilty* and *Lucky Luciano: His Amazing Trial and Wild Witnesses*). Reprint Ed., Fort Lee: Barricade, 2000.

Powell, Hickman. *Lucky Luciano: His Amazing Trial and Wild Witnesses* (formerly *90 Times Guilty*). Reprint Ed., Secaucus: NJ: Citadel Press, 1975.

Prall, Robert H. and Norton Mockridge. *This is Costello: On the Spot.* Greenwich, CT: Fawcett Publications, 1951.

Raab, Selwyn. *Five Families.* New York: St. Martin's Press, 2005.

Sann, Paul. *Kill The Dutchman! The Story of Dutch Schultz.* New Rochelle: Arlington House, 1971.

Schatzberg, Rufus and Robert J. Kelly. *African American Organized Crime.* New Brunswick, NJ: Rutgers University Press, 1996.

Schoenberg, Robert J. *Mr. Capone: The Real—and Complete—Story of Al Capone.* Reprint Ed., New York: HarperCollins, 2001.

Sciacca, Tony. *Luciano: The Man Who Modernized the American Mob.* Pinnocle Books: 1975.

Seagraves, Anne. *Soiled Doves: Prostitution in the Early West.* Hayden, ID: Wesanne Publications, 1994.

Smith, Richard Norton. *Thomas Dewey and His Times.* New York: Simon and Schuster, 1982.

Stern, Michael. *No Innocence Abroad.* New York: Random House, 1953.

Stolberg, Mary M. *Fighting Organized Crime: Politics, Justice, and the Legacy of Thomas E. Dewey.* Boston: Northeastern University Press, 1995.

Thompson, Craig and Allen Raymond. *Gang Rule in New York.* New York: The Dial Press, 1940.

Toffel, Richard J. *Vanishing Point: The Disappearance of Judge Crater, and the New York He Left Behind.* Chicago: Ivan R. Dee, 2004.

Turkus, Burton B. and Sid Feder. *Murder, Inc. The Story of the Syndicate.* Reprint Ed., New York: Da Capo, 1992.

Van Meter, Jonathan. *The Last Good Time: The Notorious 500 Club & the Rise and Fall of Atlantic City.* New York: Crown, 2003.

Walker, Mickey. *Mickey Walker: The Toy Bulldog & His Times*. New York: Random House, 1961.

Walsh, George. *Public Enemies: The Mayor, the Mob, and the Crime That Was*. New York: W.W. Norton & Co., 1980.

Washburn, Josie. *The Underworld Sewer: A Prostitute Reflects on Life in the Trade*. Introduction by Sharon E. Wood. Lincoln, NE: University of Nebraska Press, 1997.

Wolf, George with Joseph DiMona. *Frank Costello: Prime Minister of the Underworld*. Reprint Ed., New York: Bantam, 1975.

ARTICLES

Allhoff, Fred. "Tracking New York's Crime Barons," *Liberty Magazine,* Pt. 1–6, 1936.

Corina, Joe. "Mobsters: Who's Who of America's Criminals?" JG Press, World Publications Groups, Inc., 1003 <http: www.wrldpub.com>

Dail, Hubert. "Evil Consequences: New York's Meanest Killer," *Minneapolis Tribune*, 24 March 1934.

Doherty, Edward. "The Gangster: What Is to Come after Him?" *Liberty* Magazine, 21 November 1931.

_____. "The Witness Chair," *Liberty Magazine*, Undated.

_____. with Mildred Balitzer and Florence Brown. "Underworld Nights," *Liberty* Magazine, Pt. 1–3, 1936.

Gallagher, Dorothy. "The Project," *All the Right Enemies: The Life and Murder of Carlo Tresca,* 1988.

Kross, Peter. "Lucky Strikes a Deal," *World War II,* March 2003.

Lillian, Tony. "Lucky Luciana and His $12,000,000 a year Sin Syndicate," *Official Detective Stories*, September 1936.

Murray, George. "The First Underworld Peace Conference: The Legacy of Al Capone: Traits and Annals of Chicago's Public Enemies." SBN: 399–11502–1.

Pamphlet, "The History of Jefferson Market Library," NYPL, Jefferson Market Branch.

Staff, "Pretty Rita's Nice Mr. Cohen," *Minneapolis Tribune*, 22 December 1935.

Staff, "Kiki A Bride, and a Ghost is Laid to Rest," *San Diego Union*, 1935.

Feature Articles

Lieberman, Irving and William J. Keegan. "Costello Real Tammany Boss, Says District Chief," *New York Post*, 28 September 1943.

Logan, Malcolm. "Costello Reveals He Elected Kennedy, Then Named Aurelio," *New York Post*, 25 October 1943.

_____. "Aurelio Proposed Deal, Says Mayor; 'I Refused,'" *New York Post*, 27 October 1943.

Staff, "Probation Report on James J. Hines," *New York World-Telegram*, 23 March 1939.

Tagliabue, John. "How Don Calo (and Patton) Won the War in Sicily, *New York Times*, 24 May 1994.

Thompson, Craig and Allen Raymond. "Killer Ambushed in Another Drama from Gang Rule in New York," *Chicago Tribune*, 5 May 1940.

_____. "New York Gang High Jinks for Quick and The Dead," *Chicago Tribune*, 19 May 1940.

Online Articles

May, Allan, "Castellammarese War," Part 1,
<www.americanmafia.com/Mob_Report/6–10–02_Mob_Report.htm>

_____. "Castellammarese War," Part 2,
<www.americanmafia.com/Mob_Report/6–24–02_Mob_Report.htm>

_____. "Castellammarese War," Part 3,
<www.americanmafia.com/Mob_Report/7–15–02_Mob_Report.htm>

_____. "The Last Testament of Lucky Luciano Revisited," Part 3,
<www.americanmafia.com/Mob_Report/8–26–02_Mob_Report.htm>

_____. "The Last Testament of Lucky Luciano Revisited," Part 2,
<www.americanmafia,com/Mob_Report/9–2–02_Mob_Report.htm>

Pruyear, Susan C., "Women in the Legal Profession: Eunice Roberta Hunton Carter, 1899–1970," Fall 2001, Internet Article.

Other Source Materials

May, Allan, Time Line. (Unpublished)
McDermitt, Richard. *Murder, Inc.* Manuscript. (Unpublished)

INDEX

LIST OF PHOTOS

LIST OF ILLUSTRATIONS